# Think $ingle and Test Your Money-Smarts

**W**hatever their stage in life and circumstances, women need to be thinking single about their financial security. Give these true-false questions a try and see how well you are prepared for the challenge.

**TRUE OR FALSE?** *Thinking single means staying single or maintaining entirely separate financial lives even if you marry.*
**False:** Thinking single has nothing to do with the state of marriage. Rather, it's a state of mind in which you're confident of your ability to support yourself financially if necessary, and comfortable with handling money—or seeking help if you need it. You can (and should) achieve this kind of financial independence regardless of your marital status.

**TRUE OR FALSE?** *Women face unique financial situations during their lives.*
**True:** What sets women apart from men, financially speaking, is the different situations they will face during their lives, each with financial implications. They have longer life spans and more checkered careers. When they marry, they often face a special kind of financial dependency, which is not always unwelcome but can work to their disadvantage and may be discomfiting. They

often bear the main responsibility for rearing children with sound financial values, and take on the added financial burden of caring for aging family members. Then, after years of having their financial lives intertwined with others', they face years on their own following the death of husband and parents and the launching of children.

**TRUE OR FALSE?** *Men and women are equally capable investors.*
**False:** Actually, women can be *more* capable than men. In a study of investors at a large discount-brokerage firm during the 1990s, Brad M. Barber and Terrance Odean of the University of California at Davis found that women investors outperformed their male counterparts, earning 1.4 percentage points more each year on a risk-adjusted basis. What's their secret? Just as women drivers are more likely than men to ask for directions when they're lost, women investors are more likely to do research before they make an investment decision, rather than to gamble on a highflier. Once they decide on a stock, they're more likely to stick with it. They trade less often, Barber and Odean found, and the less often you trade, the better your returns because trading costs money, in the form of commissions you pay brokers. Men actually traded 45% more than women—a result that Barber and Odean attributed to overconfidence.

**TRUE OR FALSE?** *If you don't work outside your home, you can't have an individual retirement account (IRA).*
**False:** For women, one of the great features of an IRA is that you can have one even if you don't have a paying job, as long as your husband is employed. In that case, he can contribute up to $3,000 of his compensation to an account for you, besides squirreling away $3,000 in his own IRA. You can open either a traditional or a Roth IRA.

**TRUE OR FALSE?** *If you're in your 20s and unmarried, you don't need to worry about having a will.*
**False:** You may have acquired lots of things by now—a house or condo, home furnishings, a car, investments, a retirement plan. If you have definite ideas about who should get all that stuff if anything should happen to you, the only way to make sure your wish-

es will be carried out is to make a will. In the absence of a will, your state will make the decision for you, in accordance with a hierarchy that goes something like this: your parents, followed by your siblings, your grandparents, and then other relatives. You should also draft a durable power of attorney so that someone else can act on your behalf if you are incapacitated.

**TRUE OR FALSE?** *When you marry, in order to maintain your good credit rating, keep at least one or two credit cards in your maiden name or your first name and new married name—for example, Susan Smith, not Mrs. Robert Smith.*
**True,** for the reasons cited in the next answer.

**TRUE OR FALSE?** *When you marry, each partner's credit record will begin anew.*
**False:** You each carry your credit record into the marriage. If you plan to marry a man with a checkered credit history, such as a personal bankruptcy, keep your financial lives separate so that your credit record doesn't become entangled with his. Make all credit purchases in your own name and with your own accounts. Whatever you do, don't add your name to your spouse's accounts, because you become responsible for his debts. As long as you and your husband have separate accounts, your credit rating can't be affected by your husband's failure to meet obligations that are solely his responsibility.

**TRUE OR FALSE?** *Women are usually charged more than men for individual disability insurance policies.*
**True:** So, see whether your employer will let you buy individual coverage at a group discount. Such policies usually cost 15% to 25% less than individual coverage obtained on your own—and may cost as much as 50% less for women because group policies have unisex rates.

**TRUE OR FALSE?** *Life insurance is as important for women who are secondary earners in the family as for men who are primary earners.*
**True:** Although women are most often the ones who benefit from life insurance, don't underestimate your own importance and value—financial and otherwise—in supporting your family. If you

have a paying job outside the home, for example, add together both your income and your spouse's to figure your total need for coverage, and then divide it proportionately between individual policies on each spouse. Even if you are a stay-at-home parent, your loss could be a financial blow to your family if your husband had to hire someone to care for your children, run your household, manage the finances, support him in his business endeavors, or take on any of the innumerable other roles that women often perform in their homes. Your absence could mean a lower family income, a loss of attention to important family business, or a loss of flexibility at the same time that family expenses are rising and your children are growing.

**TRUE OR FALSE?** *A prenuptial agreement is just something that protects the wealthy and famous—usually men.*
**False:** You're a good candidate for a prenuptial agreement if: (1) Both you and your husband-to-be earn a high salary and have significant assets that you want to protect. (2) You have children from a previous marriage and want to be sure that they will be taken care of after your death. (3) Your new husband is paying child support for children from a previous marriage. (4) You have agreed to pay for the professional education of your soon-to-be husband and want to be assured that you will benefit from the income that he will receive in the future. (In fact, this might be one situation in which you would want to consider a prenup in a first marriage.)

**TRUE OR FALSE?** *If you stay in the work force after having children, you can expect your financial obligations to stay about the same, except for the cost of child care.*
**False:** Even if a woman chooses to stay in the work force, the family budget will take a hit, not only with the big new expense of providing for child care, but also the cost of paying for services, such as housecleaning, that may not have been required previously, or buying a second vehicle to accommodate the increasing—and conflicting—transportation demands of the family.

**TRUE OR FALSE?** *In a divorce, it's best to hang on to your home to avoid uprooting your children and maintain some stability in their world.*

**False:** Hanging onto the house might seem like a good way to keep your family situation as normal as possible under the circumstance. But it may backfire, both psychologically and financially. On your reduced income, you may not be able to keep up payments for the mortgage, insurance, taxes, and maintenance. The kids won't feel reassured if they sense you're worried about making the mortgage payment. If you keep the house and let your ex have some other asset, such as stocks or a retirement plan, you could live to regret the decision. Talk over this problem carefully with your lawyer or financial adviser, and seriously consider trading down your digs. That could ease stress and give everyone a fresh start.

**TRUE OR FALSE?** *You will probably spend as many years caring for your elderly parents as you will raising your children.*
**True:** Research by the National Alliance for Caregiving found that nearly three-fourths of all caregivers for persons over the age of 50 are women. What's more, 41% of them are caring for children at the same time they are caring for elderly adults. Even if women have brothers with whom they might share the work, daughters spend significantly more time providing care for elderly parents than sons do, according to a report on women and retirement prepared for TIAA-CREF.

**TRUE OR FALSE?** *Now that women have been in the work force for some time, they can expect to retire with about the same retirement resources as men.*
**False:** Not necessarily. Women will probably have to provide for themselves financially for more years of retirement than men will, and for many of those years women are likely to be on their own. Yet women tend to earn less than men and participate in the work force less steadily; thus they lose income and job seniority and are less likely than men to fully participate in a pension or profit-sharing plan sponsored by their employer. All of those circumstances act as a drag on women's pension assets. When women do build up funds, they tend to borrow against their balances or tap them when they switch jobs or need money.

**TRUE OR FALSE?** *You won't need to worry about the possibility of widowhood until you are well into your retirement.*

**False:** The average age of widowhood in a first marriage in the United States is 58. (It's 59 for women in second marriages.)

**TRUE OR FALSE?** *If you are covered under your husband's health-insurance policy and he dies, you and your family will be without coverage.*

**False:** If you were covered by your husband's health insurance, you can continue group coverage for you and your children for 36 months, although you may be required to pay for it. You may also be able to pick up coverage through your own employer. (If you or your children haven't previously been enrolled in your employer's health insurance plan, you may be able to join it outside the usual enrollment period due to your spouse's death.)

# Think
# $ingle!

**KIPLINGER'S BUSINESS MANAGEMENT LIBRARY**
Business 2010
Cash Rules
Customer Once, Client Forever
Fast-Track Business Growth
Hunting Heads
Parting Company
Practical Tech for Your Business
Raising Capital
Taming the Paper Tiger at Work
You Can't Fire Me, I'm Your Father

**OTHER KIPLINGER BOOKS**
But Which Mutual Funds?
Buying & Selling a Home
The Consumer's Guide to the Experts
Dollars & Sense for Kids
Financing College
Home • ology
Kiplinger's Practical Guide to Investing
Kiplinger's Practical Guide to Your Money
Know Your Legal Rights
Making Money in Real Estate
Next Step: The Real World
Retire & Thrive
Retire Worry-Free
Switching Careers
Taming the Paper Tiger at Home

Kiplinger offers excerpts and tables of contents for
all of our books on our Web site (www.kiplinger.com).

For information about volume discounts contact:

> Cindy Greene
> Kiplinger Books & Tapes
> 1729 H Street, N.W.
> Washington, DC 20006
> e-mail: cgreene@kiplinger.com
> 202-887-6431
> cgreene@kiplinger.com

# Think $ingle!

*The Woman's Guide to Financial
Security at Every Stage of Life*

## JANET BODNAR

*Executive Editor, Kiplinger's Personal Finance Magazine*

KIPLINGER BOOKS
Washington, D.C.

**Published by**
**The Kiplinger Washington Editors, Inc.**
**1729 H Street, N.W.**
**Washington, D.C. 20006**

B+T   15.95   8/03

Library of Congress Cataloging-in-Publication Data

Bodnar, Janet, 1949-
    Think $ingle!: the woman's guide to financial security at every stage of life
/ Janet Bodnar.
        p. cm.
    Includes index.
    ISBN 0-938721-99-2 (pbk.)
        1. Women–Finance, Personal. 2. Finance, Personal. I. Title.

HG179 .B5684 2003
332.024'042–dc21                                                    2002040661

This publication is intended to provide guidance in regard to the subject matter covered. It is sold with the understanding that the author and publisher are not herein engaged in rendering legal, accounting, tax or other professional services. If such services are required, professional assistance should be sought.

First Edition. Printed in the United States of America.

9 8 7 6 5 4 3 2 1

Kiplinger publishes books and videos on a wide variety of personal-finance and business-management subjects. Check our Web site (www.kiplinger.com) for a complete list of titles, additional information and excerpts. Or write:
  Cindy Greene
  Kiplinger Books & Tapes
  1729 H Street, N.W.
  Washington, DC 20006
  e-mail: cgreene@kiplinger.com
To order, call 800-280-7165; for information about volume discounts, call 202-887-6431.

*To my mother, Renie,
and my sister, Priscilla,
who have always inspired me;
and to my daughter, Claire,
whom I hope to inspire.*

# Acknowledgements

One of the benefits of being associated with the Kiplinger organization is that as an author you have access not only to a treasure trove of financial information in the pages of *Kiplinger's Personal Finance* magazine and related publications, but also to the resident experts who produce it all. My thanks to all those human resources, who are more valuable than any computer database: Priscilla Brandon, Jane Clark, Kris Davis, Fred Frailey, Mary Beth Franklin, Bob Frick, Steve Goldberg, Brian Knestout, Jeff Kosnett, Kim Lankford, Kevin McCormally, Courtney McGrath, Ted Miller, Elizabeth Razzi, Ronnie Roha, Manny Schiffres, Catherine Siskos, Mark Solheim, and Melynda Wilcox.

Thanks also to the staff of Kiplinger books:

David Harrison, for believing we had something to say to women; editor Pat Esswein, who added welcome perspective and always asked just the right questions; Norma Shaw, for her research assistance; Heather Waugh, for the polished design (and all those clever icons); copy editor Priscilla Taylor, for keeping an eye on the details and being an appreciative audience; and Cindy Greene, for her editorial support.

And thanks to all the women and men whose true stories make the financial advice in these pages come to life.

# Contents

Quiz       i

Preface       xix

Introduction       xxi

**CHAPTER 1:**

**Women Really Are Different (But Not How You Think)**       1

Your Money Personality: A Constant • The Gender Gap • Get a Grip:
Your Net Worth, Cash Flow, Goals, and Budget • The Power of Knowledge

**CHAPTER 2:**

**Single or Thinking Single: Start Out Right**       17

Five Steps to Financial Independence • 1. Pay Off Your Debt • 2. Write Your
Credit History on a Clean Slate • 3. Plump Your Cash Cushion • 4. Open a
Retirement Account • 5. Buy Peace-of-Mind Insurance • Set for Life

**CHAPTER 3:**

**Getting Married: Opposites Attract**       39

Getting Money Out in the Open • Defusing the Hot Spots • Marching
to Different Drummers • Spending Too Much • Passing the Buck • Taking
Risk—or Not • Deciding Whether to Pool or Not? • Handling Credit:
Keep Your Distance • Paying Taxes: Think Couple • Saving Marriages

**CHAPTER 4:**

**Staying Married: Don't Be a Silent Partner**       55

Stake Out Your Property • How You Hold It • What's His and What's Hers •
Keep It All in the Family • Life Insurance Made Easy • Where There's a Will,
There's Security • Your Most Precious Assets: Your Children • The Other
Pieces of the Plan • Long-Term-Care Insurance: A Lifesaver for Women •
Special Issues for Second Marriages

**CHAPTER 5:**

**Your Children: A New Financial Challenge**                    **79**

Working or Not Working? • Raising Kids on One Paycheck • Pare Your
Expenses • Borrow With Discretion • Tap Your Assets, but Address
Reality • Taking Advantage of Family-Friendly Tax Breaks • The Child
Credit (The Child-Care Credit • Child-Care Reimbursement Plans) •
Getting Help With the College Bills (State-Sponsored College Savings
Plans • Coverdell Education Savings Accounts • Prepaid College Tuition
Plans) • Teaching Kids About Money (An Eye-Opening Experience •
Hidden Expenses • Work Incentives)

**CHAPTER 6:**

**Investing: Ways to Meet Your Financial Goals**                    **99**

Women Make Better Investors • Stocks Are Gender-Neutral • Invest
for the Short-Term (Garden-Variety Bank Savings Accounts • Bank
Certificates of Deposit • Money-Market Mutual Funds • Short-Term
Bond Funds • Treasury Bills) • Invest for the Long Term • Invest With
Confidence • Keep All Things in Proportion • Invest Slowly and Steadily •
Choose Your Level of Risk • Pick Stocks (How Much Does the Company
Earn? • How Does the Price Relate to Earnings? • What Is a Company's
Book Value? • What's the Return on Book Value? • What's the Total
Return?) • Find a Stockbroker • Consider the Mutual Fund Alternative •
Different Strokes • Really Simple Investing • Invest in Bonds • Assess
the Bottom Line

**CHAPTER 7:**

**Retirement: You Won't Be a Bag Lady**                    **127**

Where Do Women Stand? • How Much Will You Need? • Consider
These Golden Opportunities to Save (Run, Don't Walk to Open an IRA •
Which IRA, Roth or Traditional? • A Retirement Plan for Stay-at-Home
Moms) • Take Full Advantage of a 401(k) • Don't Squander Your Kitty •
Plan for His-and-Her Retirement • What Can Women Expect From
Traditional Pension Plans? • How Can You Make the Most of Your Husband's
Pension? • Test the Social Security Safety Net (What You're Entitled To •
What You Can Count On) • Your Talents Are Your Greatest Asset

**CHAPTER 8:**

**Divorce: Get a Fair Deal**                                               155

Don't Go It Alone • Get Rid of Joint Debt • Who Gets What? • Don't
Count on Alimony • Know What to Expect in Child Support • Look
Beyond Child Support • Should You Keep the House? • Tap Your Husband's
Pension • Exercise Your Rights to Social Security • Revisit Your Estate
Plan • Be Informed About Equal Opportunity Divorce

**CHAPTER 9:**

**Caring for Your Parents: Help Is on the Way**                           177

Get Help From Your Employer (The Family and Medical Leave Act •
Flexible Spending Accounts • Other Employer-Provided Benefits) •
Get Help With Your Parent's Care (In-Home Care • Assisted Living •
Continuing Care • Further Help with the Options) • Get Help in Paying
the Bills (Home Care • Assisted Living • Nursing-Home Care) • Help
From the IRS • Break the Cycle

**CHAPTER 10:**

**Widowhood: Be Prepared to Carry On**                                    197

Make Settlement Easy • Sit Tight With Your Money and Say No • Take
Your Time • Manage Carefully • Take a Lump Sum or Invest in an Annuity? •
Revisit Your Investment Plan • Consider Kay's Example • Get Support from
the Widow's Safety Net (Social Security • Pensions • IRAs) • Deal with
Death and Taxes (Insurance Proceeds • Estate Tax • Income Tax • Medical
Expenses • Capital Gains) • Take Care of Yourself • Don't Panic • Don't
Underestimate Your Own Resources

**INDEX**                                                                 217

# Preface

s a wife, mother, household manager, and editor, I know what it's like to balance lots of tasks—and to let a few of them slide because I have a wonderful husband who's happy to share them. So writing *Think $ingle!* has been a revelation to me in more ways than one. I am not only the author, but as a woman I'm also the audience. In researching this book, I was my own focus group, asking questions about financial issues that concern me. And the answers I got prompted me to reevaluate my own finances in a number of ways. Here are just a few examples:

First, my husband and I both had wills, but they hadn't been updated since the birth of our third child 12 years before. After writing the chapter on estate planning, I began bugging my husband to consult a lawyer to see whether we needed to make any changes. Second, when I checked up on the status of my own pension plans with my employer, as part of the routine update recommended by our lawyer, I was shocked to find that I had never updated them to include any of my children as beneficiaries—even though I could have sworn I had done so.

Then, while I was working on this book, my own father died, and my sister and I had to help our mother adjust to the psychological bereavement and financial challenges of becoming a widow. In the chapters on caring for parents and adjusting to widowhood, I try to address the questions that all three of us—and my sister in particular, as primary caregiver—were facing. In our mother's situation, my sister and I couldn't help seeing ourselves at some point in the future. And that thought prompted us both to decide, independently, to look into long-term-care insurance.

Every woman will pass through most of the stages in this book.

Many will pass through all of them. My goal is to gather in one place answers to the questions uppermost in your mind—or the minds of women you know—at every stage. In these pages you'll find the information you need to build financial security—with your husband or on your own.

When you start your adult life as a single woman, take control of your finances and never give it up. Think single, and you can complement your husband's financial resources and knowledge instead of depending on them. Think single, and you will not have the rug pulled out from under you if you go through a divorce. You will not be left financially bereft as a widow. You will not go broke taking care of your aging parents—or yourself. Think single, and you will have enough money for a comfortable retirement. Think single, and you will never be a bag lady.

# Introduction

**O**ld myths die a slow death, so it shouldn't be surprising that a lot of people—of both sexes—still seem to feel that men have some genetic advantage over women in the skilled management of money. Late-night comics can always get a cheap laugh with stale jokes about women and money. ("I gave my wife an unlimited budget...and she exceeded it.")

But evidence to the contrary has always been out there, and it seems to be mounting. In countless households, it's the wife who manages the budget, pays the bills, initiates many financial decisions, shops for financial and consumer products, and makes investments. And if there is a spendthrift in the family, it's just as often the man of the house as the woman.

Sure, guys talk a big game about their investing success—the same way they banter and boast about cars, sports, and hunting (among other things). Men are more prone to active trading than women are—to the men's detriment. Likewise, they are more attracted to speculative investments—also to their detriment. They'll always have a great story for you about their hot stock that soared, but they'll fail to mention the 10 others that crashed and burned.

Just as men are loath to stop the car and ask directions when they're lost, they often feign greater knowledge of financial affairs than they really have. After all, men are supposed to know all about managing money, so it would look unmanly to ask the advice of others.

Women don't seem to have such hang-ups. They acknowledge what they don't know, they listen carefully, they learn sound techniques, and then they have the patience to consistently apply what they've learned. No wonder a recent study, cited in this book, found that the female customers of a major discount brokerage firm tended to outperform its male investors.

This wonderful new book, by my Kiplinger colleague Janet Bodnar, is for *all* women—whether never married, married, divorced, or widowed—who want to learn more about the right way to achieve true financial security and make their money grow... consistently, strongly, forever.

The concept of "thinking single" doesn't apply to your marital status, but to the idea of empowerment—taking individual responsibility for your own future, whatever that future holds. It means not being dependent on another person's knowledge or judgment, which might be inferior to your own.

If you have a partner in life, you will both benefit from your growing financial savvy, enabling the two of you to make better plans together than just one of you could do alone. And if you find yourself on your own—today or years from now—you'll be much better prepared.

Decades ago, women weren't encouraged to learn money management, just as women weren't generally encouraged to pursue careers and earn their own living. There were exceptions, of course. One of the most successful investors of all time was the reclusive, miserly Hetty Green, "The Witch of Wall Street." Female entrepreneurs have long distinguished themselves, ranging from Madame C.J. Walker, an African-American, to the modern marketing genius Mary Kay Ash (both of whom built empires in the cosmetics business).

But women were so rare in professional financial careers that the exceptions were all the more noteworthy—women like Muriel Siebert, of discount brokerage fame, or Julia Montgomery Walsh, a highly successful Washington, D.C. stock broker.

Women are often successful communicators and teachers, so it shouldn't be surprising that the first broadly read personal-finance journalist was a woman—syndicated newspaper columnist Sylvia Porter, whose tradition is carried on today by columnists such as *Newsweek's* Jane Bryant Quinn.

Janet Bodnar is one such skilled communicator. As executive editor of *Kiplinger's Personal Finance* magazine, she has built her career on writing and editing stories about financial subjects. The subjects might be complex, but her writing is always lucid and lively. In recent years, Janet has also emerged as America's leading authority on how to each children good money-management habits. (In the guise of "Dr. Tightwad," she has offered her advice in books and a column syndicated via *The New York Times*. You'll find her "Money-Smart Kids" column in *Kiplinger's Personal Finance* magazine, as well as on www.Kiplinger.com.)

Now Janet is applying her lifetime of professional and personal experiences—as a financial journalist, wife, and mother—to helping her fellow adult women on their journeys of financial self-discovery.

The most distinctive aspect of Janet's approach to this book is that it covers every phase of a woman's life. You can find some pretty good guides already published on money management for single women just starting out in life, women who are recently widowed, or women about to go through divorce. This new book covers all of these life stages, including great advice for middle-aged women who need to care for their own elderly parents.

Finally, there's another special group that could also benefit from this book: Men. If, as the evidence suggests, the well-informed woman might have a temperamental edge over men in handling and investing money, perhaps we men should try viewing these issues from a woman's point of view, through Janet Bodnar's knowing eyes. I, for one, have learned a lot from her already.

*Knight Kiplinger*

Knight Kiplinger
Editor in Chief
*The Kiplinger Letter* and
*Kiplinger's Personal Finance* magazine

# Think $ingle!

# Women Really Are Different (But Not How You Think)

**A** few years ago, when I suggested that *Kiplinger's* magazine do a story on women and money, the editor was reluctant. Money is gender-neutral, he argued. Any story we did on how to invest, how to plan for retirement, or where to get the best return on your money would apply equally to men and women. Furthermore, if we suggested that that was not the case—that women were somehow different—wouldn't that point of view reflect the ultimate in male financial chauvinism?

Not necessarily, I replied. If we suggested that women needed spoon feeding because they had trouble grasping such oh-so-masculine concepts as making money, we would certainly stand guilty of patronizing our readers. If instead we reflected reality—that women need specific financial advice tailored to the financial decisions they must make—then we would do our readers a service. Just as *Kiplinger's* would not recommend the same investment mix for a 20-something college grad as for a 60-something retiree, we would not

## Did You Know?

In a study by OppenheimerFunds, 31% of the men surveyed thought the wife was more likely than the husband to manage financial matters in most families, whereas 52% of the women surveyed said the wife was more likely to be in charge.

necessarily recommend the same type of retirement planning for a woman with a full-time job as for a stay-at-home mom.

The truth is, I said, that women really *are* different—but not because they're financial neophytes who are unsophisticated about money and make bad decisions about how to spend and invest it. (That's a stereotype often promoted by many self-help gurus who promise to save women from themselves and their own worst instincts.) Lack of financial sophistication can, and often does, apply to men as well as women. I think back to the late 1970s, when inflation was out of control and I had occasion to have an elective medical procedure that wasn't covered by insurance. The doctor was going to charge a fee of about $2,000, which he said I could pay off monthly. Would he be willing to give me a discount, I asked, if I paid the entire bill up front? No way, he said smugly; I wasn't going to beat him out of his fee that easily. Okay, I shrugged, but, I wondered, hadn't he ever heard about the time value of money? Given the inflationary environment in the 1970s, it would certainly have been worth his while to get his money immediately, in exchange for a small discount, instead of waiting for it to trickle in over a couple of years, when it would be worth less.

> **Thinking single is a state of mind: You're confident that you can support yourself, and comfortable with handling money— or seeking help if you need it.**

What sets women apart from men, financially speaking, is the different situations they will face during their lives, each with financial implications. They have longer life spans and more checkered careers. When they marry, they often face a special kind of financial dependency, which is not always unwelcome but can work to their disadvantage and may be discomfiting. They often bear the main responsibility for rearing children with sound financial values, and take on the added financial burden of caring for aging family members. Then, after years of having their financial lives intertwined with others', they face years on their own following the death of husband and parents and the launching of children.

In the end, my editor did agree to let me write the story for *Kiplinger's* magazine, and that article has served as the blueprint for this book.

In the Kiplinger tradition of presenting useful information in a readable style, it's my intention to cut right to the chase, giving busy women the answers they need to the questions that are on their minds, such as:

- **What, if any, is the best way to combine assets in marriage**—and to ensure a fresh start if the marriage ends?
- **In their role as caregivers,** how should women go about finding financial resources to help them?
- **What's the surest route to a secure retirement,** free from the fear of becoming a burden to your children, or, even worse, a bag lady (a concern discussed in Chapter 7)?

Another challenge to writing a book about women and money is that prospective readers are at various stages of their lives: just starting out in their 20s; making and living out commitments to partners and children in their 20s, 30s, and 40s; and possibly starting again in their 50s, 60s, or 70s because of widowhood or divorce. But life isn't static: Either by choice or by chance, at some point most women will go through most of these stages, and change can be costly. The unifying theme of this book is that wherever you are in life, if you are a wise woman you will think single.

Thinking single has nothing to do with the state of marriage. Rather, it's a state of mind in which you're confident of your ability to support yourself financially if necessary, and comfortable with handling money—or seeking help if you need it. You can (and should) achieve this kind of financial independence regardless of your marital status. Even a stay-at-home mom can save for her own retirement, make sure that her children are adequately protected by life insurance, and be an equal partner in her family's financial planning. Far from causing tension, your abilities should enhance your relationship with your husband, because each of you has your own strengths and skills that complement the other's. When you're financially independent, you can approach life's twists and turns with assurance, secure in the knowledge that you can handle any curves.

An acquaintance of mine spent years working from home as a freelance writer while her children were young. When her husband was laid off from his job, she returned to work full time to get health insurance coverage for her family and retirement benefits for herself. Soon after, her husband found a new position and she was overjoyed—but had no plans to give up her job. "I like being captain of my ship," she told me. Whatever your circumstances, you can be captain—or co-captain—of your own ship.

# Your Money Personality: A Constant

**B**efore we go further, let me reemphasize an earlier point: There is no money gene that makes men inherently more financially astute than women. While your gender is likely to influence the way you think about money, that situation is primarily a function of life experience and social conditioning. In determining your attitude toward money, your basic personality far overshadows gender, as well as income, age, career, and marital status, according to the findings of the "Women Cents Survey," conducted by the National Center for Women and Retirement Research.

So it's helpful to identify your basic money personality. See whether you recognize yourself in any of the following portraits (or perhaps in some variation thereof):

**THE ACCOUNTANT.** You keep your checkbook balanced, and one of your greatest thrills is watching your savings account grow. You blanch when your spouse or someone you know spends impulsively on a piece of furniture or a set of golf clubs. You can be a downer to live with, but you'll never be broke. For you, money means security.

**THE SOCIAL WORKER.** You regard money as filthy lucre, and the quicker you wash your hands of it the better. You are, however, willing to spend it on the people, and causes, you love. You're the one who gets suckered into hosting the family dinner every Thanksgiving, and you probably have a "save the something" bumper sticker on your car. For you, money means affection.

**THE CEO.** You lease a BMW, live in a house you can't afford, and have a closet full of designer silk suits. When your kids bring home good report cards, you write them a check. Your motto is, The one with the most toys (and the nicest clothes) wins. For you, money means success.

**THE ENTERTAINER.** Every Friday afternoon you have a couple of drinks with the gang from the office, and you pick up the tab. On Saturday night you go out to dinner with your friends, and you pick up the tab, or you host brunch on Sunday. You never balance your checkbook and can't be bothered saving receipts. You drive your accountant spouse crazy, but your neighbors and co-workers love you. For you, money means esteem.

There's nothing inherently good or bad, male or female, about these personality types. They're just distinctive. Knowing where you fit in will help you manage your money more effectively by playing to your strengths and correcting any bad habits. If you're in the social worker category, for example, there's no danger you'll become obsessed with making money. But you do need to overcome your aversion to possessing it and learn to use it as a tool that can build financial independence.

# The Gender Gap

While there may be no "money" gene, it does appear that in some ways men and women behave differently when it comes to money. The gender gap starts slowly but shows itself early. Even among children as young as 4, boys tend to have a higher income than girls—and spend more of it, according to James McNeal, an expert on marketing to children. McNeal is at a loss to explain the difference except to guess that boys are permitted more freedom in their activities than girls, and therefore spend more. "Even in Mom-only households, boys seem to be on a longer rope than girls are," says McNeal.

The disparity continues when kids become teenagers. Overall, teenage guys spend more of their own money ($59 per week) than do teenage girls ($49 per week), whereas teenage girls spend more of their parents' money ($36 per week) than do the guys ($31), according to Teenage Research Unlimited of Northbrook, Ill. Parents are more likely to pay for their daughters' cell phones and cars—possibly because girls are more adept at convincing them that it's a matter of safety over convenience. And when they enter the work force, girls between the ages of 16 and 19 earn less than boys of the same age, who tend to get higher-paying jobs,

## ⟨X⟩⏻⏻ Get a Fresh Start

You can do wonders to streamline your finances just by getting rid of paperwork you don't need. The following run-down of what to pitch, and when, will get you started. If you need more intensive help to unclutter your life and set up a financial record-keeping system that works, see *Taming the Paper Tiger at Home* (Kiplinger Books, 2002), by professional organizer and author Barbara Hemphill. Self-employed people will also want to see Hemphill's companion volume *Taming the Paper Tiger at Work*.

**Bank records.** Chuck ATM receipts after your bank statement arrives and you've matched everything up. The same goes for canceled checks and credit card receipts unless you need them for tax purposes to verify charitable contributions, business expenses, or home-improvement records.

**Tax records.** Keep the returns, but you can probably toss supporting records after 3 years. Most people are safe from being audited after 3 years from the date when the taxes were due, unless they forgot to report a big chunk of their income. If you're self-employed or have supplementary sources of income, hang on to supporting records for 6 years.

**Credit card statements.** Throw these

away as soon as your payment is posted on the next month's bill (again, unless you need them for tax purposes).

**Utility receipts.** Unless you're deducting your phone or electricity charges as home-office expenses, toss your utility receipts when you pay the bill. The stubs don't prove that you paid the bills, just that you received them.

**Mutual fund and brokerage statements.** When you sell shares, you will need to know how much you originally paid for the shares and the amount of dividends and capital-gain distributions you have reinvested. Chuck all but your first and most recent transaction reports and prospectuses. Also keep the year-end cumulative report.

**Home-improvement records.** Most people can toss them. Because you can make a tax-free profit of up to $250,000 ($500,000 if you're married) on your house when you sell, most owners won't need to worry about home-improvement expenses. You will need to keep those records, however, if you plan to rent out part of your house or to convert some portion of it into a home office. Similarly, if you think you'll live in your house for less than two years or earn a profit of more than $250,000 ($500,000 if you're married) when you sell, keep the records.

according to the Bureau of Labor Statistics.

By the time they're adults, they're showing more fundamental differences by gender. A nationwide survey of 2,000 people by OppenheimerFunds showed that whereas women are more likely than men to manage financial matters in most families, men have more confidence than women in their knowledge of investments and their ability to invest a $10,000 windfall. And more men than women said they know how a mutual fund works.

Having more confidence, however, doesn't mean that men are better money managers or investors. In fact, just the opposite appears to be true. When it comes to investing, for instance, women are less likely than men to act on hot tips and more inclined to do their homework, make a decision, and stick with it. As a result, they have a better track record as investors. A study of discount-brokerage investors by researchers at the University of California at Davis showed that during the 1990s, women's portfolios outperformed those of men.

**When investing, women are less likely than men to act on hot tips and more inclined to do their homework, make a decision, and stick with it.**

It may be that men are more willing to bluff their way through their investing lives because society expects it, or because they figure that if they lose money they can always earn more. Women, in contrast, may be less willing to take risks with their money because they're less sure of their ability to make up any losses—a reasonable presumption considering that women change jobs more frequently than men, and that the average woman spends 15% of her career out of the paid work force caring for children and parents, according to the Women's Institute for a Secure Retirement.

Nancy, a New York City financial planner, has vivid memories of the different methods her well-to-do businessman father used to teach her and her brother about money: She got an allowance, but her father doled out money to her brother "like a cash machine. I guess the implication was that I would have to look after myself, but my brother would take over the business and could always count on earning money." As a result, says Nancy, "I learned how to think before spending, but it took my brother a lot longer to learn that lesson."

## Your Cash Flow

| INCOME | TOTAL FOR YEAR | MONTHLY AVERAGE |
|---|---|---|
| Take-home pay | $ _____ | $ _____ |
| Dividends, capital gains, interest | _____ | _____ |
| Bonuses | _____ | _____ |
| Other | _____ | _____ |
| **Total income** | $ _____ | $ _____ |

| EXPENDITURES | | |
|---|---|---|
| Mortgage or rent | $ _____ | $ _____ |
| Taxes not withheld from pay | _____ | _____ |
| Food | _____ | _____ |
| Utilities and fuel | _____ | _____ |
| Insurance premiums | _____ | _____ |
| Household maintenance | _____ | _____ |
| Auto (gas, oil, maintenance, repairs) | _____ | _____ |
| Other transportation (bus, parking) | _____ | _____ |
| Loan payments | _____ | _____ |
| Credit card interest | _____ | _____ |
| Medical bills not covered by insurance | _____ | _____ |
| Clothing and care | _____ | _____ |
| Savings and investments | _____ | _____ |
| Charity | _____ | _____ |
| Recreation and entertainment | _____ | _____ |
| Miscellaneous | _____ | _____ |
| **Total expenditures** | $ _____ | $ _____ |

| SUMMARY | | |
|---|---|---|
| **Total income** | $ _____ | $ _____ |
| **Minus total expenditures** | _____ | _____ |
| **Surplus (+) or deficit (−)** | $ _____ | $ _____ |

Maybe men still have a lot to learn. In the Oppenheimer study, 44% of the men surveyed thought the husband was more likely to manage financial matters in most families, compared with 31% who cited the wife. But the women surveyed had a different point of view: 52% said the wife was more likely to be in charge, versus 28% who selected the husband.

Oppenheimer did its first gender study in the early 1990s, and in the ensuing decade the gap between men's and women's attitudes toward money narrowed considerably. Of the women surveyed recently, 64% said they are more interested in investing than they were 5 years ago. Among women ages 21 to 34, more than half reported that they were encouraged to learn more about investing while they were growing up, versus just 35% of women age 55 and over. The survey indicated a "leveling of the playing field by gender," according to Oppenheimer.

# Get a Grip: Your Net Worth, Cash Flow, Goals, and Budget

On a level playing field, the opening gambit is the same for both men and women: Gauge your position and keep your eye on the goal. To keep from fumbling your money away, nothing beats a fundamental strategy like keeping a playbook: writing down where it comes from, where it's going, and how much is left over. Even if you think you have a good grasp of your financial situation in your head, it's been my experience that putting the picture on paper (or on a computer screen) makes it more concrete and helps you spot previously hidden surprises.

I write a lot on the subject of children's finances, and I always recommend that kids make a list of their wants and needs, and match it against a list of their income and outgo. One summer I helped my 17-year-old son open a checking account for his earnings as a lifeguard, from which he was expected to pay for a senior-year training trip with his swim team. At the end of the summer he had about $1,300; after shelling out $900 for the trip he had $400 left. Nothing I could have told him about keeping an eye on his spending would have made as great an impression on him as actually seeing the precipitous decline in his bank balance.

## Your Net Worth

**ASSETS**

Cash in checking accounts        $ _____

Cash in savings accounts        _____

Certificates of deposit        _____

U.S. savings bonds (current value)        _____

Cash value of life insurance        _____

Equity in pension, 401(k),
   and profit-sharing plans        _____

Market value of IRAs or Keogh plan        _____

Surrender value of annuities        _____


Market value of house or apartment        _____

Market value of other real estate        _____


Market value of securities

   Stocks        _____

   Bonds        _____

   Mutual fund shares        _____

   Other        _____


Current value of durable possessions

   Vehicles        _____

   Household furnishings        _____

   Household appliances and equipment   _____

In the box on page 8 you'll find a worksheet for calculating your cash flow—where money comes from and where it goes. In the box above you'll find a worksheet for calculating your net worth—the total of your assets, minus your liabilities. Yes, it will take a bit of time to fill in the blanks, but there are some tricks that will make your task easier.

When calculating your cash flow, for example, you need to record your expenses, but you don't need to keep recording them indefinitely. A month or two should be enough to identify the fixed (regular) expenditures you have to make in categories such

Furs and jewelry _____

Precious metals _____

Collectibles _____

Recreation and hobby equipment _____

Loans receivable _____

Interest in a business _____

Other assets _____

**Total Assets** $ _____

**LIABILITIES**

Current bills outstanding $ _____

Credit card balances _____

Car loans _____

Taxes due _____

Balance due on mortgages _____

Other loans _____

Other liabilities _____

**Total Liabilities** $ _____

**SUMMARY** **Assets** $ _____

**Minus Liabilities** − _____

**Net Worth** $ _____

as housing and utilities, and the discretionary (fun) expenditures you like to make for things such as clothing and travel. If you're gadget-oriented, making your notations on a personal-digital assistant (PDA), or even talking into a recorder, may make the task less of a chore.

And you don't have to track every nickel. Instead, you could make a guess as to what your expenditures are, and then compare your estimates with your credit card bills and bank statements as they come in. If you find, for example, that what you had viewed as harmless shopping excursions to your favorite consignment

## A Monthly Budget Format

| INCOME | YOU | HUSBAND |
|---|---|---|
| Take-home pay | $ _____ | $ _____ |
| Other (specify) | _____ | _____ |
| **Total** | $ _____ | $ _____ |

| FIXED EXPENDITURES | PROJECTED | ACTUAL | (+) OR (-) |
|---|---|---|---|
| Mortgage or rent | $ _____ | $ _____ | $ _____ |
| Taxes not withheld from pay | _____ | _____ | _____ |
| Installment and credit card payments | _____ | _____ | _____ |
| | _____ | _____ | _____ |
| | _____ | _____ | _____ |
| | _____ | _____ | _____ |
| Insurance premiums | | | |
| Health | _____ | _____ | _____ |
| Auto | _____ | _____ | _____ |
| Life | _____ | _____ | _____ |
| Home | _____ | _____ | _____ |
| Other | _____ | _____ | _____ |
| Savings/Investments | | | |
| Emergency fund | _____ | _____ | _____ |
| Retirement or 401(k) | _____ | _____ | _____ |
| Investment fund | _____ | _____ | _____ |
| Vacation fund | _____ | _____ | _____ |
| Other (specify) | _____ | _____ | _____ |
| **Subtotal** | $ _____ | $ _____ | $ _____ |

| VARIABLE EXPENDITURES | PROJECTED | ACTUAL | (+) OR (-) |
|---|---|---|---|
| Groceries, plus food away from home | $ _____ | $ _____ | $ _____ |
| Fuel and utilities | | | |
| Gas or oil | _____ | _____ | _____ |
| Electricity | _____ | _____ | _____ |
| Telephone | _____ | _____ | _____ |
| Water and sewer | _____ | _____ | _____ |
| Household operation and maintenance | _____ | _____ | _____ |
| Automobile | | | |
| Gas and oil | _____ | _____ | _____ |
| Maintenance and repairs | _____ | _____ | _____ |
| Public transportation | _____ | _____ | _____ |
| Clothing | | | |
| You | _____ | _____ | _____ |
| Husband | _____ | _____ | _____ |
| Children | _____ | _____ | _____ |
| Medical and dental | _____ | _____ | _____ |
| Personal care | _____ | _____ | _____ |
| Spending money | | | |
| You | _____ | _____ | _____ |
| Husband | _____ | _____ | _____ |
| Children | _____ | _____ | _____ |
| Recreation, entertainment | _____ | _____ | _____ |
| Charity | _____ | _____ | _____ |
| Special expenses (eg., tuition, alimony) | _____ | _____ | _____ |
| Miscellaneous | _____ | _____ | _____ |
| **Subtotal** | $ _____ | $ _____ | $ _____ |
| **Plus fixed expenditures** | $ _____ | $ _____ | $ _____ |
| **Total** | $ _____ | $ _____ | $ _____ |

**Don't Stop Now!**

- **Consider** your money personality and how it affects the way that you spend, manage and invest your money.
- **Streamline** your financial life by getting rid of records and other paper you don't need.
- **Figure out** your current net worth, take a look at your cash flow, and create a budget.
- **Write down** specific financial goals for yourself.
- **Use** this book to help you create an informed confidence that will overcome any fear of failure or fear of the unknown.

store are in fact adding up to hundreds of dollars a month, you can focus on cutting back in that area instead of putting yourself in a budget straitjacket across the board.

The numbers alone will give you an idea of where you stand, but to figure out where you're going, you'll need to write down your goals. Do you want to buy a house? A new sports car? Save for your kids' college education? Retire early to an exotic location? In writing about children's finances, I've learned that trying to teach kids that they should save money simply because it's a good thing to do isn't effective. Kids need a reward for their efforts, whether it's a new CD system or a school trip. The same is true of adults. While "investing for the future" or "getting control of my money" may be noble goals in themselves, the motivation to save increases when you're working toward something specific.

Once you've captured your dreams on paper, you can sort them in any number of ways—short-term versus long-term, or wants versus needs, for example. Which ones move to the top of your list? (Lists have a way of nagging at you until you get them done. I am a list-maker by temperament, and one year my new year's list looked like this: new car, new house, new baby. By September I had accomplished all three.)

Be as specific as you can. Instead of writing "financial security," you might say, "I want my net worth to be $1 million by the time I'm 50." Or, "I'd like to save enough money to pay cash for a new car in three years." Someone once told me that "when we write down what we are passionate about, there seems to be some sort of power that helps us accomplish it."

Once you have outlined the picture, you can fill in the blanks. You can take that trip to Hawaii next year if you cut back on eating at restaurants. You can have a net worth of $1 million by the time you're 50 if you start putting aside 8% of your pay in a 401(k) plan when you're 25.

# The Power of Knowledge

So, you're ready to build—or rebuild—your financial future. You've gained insight into your cash flow, your net worth, and your goals, and you can create a plan to achieve them, but there's still a missing link. To identify it, let's go back to an earlier point. All the numbers aside, one of the most telling points to come from the Women Cents Survey, mentioned previously, showed that personality is critical to financial decisions. And the personality traits that have the most influence on smart money choices are:

- assertiveness
- openness to change
- optimism, and
- a spirit of adventure.

On the other hand, fear of failure and fear of the unknown are the greatest obstacles to a woman's financial success. My goal in the chapters that follow is to give you the confidence you need to be financially assertive, and the knowledge you need to be independent.

# Single or Thinking Single: Start Out Right

Michelle, a single woman in her 20s, acquired an Ivy League degree but didn't pick up much financial education along the way. Neither her parents nor her peers ever discussed money. "At home I never saw my mother with money," she recalls. "It was always, 'Go ask your father,' even to get change for the ice cream truck." At school, "most people had money, so it was déclassé to talk about it." Because she was on a scholarship, Michelle was "ashamed" to bring up the subject.

Once she had graduated, Michelle landed a job on the assignment desk of a network news organization—a high-profile position with a low-profile paycheck that barely covered rent, student loans, and credit card debt (and left very little room for a "Sex and the City"-style wardrobe). Michelle also had a weakness for ATMs. "My downfall is knowing that I can walk up to a machine, punch buttons, and get cash."

Given her background and habits, Michelle seemed to be setting herself up for a long slide down the slippery slope of financial woes. But she pulled herself back from the

### Did You Know?

At some point in their lives, 90% of women in the U.S. will be managing money on their own because they've been divorced or widowed or have never married.

brink with a simple move: She bought a budgeting book. "Before I get my paycheck I fill in what I anticipate spending, and then what I actually spend," says Michelle. "It's really eye-opening, and it keeps me from getting out of control."

Women like Michelle have more at stake than ever when it comes to taking control of their finances. Single women in the U.S. who have never married, live alone, and have full-time jobs actually earn, on average, 28 cents per hour more ($17.26 per hour) than their single male counterparts, according to a recent study by the Employment Policy Foundation. That's true across the full spectrum of occupations, education levels, and age, and it represents significant progress over the past 20 years or so. In March 1981, single women, on average, earned only 93 cents compared with every dollar of hourly wages earned by men. (With regard to earnings, single women tend to do better relative to men than women as a whole because the distractions of marriage and children are factored out.)

Although it's critical to lay a strong foundation when you're just striking out on your own in your 20s, the basic principles of smart money management are just as applicable if you're a 30-something trying to get out of debt, a 40-something recovering from divorce, or a 50-something planning for retirement.

On the preceding page, we've highlighted one of the most startling statistics I've seen regarding women and money, which is that, at some point in their lives, most women in the U.S. will be managing money on their own because they've been divorced or widowed or have never married. Consider these supporting facts:

■ **Never married.** Of American women who are ages 25 to 29, 29% have never married; of those ages 30 to 34, 16% have never married; ages 35 to 39, 12%; and ages 40 to 44, 9%, according to the National Center for Health Statistics (NCHS).

■ **Divorce.** About 40% of first marriages end in divorce, according to the U.S. Census. (Among first marriages, 33% end in separation or divorce within 10 years, and 43% end in separation or divorce within 15 years, according to the NCHS.)

■ **Widowhood.** The median age of widowhood for women in a first marriage is about 58 years; in a second marriage, it's 59 years, according to the U.S. Census.

Even women who are married or in relationships need to maintain their financial independence, so that if anything happens to a spouse or partner the women will not face financial disaster as well as personal tragedy. (See Chapters 8 and 10 for advice on how to survive divorce and widowhood.) Whatever your age or life situation, think single. And the sooner you start, the better off you'll be.

# Five Steps to Financial Independence

Tracking your cash flow, figuring your net worth, and creating a budget as outlined in Chapter 1, will help you get a grip on where your money comes from and where it's going. Now you're ready to take your first steps toward financial independence.

## 1. Pay Off Your Debt.

When you're in college, says Michelle, "you don't even have to apply for credit cards. Companies send them to you. It's so easy to get behind." Michelle knows whereof she speaks. In 2001 more than 80% of college students in the U.S. had credit cards, up from 67% in 1998, according to a study by Nellie Mae, a top originator of student loans. What's more, the average credit card balance among college students in the U.S. rose from just under $2,000 to more than $2,300.

Once acquired, that burden is hard to shake—especially if it comes on top of student loans. Graduating students have an average of more than $20,000 in combined education loans and credit card debt, according to Nellie Mae. Added to a new-car loan, that much indebtedness often puts young people in a hole they find it tough to climb out of.

There are plenty of women in that hole. A survey by OppenheimerFunds found that 47% of single Gen X women, ages 21 to 34, had credit card debt, compared with 35% of single men. The typical single Gen X woman with credit card debt has an outstanding balance of $2,300—the equivalent of four weeks of take-home pay.

Partly as a result of these spending patterns, significantly more single young women (53%) say that they live from paycheck to

## How Much Debt Can You Handle?

One long-standing rule of thumb is that monthly payments on installment debt—credit card balances, car loans, and other borrowing, excluding a home mortgage—should not exceed 20% of take-home pay. Most mortgage lenders stipulate that your monthly housing payments (principal, interest, taxes, and insurance) should not exceed 28% of your gross pay. When you add that payment to the rest of your installment debt, the figure should not exceed 36% of your monthly gross pay.

paycheck than do single young men (42%). And 30% of all bankruptcy petitions are filed by single women, compared with 26% by single men.

I may be whistling in the wind, but the best way to break the debt-to-bankruptcy cycle trend is to avoid credit cards in college—advice I always give to college students and their parents. Students don't need them, not even for emergencies—and it's too easy to define an emergency as buying a must-have outfit for a weekend event, or treating your dorm-mates to pizza during a mid-term study marathon. You don't want to end up paying the bill long after the outfit has been discarded and the pizza has been consumed. Say you spend $400 on those new clothes, and pay for them in $15 monthly installments on a credit card charging 21% interest. It would take more than three years to pay the bill in full.

But if you're already in trouble, here are the secrets to digging your way out:

**Stop using your credit cards,** even if, to avoid temptation, you have to cut them up or do something hokey like putting them on ice in the freezer. Henceforth, pay cash. Period.

**Pay off your bills,** using whatever strategy makes you feel that you're making progress. If credit card balances are your nemesis, move them to a low-rate card. Even if that rate is only temporary, it will give you breathing room while you concentrate on paying off the balance. Remember, however, this strategy will work only if you don't charge any more.

**www.**

## Help With Debt

Do you need assistance to get out of debt? Credit counseling may provide the answer you need.

**The National Foundation for Credit Counseling** (800-388-2227; www.nfcc.org), or **the Association of Independent Consumer Credit Counseling Agencies** (703-934-6118; www.aiccca.org). To find a program in your area, check out groups that are members of these agencies. They can usually get card companies to lower your interest rates and eliminate some late fees. You make one monthly payment and the agency distributes it to your creditors. A good program will also help you create a budget. It usually takes about

five or six years to become debt-free. These credit-counseling agencies charge debtors very little—an average of $11 per month, says Joy Thormodsgard, vice-president of the NFCC. They get paid primarily by the credit card companies—which typically pay them 9% to 15% of the money they collect.

**The Consumer Credit Counseling Service.** This is one of the largest non-profit counseling services in the U.S., with nearly 2,000 offices throughout the country. Some CCCS offices offer a free debt repayment plan; others charge a nominal fee based on what you owe creditors. To locate the office nearest you, check your local white pages.

**Tackle your most expensive debt first.** Financially, that makes the most sense. That's what Rebecca did. When she returned to school in her late 20s to complete her college degree, she racked up $20,000 in student loans, on top of a car loan. After graduation, she took advantage of programs to consolidate her student loans with a single lender at an attractive rate, and extended the term from the standard 10 years to 20 years. That reduced her monthly payments, so that she could put more cash toward her more expensive car loan. Once the car loan was paid off, she put the extra money toward the student loans, and still repaid them in 10 years. "I understood debt a lot better when I went back to school the second time," says Rebecca. (For more information about dealing with student loan debt and to use various loan repayment calculators, visit www.salliemae.com and www.nelliemae.com, or consult *Take Control of Your Student Loan Debt,* by Robin Leonard and Deanne Loonin and published by the Nolo Press.)

## The Major Credit Bureaus

- **Equifax** (P.O. Box 105496, Atlanta, GA 30348-5496; 800-997-2493; www.equifax.com)
- **Experian** (National Consumer Assistance Center, P.O. Box 2104, Allen TX 75013-2104; 800-397-3742; www.experian.com)
- **Trans Union** (Consumer Disclosure Center, P.O. Box 403, Springfield, PA 19064, 800-888-4213; www.transunion.com)

Although it's smart to knock off your more expensive debt, that may not be the most effective strategy for you. One couple I interviewed paid off $35,000 in credit card debt on 20 cards in just 2 years by taking them one at a time, starting with the smallest balances regardless of the rate. Paying off their bills more quickly gave them a psychological lift. As long as they could see they were making progress, they had an incentive to keep going.

**Don't carry a balance from month to month.** Once you have your bills under control, you can pull out your card again to use as a convenience—but only if you make up your mind to pay the bill in full each month.

## 2. Write Your Credit History on a Clean Slate.

Using credit rashly can make your life a misery. Using it wisely can make your life a breeze, paving the way to everything from renting a car to buying a house. In fact, it's particularly important for women to build a credit record in their own name that will last a lifetime and be unaffected by their marital status.

The Equal Credit Opportunity Act prohibits discrimination on the basis of gender (or marital status) during any part of a credit transaction. So, for instance, creditors can't discourage you from applying for credit because you're a woman, and must not consider gender in any credit-scoring systems they use for evaluating credit-worthiness. (For more on women's credit rights, see page 48.) But the law doesn't guarantee that you will get credit. You'll have to do that on your own.

As mentioned earlier, it's sad but true that one of the easiest ways to get a credit card is to apply as a college student. Even though students generally have no credit history and no income, they do have parents who presumably are willing to bail out their kids if they get into trouble. To avoid the pitfalls I mentioned earlier, I generally recommend that students not apply for a card until they're at least juniors or seniors, or just about to graduate. That way, they have time to build maturity and develop money management skills.

If you're among the minority who resist the pressure to get a credit card while in college— and I salute you—you may find that you're considered a risky credit prospect after you graduate.

**The best way to get credit is to incur debt, so that card issuers can gauge how reliable you are when it comes to repaying. Start with your bank or credit union.**

Take Barbara. A full-time teacher with her own apartment, she paid her bills on time each month, and her only outstanding debt was a small amount on a student loan. Yet at the age of 27 she still didn't have a credit card. She once responded to a card offer through the mail, but was turned down—ironically, because she had no history of repaying debt. "I was so discouraged I didn't bother trying for a while," says Barbara. When she finally received a mail solicitation from Capital One, a major card issuer, she applied for and got her first Visa—with a $200 credit limit.

The best way to get credit is to incur debt, so that card issuers can gauge how reliable you are when it comes to repaying. But that doesn't mean you're out of luck if you're starting fresh. Competition is so fierce among card issuers that you may be able to establish a satisfactory credit history in as little as six months. If you play your cards right, you may even be able to get credit immediately.

Apply first at the bank or credit union where you have a checking or savings account. As long as you're employed full-time and haven't bounced any checks, your bank will probably be willing to issue you a card with a low credit limit—say, $200, as in Barbara's case—and gradually ratchet up that limit if you pay your bills on time. The longer you've lived at your current address or worked for the same employer, the safer a risk you are.

If your bank isn't willing to issue you a card right away, you

## Cards to Avoid

If you're in the market for credit, don't be conned by Web sites that promise to get you a card, or that charge exorbitant or unnecessary fees. Some cards charge an application fee, a processing fee, and an annual fee—and if you're late paying those charges, the issuer slaps on a penalty and charges interest retroactively. It's possible to have a credit line of $500 and a balance of $450 before you've even used the card. Unless the charge is an annual fee, or a bank deposit for a secured card from a reputable issuer, don't prepay for a credit card.

can build a credit history over several months with a department store or gasoline card (both of which are easier to get) or even with a small bank loan, as long as your payments are reported to the credit bureaus that keep track of your credit history (see the box on page 22). Some major banks have programs to help you establish good credit by making you a loan that you repay before getting the money. After repaying a $500 loan, for example, you'll have $500 plus a good payment record—and the rest will be credit history.

First-time cardholders with limited or no credit history rarely qualify for low interest rates. But you can always renegotiate the rate after 6 months. And, remember, if you pay your credit card bill in full each month, the interest rate won't matter.

Don't shop for several cards at the same time. That mistake—called shotgunning your credit—is sure to sabotage your chances. Card issuers checking your credit report will see the other inquiries and assume the worst—that you'll get all the cards and use the entire credit limit. If issuers think you have too many cards, they'll be less confident that you'll be able to pay your debts. And being rejected for a credit card can also hurt your chances of being accepted for one in the future.

*Note:* Those direct-mail offers promising that "you've been preapproved" for credit really mean that you've been preapproved to apply for a card. You can still be turned down.

One of the fastest ways to get credit is to apply for a secured card, which requires you to deposit money in a savings account or a certificate of deposit—$200 to $500 is common—that is frozen while you have the card. (I often recommend secured cards for college students. Putting up some of their own money in order to get the card makes the point that credit has a cost, and protects them if they get into trouble.) A couple of lenders that issue secured cards are Capital One (800-445-4523) and Amalgamated Bank (800-365-6464). To find other lenders that issue secured cards, check online at CardWeb (http://www.cardweb.com/cardtrak/surveys/secured.html), an online source of information for consumers about credit, bank, and many other varieties of "payment" cards. Just make sure that the issuer will eventually upgrade the card to one that is unsecured. Capital One, for instance, will upgrade a card after 6 months for customers in good standing.

Sometimes customers who have bad credit ratings or habitually bounce checks are forced to use secured credit cards, which can be a red flag to other credit issuers. To avoid tarring good applicants with the same brush, some lenders, including Capital One and Amalgamated, report all the cards they issue as unsecured. Before applying for a secured card, find out how it will be reported to the credit bureaus. Avoid issuers that deal exclusively in secured cards and don't offer the option to upgrade.

## 3. Plump Your Cash Cushion.

The car breaks down. The roof springs a leak. You have an unexpected medical bill. You lose your job. Those are the rainy days for which, financial experts will tell you, you should have enough cash tucked away to cover 3 to 6 months' worth of living expenses. You probably won't be surprised to learn that most people don't follow that advice. Only 38% of Americans actually keep that much savings on hand, according to a survey by Lutheran Brotherhood, a financial organization sponsored by the Lutheran Church. Young adults are especially short of cash, with just 30% of them reporting they have a cushion that would last at least three months.

It's not that young adults don't save. Because they have doubts about the future of social security, members of Generation X (adults between the ages of 24 and 35) have started saving for retirement earlier than previous generations. But apparently they don't worry much about emergencies, assuming that they can always fall back on borrowing against their credit cards or retirement accounts.

## Ten Ways to Stay on Top of Your Spending

Can't seem to save? Welcome to the club. No matter what your income, your spending level has a funny way of rising to meet it. Truth to tell, the best way to get your finances under control is to trick yourself into spending less and saving more. As I pointed out in Chapter 1, everyone has different styles and ways of managing money. Know yours, so that you can play to your strengths and compensate for your weaknesses. For example, some people prefer using cash rather than plastic because they can actually see what they're spending—and stop when they run out of money. Others prefer using credit or debit cards because they get a written record of their expenditures, and cash tends to burn a hole in their pocket. There's no "right" system that works for everyone. For starters, follow these 10 easy tips:

1. **Start an automatic savings or investment plan** with a bank, mutual fund, or your retirement plan at work so that money is taken right off the top of your salary, before you even see it.

2. **Have your paycheck deposited directly to your savings account** rather than to your checking account. Psychologically, it's tougher to take money out of savings.

3. **Go to the ATM no more than once a week,** and make your cash last till the next time.

4. **When you make a credit card purchase,** subtract the amount immediately from your checking account so that you're not surprised when the bill arrives at the end of the month.

5. **If credit is a chronic temptation,** pay for purchases with some form of

That attitude creates a false sense of security. Financing a calamity with a credit card that charges 19% or 20% interest lands you in a vicious circle of more debt and little savings. It's equally risky to borrow from your 401(k) or other retirement plan. By taking money out of your retirement fund, you're crippling its ability to grow. And if you lose your job or leave it before you're fully vested in your company's retirement plan (for more on vesting, see page 142), the loan is considered a distribution from the plan, so that you'll end up paying both taxes and a penalty.

But let's face it. The prospect of stockpiling enough cash to cover three to six months' worth of living expenses can deter the most dedicated savers—and it's even tougher if your income is low and you have a lot of debt.

The solution is to aim for a less-daunting alternative, say, a

cash—hard currency, check, or debit card—which limits the trouble you can get into.

6. **If you can't decide between two items** in a store, give yourself a 24-hour cooling-off period before you buy either. Chances are you won't go back. As a bonus, take the money you would have spent and deposit it in your savings account.

7. **If you tend to misplace credit card receipts or forget to record debits,** buy yourself a couple of eye-catching storage bins or baskets into which you can toss the receipts. That simple step will help you get organized; you can sort them out later, and you'll know where to find them.

8. **Don't make yourself crazy trying to track every nickel you spend.**

Estimate what you're spending in certain categories each month, then compare your estimates with your credit card or bank statements to see where your spending is out of line, and where you can cut back.

9. **Get a fun savings bank**—even a decorative glass jar will do—into which you can toss spare change, and watch your money grow. Deposit it eventually in your savings account, or reward yourself with a dinner out or some small splurge.

10. **If you finish paying off a loan or credit card balance,** keep writing the check but send it directly to a savings or investment account (or have the investment company automatically withdraw money from your checking account).

month's worth of expenses. As your income rises, beef up your cash reserve to cover longer periods and reflect any increases in your spending, such as higher rent.

A cash reserve should be your first saving priority, even if it means delaying contributions to a retirement plan. If you have credit card debt, consolidate it at the lowest possible interest rate, stop using the card, and make the minimum monthly payment so that you can use your available cash to build up the equivalent of a month's living expenses. After that, allocate savings toward other goals, such as paying down that debt or opening a retirement account.

Once you have the money saved, keep it where you can get your hands on it. The stock market is far too risky for money earmarked for an emergency. Even a bank certificate of deposit,

# How to Pocket More Cash

If you must shop till you drop, at least don't drop more cash than you have to. Every dollar in your pocket is money in the bank—or your IRA.

**Find fashion for a song** at consignment stores, which accept items from individuals, resell them within a certain time, and then split the proceeds with the consignor. You may be able to find never-worn designer duds for as much as 70% off. Tips: If you see something you really like, buy it promptly, because it won't last. And always shop in a neighborhood better than your own.

**Join the club.** The secret to saving money at warehouse stores such as Costco or Sam's Club is not to get carried away. Bring a list and a calculator, pay cash, and, if possible, forgo the cart. Look for products that have been marked down (though they aren't necessarily advertised as such—at Costco, sale items have prices ending in 77 cents; at Sam's Club the sale tipoff is 91 cents).

**Clear savings** of up to 50% by ordering disposable contact lenses by mail or through the Internet (eg., www.visiondirect.com or www.contacts.com), or by buying them at a warehouse club.

**Tie the knot abroad.** You can plan an overseas wedding for as little as $5,000, compared with the $20,000 average cost of a wedding in the U.S. The $5,000 includes the ceremony and a reception with dinner for 10, plus a consultant's fee. It doesn't include airfare or lodging for you or your guests—but you'll save on the cost of a honeymoon. After all, you're already there.

**Drive a "gently used" car** coming off a short lease. You can get a low-mileage model from upscale manufacturers such as Acura, Jaguar, Volkswagen, and Volvo that comes with warranty protection and costs thousands of dollars less than the new version.

**Fly into and out of airports** that are slightly off the beaten track, such as Baltimore (30 miles from Washington, D.C.) and Burbank (18 miles from Los Angeles). Find such airports on Expedia.com and Orbitz.com, and save hundreds of dollars on your airfare.

**Cut off high-priced long-distance phone charges** with a prepaid calling card from Costco or Sam's Club, or search for a low-cost plan at www.saveonphones.com.

which locks up money for a set period, is too restrictive, because you'll forfeit any interest earned if you withdraw the money early. Essentially, you have two good options for parking your emergency cash: a savings account at a bank or credit union, or a money-market mutual fund. Banks sometimes offer free checking as a perk with their savings accounts, but these typically pay a meager rate of interest. Credit unions generally offer a better deal.

Your best bet is money-market mutual funds, on which the going rate is likely to be higher than a bank's. Money-market funds pool the money deposited in the fund and invest it in forms of debt with short maturities, such as commercial loans and short-term CDs. Unlike bank accounts, money-market funds aren't federally insured, but they're considered extremely safe. On the few occasions when loans in a fund's portfolio have defaulted, the mutual fund company has absorbed any potential losses.

Choose a money-market fund with the best interest rate available, low fees, and a feature that lets you write checks. Most funds restrict the number of checks you can write and set a minimum amount per check—often $500. If the fund does not let you write checks, see whether money can be wired to your checking account in an emergency.

You generally need a minimum of $1,000 to open an account, but funds sometimes let you in for $250 or less.

Search for funds at www.Imoneynet.com, which offers a money-fund search engine that lets you use criteria such as minimums needed to open an account and check-writing requirements.

## 4. *Open a Retirement Account.*

"Saving is never easier than the day you start the job," a financial adviser once told me. Saving is especially important for women because they tend to move in and out of the work force even as they have to plan for a longer life span.

Yet whenever the issue of saving comes up, the response is immediate: How can I save money, especially for retirement, when I barely have enough to make ends meet now? This is a universal refrain that cuts across ages and income groups. The more money you have, it would seem, the more ends you have to meet.

In the OppenheimerFunds survey, fully half the single Gen X women said that at this point in their lives, money is for spending and not saving. Three out of four said it was important to "look successful," and 54% said they were more likely to accumulate 30 pairs of shoes than to accumulate $30,000 in retirement savings.

## Little Things Add Up to a Lot

Consider the case of two young women, Teri and Toni. As soon as Teri gets her first job at age 22, she begins contributing $3,000 a year to an IRA. She makes annual contributions for 9 years. Then, at age 31, with a new home and young children claiming her attention and her income, she stops, letting her money sit in the account.

Toni spends her 20s building her career (and a designer wardrobe to match). At age 31 she gets retirement religion. She begins contributing $3,000 every year to an IRA, and doesn't stop. If both Teri and Toni earn an average annual return of 9%, who will have more money at age 65?

Incredibly, Teri. Even though she stopped contributing after 9 years and $27,000, her kitty will grow to $854,000. Toni, in contrast, who saved $3,000 a year for 34 years, or $102,000 in all, will have only $647,000—a stunning illustration of how compound interest can work its magic if you start saving early (and the best argument I know for diverting part of your clothing budget to retirement savings).

Let me let you in on the dirty little secret of saving: Very few people, no matter what their income or age, have the self-discipline to save on their own. The only way to do it successfully is to have someone do it for you, off the top of your paycheck, so that your earnings don't burn a hole in your pocket.

To fund your emergency cushion, for example, you can arrange for your bank to automatically deduct a certain amount from your pay and deposit it in a savings account. Once you have enough saved to cover at least a month or two of your expenses, think about using regular savings contributions to open a retirement fund.

If you have access at work to a 401(k) retirement plan—or a 403(b), the nonprofit equivalent—take advantage of it. Your employer will automatically deduct the contribution from your pay so that you won't have to think about it. As a bonus, you won't have to pay taxes on the amount of your income that you contribute. And when you invest the money, you won't owe any tax on the investment earnings as they accrue; as a result, your savings will compound and grow faster than if some of the earnings went to pay taxes. In fact, you won't owe taxes at all until you withdraw the money when you retire.

Put in as much as you can, especially if your employer matches your contribution. That's free money—and who among us can afford to turn down free money? Don't worry if you can't afford much at first. Even a small amount can grow into a comfortable kitty, given enough time (see the box at left).

If you don't have access to a 401(k), open a Roth IRA, to which you can contribute as much as $3,000 a year (so long as your income on a single return is less than $95,000). You won't get any tax deduction for your contribution. But, as with a 401(k), you won't owe taxes on your investment earnings as they accrue. And best of all, you won't owe any taxes even when you begin withdrawing money at retirement.

**Assets you won't need for a long time— 10 years or more, or even 5 years or more—should be in the stock market.**

What should you do with all the money you're saving? Assets you won't need for a long time—10 years or more, or even 5 years or more—should be in the stock market. Despite the market's daily ups and downs, stocks and stock mutual funds still promise the highest returns over the long term. As a good basic investment, I recommend a broad stock-market index fund that lets you, in effect, buy a share in virtually every company that's traded. One example is Vanguard's Total Stock Market Index fund (800-635-1511), which has a minimum investment of $3,000 for regular accounts and $1,000 for IRAs; another is TIAA-CREF Equity Index (800-223-1200), with a minimum investment of $1,500 (or $50 a month if you participate in the automatic-purchase plan; for more on such plans, see page 116 of Chapter 6). A broadly based index fund is a good deal even for experienced investors, because it's difficult, if not impossible, to predict which small piece of the market will be the next big winner, or which money manager will consistently be able to turn in a better performance than the market.

"Nobody's smart enough to beat the market except for a few times when they hit it lucky," says Rhonda. Every month she puts 10% of her salary into a 401(k) plan that is almost entirely invested in an index fund. Although she's interested in the stock mar-

## Insurers on the Net

To meet your insurance needs, you can find insurers on the Net at:

- **www.instantquote.com**
- **www.quotesmith.com**
- **www.consumerquote.com**
- **www.masterquote.com**

ket overall, she doesn't keep close enough track of market minutiae to be able to say, as she puts it, "Aha! Fund X is going into a slump because the manager has invested in the petroleum industry because the stocks are cheap, or whatever the reasoning is." With her index fund, says Rhonda, "you know why it's going into a slump because you're reading about the market in the paper."

Over your lifetime, you will have to allocate savings to lots of different purposes—an emergency fund, a new car, a new house, your kids' college education—but always make it a top priority to save for yourself, by funding your own retirement. If you don't take care of yourself, who will?

## 5. Buy Peace-of-Mind Insurance.

Your rainy-day fund can help shelter you from a brief shower, but what if you're swamped by a longer-term financial crisis, such as an illness or a health problem, or an accident that temporarily keeps you from working? You don't need life insurance if you have no dependents who count on your income. But you do need health and disability insurance because *you* depend on your income.

**HEALTH INSURANCE.** Lots of young women can identify with Jessica, who graduated from college and started a new job that did not provide health benefits. On her entry-level salary, she didn't think she could afford to buy health insurance on her own. At first, Jessica got coverage under her parents' policy, which insures adult children for up to 6 months after they graduate from college. But when that coverage expired, she joined the ranks of 20-somethings who are uninsured, and she has lots of company. Nearly one in three young adults between the ages of 18 and 24 has no health insurance—the highest proportion of any age group, according to the U.S. Census Bureau (the rate is about one in four among adults between 25 and 34, the second-largest uninsured group). They're gambling on their youth to keep them in good health. But if you lack insurance, a single accident or unexpected illness could wipe out your savings and put you in debt for years.

Without group coverage through your employer, or during an interim period before your employer's coverage kicks in, you have several options:

**If you're a recent grad,** check to see whether your parents' policy still covers you. Most insurance plans will cover adult children if they are full-time students or until they turn 23.

**Even after your parents' coverage expires,** you may be eligible to extend it for up to 36 months under COBRA (the Consolidated Omnibus Budget Reconciliation Act). You must apply within 60 days of losing coverage, and—here's the kicker—you have to pick up the cost of the premiums, along with a 2% administration fee. But any preexisting conditions would be covered.

*Note:* You can also extend health coverage under COBRA if you lose your job, or if your husband loses his job and you were covered by his insurance. Your employer or insurer can help you with the details.

**If you need insurance for only a limited time**—say, before you start working, during any probationary period as you begin a job, or while you're between jobs—it may be more economical to buy a stopgap health plan, which lasts 1 to 6 months. A couple of insurers—Fortis Health (800-211-1193) and Golden Rule (800-444-8990)—are the leading providers of these plans.

**If you're going to need insurance indefinitely,** say, because you are or expect to be self-employed, it makes sense to bite the bullet and buy an individual policy through an insurance agent or directly from an insurer. You may be able to obtain group coverage through a professional association to which you belong, such as those frequently organized by freelance writing and editing

## Thirty-Something Financial Checkup

Being 35 and still single—with prospects of remaining that way—means you need to consider basic financial issues from a new perspective:

**Your credit.** By this time you've probably got credit cards of your own—possibly too many of them. If you spent your 20s on a buying binge, now's the time to pay down that debt, so that you can put the money toward other things that are becoming more important in your life.

**Your home.** If you have been putting down roots in a job or a geographical location but are still renting an apartment, consider buying a home of your own—primarily as a place to live, but also as a source of tax breaks (to help offset your growing income) and a real estate asset (to help diversify your portfolio).

**Your assets.** You may have acquired lots of things by now—a house or condo, home furnishings, a car, investments, a retirement plan. If you have definite ideas about who should get all that stuff if anything should happen to you, the

only way to make sure your wishes will be carried out is to make a will. In the absence of a will, your state will make the decision for you, in accordance with a hierarchy that goes something like this: your parents, followed by your siblings, your grandparents, and then other relatives. You should also draft a durable power of attorney so that someone else can act on your behalf if you are incapacitated. For a more detailed look at estate planning, see Chapter 4.

**Your parents.** They may still be relatively young themselves, but if it looks as if you would be their primary caregiver, encourage them to look into buying long-term-care insurance (see Chapter 4)—or buy it for them, especially if you have access to coverage as a benefit through your employer.

**Your retirement.** If you didn't start saving in your 20s, you haven't missed the boat. You've still got 30-plus years until you leave the work force—plenty of time to build yourself a comfortable retirement kitty. But start now.

professionals. You can cut costs by raising your deductible (the amount you must pay out of pocket before the insurer will begin to pay on any claims), or by passing up expensive options such as prescription-drug coverage. Even if you skimp on certain types of coverage just to afford the premiums for major medical care, such as an expensive hospital stay, that's far better than having no protection against catastrophe.

**You can also keep your fingers crossed**—or find a new job. That's what Jessica did, switching to an employer that provides health benefits. If you are currently job hunting, be sure to consider the value of any health-insurance benefits when weighing job offers.

**DISABILITY INSURANCE.** Although she doesn't recall its critical events, that day—Memorial Day, 1995—is burned into Deborah's memory. She was enjoying a holiday weekend getaway in Florida with her boyfriend when the SUV in which she was riding flipped over. Deborah wasn't wearing a seat belt. She was thrown from the back seat and broke her neck, rendering her unable to walk and impairing her movement from the waist up (an injury similar to that of actor Christopher Reeve). She was 28 at the time.

Fortunately, Deborah, a lawyer, had a group disability insurance policy through her employer. The policy replaced 60% of her income, up to $5,000 a month, for total disability, and took effect after a 90-day waiting period—a fairly typical policy. It was enough money to pay for her rent and the services of home health aides, but not enough to cover utilities, groceries, or any kind of entertainment. "My parents filled in quite a bit," she says.

Before her accident, Deborah had paid little attention to how she would cover expenses in case of a catastrophe. "I knew I had long-term-disability insurance, and who ever thinks of it?" While many workers, like Deborah, have some coverage through their employer, don't assume that you do. Only about 40% of workers in medium-size and large companies are covered, and even fewer employees of small companies. Women are more likely than men to work for an employer that does not offer coverage. The typical 60% maximum coverage may not include income such as overtime, bonuses, commissions, or pretax contributions to a retirement plan. Even if it does, you'll owe income tax on benefits from a policy purchased by your employer, which could be a big bite.

You'd be wise to supplement an employer-paid policy with disability insurance you've purchased on your own, bringing total coverage to 80% or 90% of take-home pay. But individual policies can cost a lot. See whether your employer will let you buy individual coverage at a group discount. Such policies usually cost 15% to 25% less than individual coverage obtained on your own—and may cost as much as 50% less for women because group policies

## ◉⊐▮▶ Buying a Home Alone

If you're single and thinking about buying a home of your own, the simplest way is to go it alone. Making the purchase with another person—whether it's a parent, sibling, or partner—as a co-buyer raises all sorts of complications regarding such things as who's entitled to tax breaks on mortgage interest, how to dispose of your share of the property, and how to make sure you get your rightful share of the proceeds if the property is sold. If money is an issue, adjust your sights to find a home that fits into your budget. Or buy the home on your own and consider taking in a roommate afterward to help you pay the mortgage. (In that case, however, keep in mind that you will have to qualify for a mortgage based on your own income, not any rental income that you hope to have.)

have unisex rates. (Women are usually charged more than men for individual disability policies.)

In some cases, women are less likely to have disability insurance because they may consider their husbands to be the main provider for the household. However, government statistics show that women who work outside the home are three times as likely as men to miss work because of a disability-related illness (it's mainly because women are more likely to experience pregnancy-related disabilities).

When tragedy struck, Deborah had lots of support systems in place—her family, her employer, and her insurance—and she eventually returned to her job, although with a reduced workload. "Before, I was making a very nice salary for a 28-year-old single woman," she says. "I worked hard, but there was not much I denied myself. Now, I'm making ends meet, but I need all my money. There's no play money there."

# Set for Life

Look at what you have accomplished so far. You have paid off your credit card debt. You have a clean credit record in your own name. You have a rainy-day fund to pay for emergencies. You have a long-term savings plan that will put your assets to work mak-

## Don't Stop Now!

- **Figure** out how much debt you are carrying month to month and look at ways to pay it off.
- **Order** a copy of your credit report and take steps to improve your credit status.
- **Start** or beef up your savings for emergencies and retirement.
- **Purchase** health and disability insurance coverage or reconsider the adequacy of what you have.
- **Look into** buying a home of your own if you haven't already done so and you're reasonably settled.
- **Make** a will or revisit a previously written one. Does it reflect your current situation?

ing money for you automatically—and lay to rest the specter of the bag lady once and for all. You have peace of mind should anything happen to you that makes you physically unable to work.

If you don't feel you can finance all of these strategies all at once, don't worry. Do as much as you can, setting priorities and doling out your money in small parcels, building as you go along. What you can't afford today, put on your to-do list for later (remember, when you write it down, it tends to get done). What's important is that you get a psychological lift, and that you feel comfortable enough to sleep at night. So, for example, if you want to get the credit card monkey off your back, concentrate your resources there until you make a notable dent in what you owe. If you're trying to save for a short-term goal like a new car, feel free to divert some of your retirement funds in that direction. (But please don't stop saving for retirement altogether. Even if you're only putting away 1% of your income, compounding over time can be significant—especially if your employer is matching that 1%.)

The point is that once you have a plan going, you can breathe more freely. Want to splurge on a new outfit? Go ahead. With your debt paid off and your saving on autopilot, you have nothing to feel guilty about. On the contrary, you're well on your way to being set for life. Think single!

# 3

# Getting Married: Opposites Attract

I was once asked to talk about finances to a small group of engaged couples attending a marriage preparation program. As I spoke to the couples and observed them together, I felt as though I were watching a scene from an "Oprah" show focusing on dysfunctional couples. What I saw were three textbook examples of how money and marriage don't necessarily mix well.

One man, Don, expressed annoyance that his fiancée, Louise, spent weekends at the mall shopping with her mother—a colossal waste of time and money, in his opinion. Louise shot back that she had a job, and if she chose to spend her own money, and her Saturdays, at the mall, that was her business. She also pointed out that her shopping didn't cost any more than what Don was spending on his hobby, golf.

Then there were Carlos and Maria. Although they weren't married, they had been together for some time and had two children. Their financial relationship was a traditional one, in which he was the

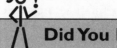

| Did You Know? |
| --- |

More than a third of married women (36%) confess to having kept a secret about money from their husbands, and 42% of married men have kept such a secret from their wives, according to a poll conducted for *Reader's Digest*. What do they hide? The price of something they've bought tops the list, cited by 48% of both women and men.

breadwinner while she stayed home with the kids. He couldn't resist needling her about having no income of her own and complaining that she couldn't seem to run the household on the money he gave her. Maria retorted that she kept the household accounts and knew where every penny was going—and if they didn't have enough to buy everything they wanted, it wasn't her fault.

Sitting on the other side of the room were Peter and Gabrielle, recent immigrants to this country. She was spending a lot of time and money scouting out native markets so that she could re-create the meals he was used to eating at home. But what she considered her thoughtfulness he considered a wasteful extravagance—a revelation that appeared to take her by surprise.

I couldn't help wondering whether any of these couples had a chance of success in marriage, given such obvious differences about money—and, especially, their apparent unwillingness to compromise. It wasn't a question of, "Can these marriages be saved?" but, "Should these marriages take place?"

## Getting Money Out Into the Open

What went on in the room that night is typical of scenes in households all over America. Merging assets and combining money-management styles that often conflict are among the greatest challenges married couples face, yet they're often ignored. In the excitement of preparing for the wedding and figuring out how to pay for it, many couples simply overlook the other financial implications of plighting their troth.

Women often assume that their husbands will think the same way they do, handle money the same way, and have the same goals (and if they don't, we can always change them, right?). Or, concerned about making the marriage work, women are reluctant to address nitty-gritty details that make it seem more like a business relationship than a love match.

The situation is exacerbated by the fact that when it comes to money, as in so many other aspects of our lives, opposites attract. If disagreeing about money were sufficient grounds for ending a relationship, we'd be a nation of celibates. And if you do happen to marry someone whose financial habits are like yours, the two of you will tend to drift in opposite directions.

Pair a couple of spendthrifts, for example, and one will probably take on the role of saver, if only to preserve the family assets. On the surface, one husband and wife I know apparently agree on what constitutes the good life: They own a hillside house with a view, belong to a golf club, and travel abroad whenever they can. But the wife once confided to me that all this spending makes her nervous. "I like to know where my money is coming from, so if I want to buy something, I save for it," she said. "My husband lives closer to the edge. If he wants to buy something, he's willing to borrow. That makes me crazy."

For the sake of keeping peace in the relationship or preserving the marriage, women are often inclined not to make waves. But ignoring fundamental differences can be perilous. Money issues are the leading cause of divorce in the U.S. Marriage counselors tell me they spend the bulk of their time giving financial advice. Even divorce doesn't solve the problem. "Money is the glue that holds couples together, whether they're married or divorced," says one marriage and family therapist. (In fact, divorce may make things worse. See Chapter 8.)

**Getting financial issues out in the open with a husband or husband-to-be is especially critical if you've already taken pains to lay a foundation of financial independence.**

Getting financial issues out in the open with a husband or husband-to-be is especially critical if you've already taken pains to lay a foundation of financial independence as described in Chapter 2. You don't want to jeopardize what you've worked so hard to build, and you want to let your husband know what you've accomplished. The trick is to address the subject in a way that's not threatening either to the relationship or to your own financial well-being—to think single while you're in a relationship.

That doesn't necessarily mean keeping your assets scrupulously separate, or setting out the terms of your marriage in a prenuptial agreement (although it could mean both). At a minimum, it does mean talking about money early on and being willing to compromise. Don't be afraid to take the initiative. Your relationship will be stronger if you make the effort, and so will your finances. If you neglected to have "the talk" before you married, and now you're muddling through financially, it isn't too late. If, heaven forbid, the relationship should end for any reason, you don't want to add financial disaster to emotional trauma.

# Defusing the Hot Spots

Communication and compromise are obviously critical to resolving money disputes with your husband. But you also need some practical money-management techniques to cool off some of the hottest issues:

## Marching to Different Drummers

You want to save for a house, but your husband has his sights set on a new sports car. It's okay to have different goals, so long as you don't assume that your husband's are the same as yours. If you're going to dream, dream out loud, so that you can each adjust your plans. He may have to agree on a less expensive car— and you may have to resign yourself to renting an apartment for a few more years.

Finances are a key element in the premarital counseling program of the Marriage and Family Therapy Clinic at Colorado State University. Couples are asked, for example, to create a budget, both for the immediate future and for five years into the marriage. "That forces them to consider whether they'll be making mortgage payments or supporting a child," says one therapist.

## Spending Too Much

Sometimes a spender is in conflict with a saver, and sometimes two spenders stroll hand in hand to the brink of bankruptcy. In either case, write down your goals—a house, the kids' college education, a trip abroad, early retirement—and work out the numbers to see whether you're on track toward achieving them. (You can use the tools provided in Chapter 1 for this.) Once you see where you stand in dollars and cents, one spouse may be convinced that you need to spend less, or the other may feel more comfortable about spending more.

Mara and Keith, for example, have set up automatic savings plans to pay for their children's college education and for their own retirement. With their savings already put aside, they feel comfortable about spending—even if it's on different things, such as the new bedroom furniture that Mara wanted and the new computer that Keith purchased. "We take turns," says Mara.

Another solution is to allow each of you a slush fund to spend as you wish, with no questions or recriminations. Or agree that on purchases above a certain amount—say, $500 or more—you'll consult with each other before buying impulsively.

## Passing the Buck

Whether by design or default, one spouse generally ends up as the keeper of the books—a situation that can make the book-keeper bitter at being stuck with a thankless task, or make the other spouse resentful about being out of the loop. One financial planner tells of a situation in which a husband had turned over money-management responsibilities to his wife, along with an implied warning: You handle everything, but if anything goes wrong, I'll have something to say about it. "She was really feeling the pressure," says the planner. "It was a challenge even to drag him in to see me, but once he got involved it took all the stress away from her."

Sometimes the solution is as simple as taking turns managing the checkbook, or having regular conversations so that the spouse who doesn't keep the books at least knows what's going on—anything but letting the situation fester.

Finding fault with your spouse's behavior is counterproductive. Olivia Mellan, a Washington, D.C., psychotherapist who specializes in money issues, recommends role reversal as a good way to resolve any financial differences between wives and husbands. Each spouse does something characteristic of the other. A hoarder might indulge in a spur-of-the-moment purchase, for example, or a spender might slip some money into an envelope and put it aside. Then they compare notes and reward themselves (not necessarily with money).

And if all else fails, you can always hire a bookkeeper.

## Taking Risk—or Not

One of you treasures the safety of a bank CD, while the other wants to take a flier on biotech stocks. Often, though not always, it's men who are the risk-takers—sometimes to a fault—perhaps because they feel more confident in their ability to earn back any losses (or

## Golden Rules for Fending Off Fights

For richer or poorer, in good times and bad, it's possible for spouses to avoid, or at least defuse, many of the most common disputes about money by adding the following resolutions to your marriage vows:

**Talk about money openly and matter-of-factly.** Silence is not golden and could lead to unpleasant surprises later.

**Settle the issue of joint versus separate checking accounts.** Either system will work if you both accept it. Or both of you could chip in to fund a third kitty for household expenses.

**Designate which spouse will pay bills, balance the checkbook, and handle investments.** Whether you pool your money or keep separate accounts, someone has to do the financial housekeeping. Know where your money is. Even if your spouse is the numbers whiz, you can't afford to tune out. Touch base periodically so you know how much you owe on your credit cards and how much is in your retirement accounts.

**Don't begrudge your spouse small indulgences.** Each of you should have some money to spend, with no questions asked or explanations required.

**Consult with each other on purchases above, say, $500.** That counts as a big indulgence, and your partner deserves a say in the matter.

**Don't criticize your spouse about money in front of others.** Talk openly, but talk privately.

**Coordinate your responses when your kids ask for something,** so they don't play one parent against the other. If Mom says no, Dad says no.

**Discuss your goals regularly,** preferably at a time when you're not under the gun to solve a money problem. Even when you keep separate accounts, you need to coordinate financial plans—if you hope to retire together.

perhaps because they think that's the macho thing to do).

You can come to terms with different tolerances for risk if you both realize you don't have to put all or nothing on the line. To control an impulsive, even reckless, investor, set a limit on how much he or she can risk—say, 10% of your assets. If you're reluctant to move beyond the safety of a bank, take it one step at a time by investing in a relatively safe blue-chip company instead of an aggressive-growth mutual fund (to become more comfortable with these and other investments, read Chapter 6). If you each have your own IRA or 401(k) tax-favored retirement plan, each of you can decide how to invest your own money there.

If you still can't reach an amicable agreement on the issue of risk, you might seek help from a neutral third party, such as a financial planner, who can recommend appropriate investments to meet your needs and act as a buffer to absorb some of the worry—and any blame.

## Deciding Whether to Pool or Not

Right from the beginning of their marriage, Susan and Shane chose to merge their bank accounts and make joint decisions on how to spend and invest their money. Susan eventually quit her job to stay home and care for their two daughters, but she continued to manage their joint checkbook. Their finances were so intertwined that when Susan eventually opened a small business selling antiques and decorative items, her start-up money came from their joint personal checking account.

Contrast Susan and Shane's approach with that of Debra and David, who employ a separate-but-equal money-management system in their marriage. They maintain two checking accounts, where their paychecks are deposited electronically, and a joint household account to which they contribute regular amounts each month. "We decided early on that what was mine was mine and what was his was his, and we'd split our expenses down the middle," Debra says. "I paid the mortgage since the house was in my name [she had bought it before their marriage], and he reimbursed me for his share. We did the same thing for the utility bills and credit cards."

To pool or not pool? There's no single right answer to that question so long as at least one of you is responsible for paying the bills and you're both comfortable with the system you've chosen. For the sake of convenience, expect to meet each other halfway. It's easier to pay household bills from a joint account, for example. Nowadays, with the tendency for both spouses to be employed when they marry and to continue working, it's understandable if you each want to have a savings or checking account of your own, at least at first, from which you can spend money with no questions asked.

## A Commonsense Budget Tool

For those who want a paper-and-pencil alternative to financial software, *The Budget Kit: The Common Cents Money Management Workbook* (Dearborn Financial; $16.95) is a clearly explained and easy-to-use tool for recording your actual expenses and anticipating future ones month by month. If creating a budget has seemed overwhelming, this is a great place to start—and you can use it at the dining room table.

Avoid slipping into an arrangement in which your husband's income is earmarked for "essential" expenses, such as the mortgage, the car, and life insurance payments, while yours goes to pay for "extras," such as vacations, entertainment, and household furnishings. And don't fall into the pattern of taking over management of day-to-day concerns while your husband makes the big decisions about saving for college and investing for retirement. Even if you maintain separate accounts or take on different tasks, you need common goals and open discussion in order to be full partners. In the event of death or divorce, you don't want to face any nasty surprises—such as finding out that your husband didn't have life insurance, or that you're being audited by the IRS as a result of a tax return that you signed but didn't bother to read. You don't want to have to get up to speed on financial details at a time when your life is in such turmoil. Here's how two couples settled on different solutions to the issue of pooling their resources and setting goals:

■ **Before they married, Cathy and Jack** agreed on a commitment to live debt-free. "You just can't spend more than you have," says Cathy. In the 18 months before their wedding, Jack led a spartan lifestyle so that he could pay $1,000 a month on his student loans—and wipe out that $16,000 debt by the time he and Cathy married. After their marriage, they decided on two major financial goals: purchasing Jack's car when its lease expired and buying a home in a year or two. They even put a rough budget on paper, "but it's not like we examined and reexamined it," says Cathy. Fundamental to their plan was a 10% tithe to their church. That and living expenses came out

www.

## Unusual Wedding Gifts

Looking for a wedding present that's sure not to be duplicated? Think tax software, such as *TaxCut* ($14.95), to help the happy couple celebrate their first tax season together. It's not sexy, but it's right up there with bath towels and dinnerware for usefulness. How about throwing in a tastefully designed file cabinet with at least two drawers, a stack of hanging file folders—and a copy of this book? Think of it as the gift that keeps on giving—potential tax refunds, a well-organized merger, and marital peace.

of a joint checking account, which Cathy managed.

■ **To take the pressure off themselves, Avril and David** sought the help of a third-party adviser after they were married. Because David was in graduate school at the time, "he wanted me to be more conservative," says Avril. "He was right, but I never had to think of a 'we' before." A financial planner helped them set their goals: to buy a home and to have a child within a few years. They also set up a joint household account, but Avril kept a savings account in her name; she continued to work while David was a student, and it was important for her to control money of her own.

Remember, there's no right or wrong way to do these things—just the way you feel comfortable with. If your husband likes to play around with a money-management software program such as *Quicken* but you prefer to work with pencil and paper, don't automatically assume that his way is better. A friend of mine recalls that when her husband started using *Quicken*—before they had kids—she felt completely out of the loop. "I didn't want to sit in front of the computer after my workday," says Jean. "I didn't want to learn how to use the program, and I found the reports overly complicated and not especially helpful. But my husband just loved those pie charts." Then the kids came, and her husband, John, never seemed to have time to enter the data. "We gave up on tracking dollars and cents for awhile," says Jean. "Suffice it to say, that was *not* good." Ultimately, Jean took over the bookkeeping for the family, working in a budget book because "it's simple to use—anywhere—and it's easy to show John where we stand."

## The Credit Rights of Married Women

When you apply for credit, women who are or have been married are protected by a number of provisions in the Equal Credit Opportunity Act:

**If you and your husband apply jointly for credit,** creditors must consider your income, even if it's from a part-time job, in the same way they consider your husband's income to determine how creditworthy you are and how much you can borrow. For instance, if you're applying for a mortgage, the lender must include your income—even if you just work part-time—when calculating how big a loan you can qualify for.

**If you are married and independently creditworthy,** creditors must permit you to open and maintain credit accounts in your maiden name (if you retained it), in your first name and married surname, or combined surname, whichever you prefer. For example, Susan Brown who married James Hanson can get credit as Susan Brown, Susan Hanson, or Susan Brown Hanson. That way, you maintain a separate credit identity and record, which continues even if you become widowed or divorced.

**A creditor can't require you to provide** a co-signature—your husband's, for instance—on your loan or credit account, unless the same requirement is imposed on all similarly qualified applicants—that is, others whose income, existing debt obligations, and credit history are comparable to yours. Thus, if you apply for credit independently, you have to be judged on your own merits.

**When creditors pass along information about your account** to credit bureaus or other agencies, they must report all information on joint accounts in both your name and your husband's if both of you use the account and are liable for it. This practice ensures that both of you build a credit history in the account.

**Creditors can't ask for information about your husband unless** (1) he will be liable for or will use the credit account or loan; (2) you live in a state with community-property laws; (3) you're relying on alimony provided by him as part of the income listed in your credit applications; or (4) you're applying for a student loan. Again, this provision protects your independence in applying for credit. Your application isn't contingent on your husband's income unless it's pertinent.

As Jean's case illustrates, systems of money management can evolve over time as the roles, goals, and dynamics of your marriage change. For example, if you were initially loath to merge your finances but your marriage has developed into a strong relationship, you may feel more comfortable about pooling your funds. After 7 years of marriage, Debra and David, the aggressively independent couple mentioned earlier, finally purchased their dream home—together.

## Handling Credit: Keep Your Distance

When Susan and Shane were first married, they did have "one huge fight" about money, Susan recalls. "It was about Shane's credit card bills. I realized we were probably still paying for dates with his old girlfriends before he met me." Shane had about a dozen credit cards when the couple got married. With Susan's help, he paid off all the balances. They now use one Visa card, which earns frequent-flier miles, for routine purchases, and discuss major outlays in advance—and usually pay the bill in full each month.

Not every credit horror story has such a happy ending. An acquaintance of mine, who happens to be a credit counselor, once confided that she cringed every step of the way when she walked her daughter down the aisle because she knew how much her future son-in-law owed—and how much of her daughter's earnings would have to go toward paying off his debts.

The moral here is that you need to be fully aware of your intended's credit habits and history before you agree to marry. It may sound hopelessly unromantic, but it can be just as important for each prospective spouse to see the other's credit report as it is to take a blood test before you get a marriage license.

If the news is bad, consider the possible consequences of walking down the aisle with someone who has been irresponsible with his (or her) finances. There used to be a motto for women seeking heterosexual mates—"Single, straight, and solvent"—and the advice still goes. If the two of you want to buy a house, for example, a personal bankruptcy, or even a checkered credit report, can kill your chances of getting a mortgage.

In the end, if you are fully aware of someone's financial drawbacks as a mate, believe they can ultimately be overcome, and choose to go through with the marriage, at least use the following strategies to keep your financial lives separate so that your credit record doesn't become entangled with his:

## Keep Your Name?

**Q.** *Rather than take my husband's surname, I decided to keep my own. Will that cause us problems with the IRS when we file a joint return?*
**A.** It shouldn't. The tax form provides separate lines for each spouse's name and social security number.

■ **Make all credit purchases in your own name and with your own accounts.** Depending on the extent of your husband-to-be's credit problems, you could discover that it's easier for you to finance a home as a single woman with a good credit history than as a married couple with your husband's name on the loan application.

■ **Whatever you do, don't add your name to your husband's accounts,** because you become responsible for his debts. So long as you and your husband have separate accounts, your credit rating can't be affected by your husband's failure to meet obligations that are solely his responsibility.

If your husband has good credit, and the two of you intend to make shared purchases together, open a new joint account. Even if the two of you have spotless credit records, it's best to follow the example of Cathy and Jack and pay off all your debts before you marry so that you can start with a clean slate. Then use your card as a convenience rather than as a means of buying things you couldn't otherwise afford. That way, you can pay your bill in full each month and keep your charges from spiraling out of control.

Whether you have individual or joint accounts when you marry, use your maiden name or your first name and new married name—for example, Susan Smith, not Mrs. John Smith. That way, you will continue to build a credit rating in your own name—we'll assume it's a good one, because you've followed the advice in this book—and you'll continue to have access to credit even if something should eventually happen to your husband.

## Paying Taxes: Think Couple

One area in which you don't want to think single is taxes. Despite all the talk about the so-called marriage tax penalty, which could force you to pay more tax together than the two of you paid singly, most couples are better off filing jointly rather than separately. And many couples will actually get a marriage bonus. (Moreover, relief from the marriage tax penalty is on the horizon, but not until 2005, when adjustments will begin to hike the standard deduction for couples.)

Whether matrimony proves for better or for worse on the bottom line of your tax return depends on how much each of you earns. If one of you has little or no income, marriage is sure to cut the family tax bill. But if you and your husband have similar incomes, you're likely to pay more tax as a couple. And the higher your incomes, the more painful the bite.

Although far from romantic, cranking the income tax consequences of marriage into your wedding plans could pay off handsomely. No matter when you get married during a calendar year, Uncle Sam considers you married for the whole year. So, if you're going to be hit by the marriage-tax penalty, consider forgoing that year-end wedding with all the holiday trappings and wait till after New Year's to tie the knot. By postponing the ceremony for just a few weeks, you can enjoy one more year of blissfully unwedded tax bills. And you'll have the whole year ahead before your first joint tax bill comes due.

**While you're filing for a marriage license or taking care of other legal forms, ask your employer for a new W-4 form and adjust your withholding, too.**

While you're filing for a marriage license or taking care of other legal forms, such as changing the name on your driver's license, ask your employer for a new W-4 form and adjust your withholding as well. If each of you has been claiming one exemption, for example, one or both of you might reduce that to zero. That way, more money will be withheld from your salary for taxes during the year and you'll be less likely to have to write a check come April 15.

If you are going to be hard hit by the marriage penalty, you don't have many other options. Legally, you can't continue to file as a single taxpayer. I once received this e-mail from a young woman named Debra: "Suppose that when a couple marries, the woman takes the man's name, except she keeps her maiden name on her W-2 and social security card so they can keep filing their taxes under 'single,' not 'married.' That way they can get the lower tax rate instead of filing jointly, which will cost them more taxes. What are the repercussions of doing this?"

Debra gets credit for some creative accounting, but unfortunately her plan is illegal. The law says that if you are married at the end of a calendar year, you are considered married for tax purposes, giving you a choice only between married filing jointly and married filing separately. Single is not a legal option.

Although legal, filing separately almost never makes sense on the federal tax return, but it can sometimes cut your state tax bill. For federal tax purposes, the rare circumstances in which filing separately can pay off usually involve a husband and wife with similar incomes who, by splitting that income on separate returns, can claim deductions that they wouldn't qualify for on a joint return—as in the case of significant medical bills, for example. Medical expenses are deductible only to the extent that they exceed 7.5% of adjusted gross income. Thus, splitting income on separate returns might squeeze out a bigger medical deduction for one spouse.

But filing separately could cost you many other advantages of filing jointly. On separate returns, for example, you can't claim the child-care credit (which is discussed on page 87 of Chapter 5).

# Saving Marriages

L et's return to the three financially dysfunctional couples I met in the marriage preparation class and reconsider the questions I posed at the beginning of this chapter: Can their marriages be saved—or should they even take place? The answer is yes—if the couples are willing to follow the advice you've just read.

For Don and Louise, who chafe at each other's spending habits, the solution is separate "slush fund" accounts with an agreed-upon amount of money each can spend with no questions asked. But they should have a single account for household expenses, and they should consult with each other about major household purchases above a certain amount.

Carlos and Maria, whose relationship is strained because Carlos, the breadwinner, criticizes Maria for being unable to stay

## Don't Stop Now!

- **Discuss** your financial goals and compare your credit habits—and possibly your credit reports—before you marry.
- **Identify** your money-management styles and agree on some new strategies for handling them that both of you find satisfactory.
- **Track** your spending—whether on paper or electronically—in a way that works for both of you.
- **Pay off** your credit-card debts before you marry so that you can start fresh.
- **Anticipate** the marriage penalty: Adjust your wedding date (if you can) and your withholding.
- **Reverse** your financial roles occasionally so that neither of you is left out of the loop.

within the allowance he gives her, could benefit from role reversal. He should become more familiar with the bills she's struggling to pay. She might consider a part-time job, which would help the family finances and increase her standing in the relationship.

Peter and Gabrielle need to talk more about their goals to make sure they're in the open, and in sync. Gabrielle assumed that Peter would want her to re-create the meals, and the environment, of his home country. If that's not important to him, and apparently it isn't, she'd be better off spending time and money on other goals that have a higher priority with both of them.

In each relationship, communication and mutual respect would go a long way toward making a successful marriage.

# Staying Married: Don't Be a Silent Partner

A greeing on a system to merge your assets and manage your credit should get your marriage off to a good start. Assuming that your union thrives, you'll be faced with more complex financial challenges and decisions: how to acquire assets and pass them on later to meet your financial goals as a couple.

For women, who are often in the position of earning less than their husbands—or even depending on them financially at some point—a big concern is getting their fair share of the property and not being left high, dry, and broke, with children to support, if anything happens to their husband. And, despite that concern, women often by choice or default find themselves out of the loop—in terms of participation in decision-making or knowledge of those decisions.

Let me say right off the bat that in making that observation, it's not my intention to engage in any kind of male-bashing. The marital division of financial labor isn't necessarily sinister, nor does it usually reflect an intentional effort to somehow keep women in their place. From my observations, it's

## Did You Know?

If a husband or wife dies, many of his or her assets will pass directly to the surviving spouse without benefit of a will and will avoid probate—if each spouse has named the other as his or her beneficiary.

just a fact of married life, which men often don't notice and women take for granted.

A typical example is a friend of mine named Julie, a busy, stay-at-home mother of three who decided to go back to school full-time to get a master's degree in education. To give Julie time for her studies, her husband, Dave, had leaped into the breach to help ferry the kids, fix the meals, and handle the family finances. When I mentioned that I was writing this book, Julie, this educated, talented woman accustomed to juggling multiple tasks, looked at me guiltily and said, "I know I should be interested in all that financial stuff, but it's easier to leave it all to Dave."

Often "letting Dave do it" works out just fine. But there's always the chance that you may end up in a situation like Caroline's, unexpectedly widowed at the age of 32. Before Caroline and her husband met, he had named his mother as the beneficiary of his retirement account and had never bothered to change it after marrying. When he died, there was nothing Caroline could do to get access to that money for herself and her young daughter.

The moral: Much as you may love your husband, thinking single means never depending on him alone to plan for your future, or your family's—especially because he isn't necessarily any more financially knowledgeable than you are.

# Stake Out Your Property

If you have assets when you marry, it's smart to keep them in your own name. As you acquire property during your marriage, you'll probably hold much of it jointly with your spouse, but the longer your marriage lasts—and the more financially successful you are—the more it will make sense to split up your assets again.

## How You Hold It

To make sure that you're getting a stake in the property you acquire as a couple—and to keep tabs on what's going on with your finances—pay attention to the way in which you and your husband own property.

First, let's clear up some legalese. What's generally known as "joint ownership" is actually shorthand for two different ways of owning property:

■ **joint tenancy with the right of survivorship, and**
■ **tenancy by the entirety.**

Although joint tenancy is more common, tenancy by the entirety can give you a bit more protection because neither of you can divide the property without the other's consent. Also, the property is protected against your husband's creditors, as long as you didn't also sign the debt. But not every state recognizes tenancy by the entirety (a lawyer can tell you whether yours does).

Both forms of joint ownership provide a survivorship feature that's especially attractive to married couples. If your husband dies, you automatically become sole owner of the property. The property bypasses the legal process of probate—the sometimes costly and time-consuming court-supervised process for settling an estate—avoiding delays and usually trimming the costs of that final accounting process.

Offsetting the advantages are a few potential problems:

> **Though joint ownership is called the poor man's (or woman's) will, or mini estate plan, it is no substitute for a will.**

**For one thing, control of jointly held property is sometimes muddled.** Depending on what's involved, you or your husband may be able to dispose of it without the other's knowledge—as is generally the case with the entire balance of a joint checking or savings account. Or each of you may be hamstrung, unable to sell the property without the other's consent—a situation that can apply to a home or to stocks and bonds.

**Despite what many people think, joint ownership is no substitute for a will.** Sometimes joint ownership is called the poor man's (or woman's) will, or mini estate plan, because it guarantees that the surviving spouse will get the property when the other dies. But you may not want your husband to automatically inherit the property. Say, for example, that you and your husband buy a cottage in the mountains. If you take title as joint owners and you die first, your share disappears and your husband automatically becomes sole owner. That could mean unintentionally disinher-

## Six Things You Both Need to Know

Over the years, most couples cobble together some sort of arrangement for sharing financial information that works for them. But beyond the month-to-month bill-paying and budgeting, there are some important documents that are easy to overlook even though they can affect your long-term finances:

1. **Retirement plans.** Take the time to fully acquaint each other with employer pension plans, 401(k) accounts, IRAs, and social security benefit statements. You need to coordinate them if you hope to retire at approximately the same time.

2. **Credit card documents.** Even if you each have your own credit cards, it pays to know how much you both owe—especially if you're sharing joint checking and savings accounts. It's also wise to keep a record of the account numbers, in case one of you loses your wallet and the accounts must be canceled.

3. **Power of attorney.** If you have assets that you don't own jointly, each of you should have power of attorney for the other, just in case one becomes ill or otherwise unavailable to manage his or her assets.

4. **Wills, trusts, and life insurance.** Your lawyer can keep a copy of your will, and you might want to keep your own copy at home in a fireproof box or safe. But don't lock up wills and insurance documents in a bank's safe-deposit box. The bank may delay access to the documents when one of you dies, which is just when the other partner will need them.

5. **Health insurance policies.** If you and your spouse are covered under different insurance plans, familiarize yourself with any preadmission hoops that you must jump through, in case you have to act on your spouse's behalf.

6. **Business loans.** If one of you owns a business or is a partner in a professional firm, you should both know about any personally guaranteed loans. Household assets could be hit if the business can't repay the loan.

iting someone else, such as a son or daughter.

Also, if the inheriting spouse later dies without a will, the property will be divvied up according to the state's scheme of who should get what.

*Note:* It is possible to co-own property without being joint owners. If you take title as "tenants in common," you and your husband will have the same ownership rights during your lifetimes, but neither of you will have right of survivorship and your will will control what happens to your share of the property if you die. You have the right to pass it along to whomever you name as the beneficiary rather than having your husband inherit it automatically.

**Then there's the tax question.** The tax bill passed by Congress in 2001 will gradually eliminate the federal estate tax by 2010 (though it may be reinstated in 2011). In the meantime, you're entitled to certain tax breaks to minimize the tax if you're affected (the tax-free amount is sufficiently high that most people aren't affected, by the way). But you can't take advantage of those breaks if you hold everything jointly. You'll have to think single, retitling your assets to hold some in your name and some in your husband's (more on this subject a little later in the chapter).

## What's His and What's Hers

You may end up deciding that the best course for you and your husband is a careful mix of joint and individual ownership, depending on the property involved. Especially if your assets are substantial—or if you have specific concerns about taking care of your children or maintaining an equal mix in case the marriage should break up—get help from a lawyer who is well versed in federal estate and local property laws.

**SAVINGS AND CHECKING ACCOUNTS.** As I mentioned earlier, joint household accounts are convenient and make practical sense, although you may want to keep some money in an account of your own if you want to make independent spending decisions.

**YOUR HOME.** The survivorship feature of joint ownership is especially appealing here: If you're living in the house together, you automatically inherit it. That's why it usually makes sense to own your home jointly, especially if you live in a state that recognizes tenancy by the entirety. In contrast to regular joint tenancy, creditors of one spouse can't touch property owned as tenants by the entirety (although creditors of joint debts can). That gives you some protection if, for example, one of you is in a profession with high liability risks, such as doctor or lawyer. Your property won't

## A Note on Community Property

If you live in Arizona, California, Idaho, Louisiana, Nevada, New Mexico, Texas, Washington, or Wisconsin, you have to deal with a special twist to the ownership question. In these states, salaries and assets acquired during the marriage are generally considered community property, which means they are owned 50/50 by each spouse. This can be an important protection (or irritant, depending on your point of view) in case of divorce.

In case of death, community property doesn't carry the right of survivorship; as a result, if your husband dies first you don't automatically assume full ownership. Your husband's half is disposed of by his will, or by the state's rules for people who die without a will.

Community-property states usually permit couples to set up other types of ownership, either separate or joint, if you prefer it for estate or tax purposes. Check on local laws that apply to your circumstances. If you move to a community-property state from another state, or vice versa, be sure to review ownership arrangements and estate plans.

be at risk unless someone is suing both of you.

Also, with tenancy by the entirety, one spouse can't sell the house without the other's consent.

If your estate is large enough to be affected by the estate tax, you might want to steer clear of jointly owning the family home. In such a case, talk with your lawyer about individual ownership for estate planning purposes, as discussed later in this chapter.

**YOUR CAR.** Consider keeping your car and other vehicles in individual names. When you own a car together, one spouse's accident that results in damages in excess of insurance coverage can put other jointly owned property at risk if the other party decides to sue you for the uncovered damages.

**STOCKS AND BONDS.** If you own stock certificates registered in both names, both signatures are required to sell the stocks—which could be either an inconvenience or a protection. Investments that are held in "street name" (the name of your brokerage firm) can generally be dealt with by either of the joint owners without the other's agreement.

As an example of how all this might work in real life, consider the case of Kathleen. Happily married for 22 years, she and her husband own their own home and investment accounts together. But Kathleen, who has three children from a previous marriage, keeps her name alone on money she inherited and on the deed to a cherished oceanfront vacation home that has been in her family for years. "I want to pass that money and the house on to my children," she says. She'll do that by bequeathing the assets in her will. If they were jointly owned, at her death her husband would control who gets what. "I feel secure knowing that what I want to happen will happen," she says.

# Keep It All in the Family

E state planning is a fancy term that means distributing your property and planning for your children and other heirs after your death. Don't make the mistake of thinking about it as something only "rich people" have to worry about. It's true that most people will never have to pay the federal estate tax. In 2003 the estate tax doesn't kick in until you have assets of more than $1 million. That number gradually rises to $3.5 million in 2009, and the tax is scheduled to disappear entirely in 2010, although possibly for just one year. But if you and your spouse add up the value of your house, pension plans, insurance policies, and other assets, you may be closer to the threshold than you think.

And estate planning isn't just about financial assets. If you have children, your wealth is incalculable. It's critical that you specify how the children should be taken care of in your absence, and how your family's finances should be handled on their behalf.

As one lawyer explains it, estate planning is about "the who, what, when, and how":
- **Whom do I love?**
- **What people and organizations do I want to help?**
- **What do I want to have happen if I die, retire, or become disabled?**
- **When do I want to transfer property?**
- **How do I want to accomplish all of that?**

All those questions are important no matter how big your estate is, especially if you have children.

In the heart of every married woman lurks the fear that her husband will die prematurely, leaving her and the kids in desperate financial straits. Yet we're often reluctant to talk about our fear, perhaps worrying that just saying the words will make them a reality. Sometimes we simply assume that our husbands have taken care of things.

Do not assume anything. Talk to your husband about what arrangements both of you should make in the event of his death, or yours. If he's reluctant, try bringing up the subject in a roundabout way by mentioning someone else you may have heard or read about who was left in a difficult situation. Tell him that you know that he'd never want anything like that to happen to you and the kids.

Some husbands go to the other extreme, making plans in the event of their death but neglecting to fill in their wives—possibly as a way of trying to protect them. But you don't want to be left in the dark about any arrangements your husband has made, or be put in the awkward position of having to ask the trustee of his estate for money, like a child asking for an allowance. Be informed, not ignored.

## Life Insurance Made Easy

Start with life insurance, which is the first step in estate planning, even if you don't usually think of it in those terms. The main purpose of life insurance is to take care of the people who depend on you and would suffer financially if you weren't around to provide for them. When you were single, chances are no one would have suffered a serious financial loss as a result of your death, so you didn't need life insurance.

That's still probably true when you marry, especially if each of you continues to work. Besides, you each may already have coverage through your employer. However, if you buy a house together and you're depending on both incomes to pay the mortgage, each of you may need to buy life insurance or beef up your existing policies.

Once you have children, life insurance becomes a priority. Women are particularly vulnerable if they're stay-at-home mothers almost completely dependent on their husband's income. But even working mothers could be at a serious financial disadvantage if they are left to bring up a family alone.

Take the case of Sharon, a stay-at-home mom and the mother of triplets. When her daughters were 18 months old, her husband, Dan, died suddenly. He was only in his 30s— and with all the preparations Sharon and Dan had made for the birth of their triplets, they had not bothered to purchase life insurance. To support her children financially, Sharon was forced to depend on her family and on the fundraising efforts of support groups for parents of multiple children. She was fortunate in having that support available to her. But with life insurance she would have had independence and security, without having to rely on the kindness of strangers.

**To keep things even simpler, buy term life insurance, which is the easiest type to understand and the least expensive kind you can buy.**

For a calculator to figure exactly how much life insurance you need, go to www.Kiplinger.com. Right now, we'll use this rule of thumb: Insurance coverage should equal 5 to 10 times your total household income (including any coverage you have through your employer). To make things simple, let's split the difference and recommend buying insurance equal to about 8 times your annual income.

To keep things even simpler, buy term insurance, which has twin virtues. First, it's the easiest type of insurance to understand— it's pure insurance, with no savings features or complicated (and potentially misleading) projected future values based on the investment of your premiums (the money you pay in). Second, it's the least expensive kind of insurance you can buy. To price policies, go to InsWeb (www.insweb.com) or to www.Vanguard.com. Vanguard, the mutual fund company, sells policies only to its shareholders, but the deals are so good that it may be worth opening an account to get access to low-cost insurance.

Although women are most often the ones who benefit from life insurance, don't underestimate your own importance and value—financial and otherwise—in supporting your family. If you have a paying job outside the home, for example, add together both your income and your spouse's to figure your total need for

## Who Gets What?

Just as important as setting up a will is reviewing the beneficiary designations on insurance policies and on pension and profit-sharing plans, IRAs, 401(k)s, and Keogh plans. Proceeds of life insurance policies and balances in your retirement accounts go to whomever you've named on the beneficiary designation forms; these proceeds and balances are not covered by your will. Failure to update beneficiary designations could put you in the position of Caroline, mentioned earlier, whose husband neglected to name her as the beneficiary of his retirement plan after they married. Instead, his mother got the money.

In addition, property owned as joint tenants with the right of survivorship goes automatically to the surviving joint owner. You can't give it away under your will.

coverage, and then divide it proportionately between individual policies on each spouse.

Even if you are a stay-at-home parent, your loss could be a financial blow to your family if your husband had to hire someone to care for your children, run your household, manage the finances, support him in his business endeavors, or take on any of the innumerable other roles that women often perform in their homes. Your absence could mean a lower family income, a loss of attention to important family business, or a loss of flexibility at the same time that family expenses are rising and your children are growing.

Recalculate your life insurance needs at various points in your life. You may need more coverage, for example, if you have another baby and family expenses increase, or if you decide to return to work and your contribution to household income increases. On the other hand, once your children finish college and are less dependent on your income, you may need less insurance—or none at all.

## *Where There's a Will, There's Security*

The next step in estate planning is writing a will that sets out your plan for how your assets should be distributed and your children should be provided for. If you die without a will—intestate, as lawyers call it—your state's one-size-fits-all plan kicks in, and it may not be tailored to your or your children's needs.

For example, as the surviving spouse, you may get only one-third or one-half of your husband's assets, with the rest going to your children. (A nonmarital partner will get none of her partner's assets.) If your children are minors, a court will supervise you when you spend their money on their behalf. Your children will get their share outright, to do with what they will, when they reach majority, usually at the ripe old age of 18. If you have no children, you'll typically share your husband's estate with his parents and siblings. Perhaps worst of all, if you and your spouse both die, the state decides who will raise your kids, on the basis of a court investigation of potential candidates.

Estate planning lets you call all these shots. You can divide your property just about any way you like. (One exception: A spouse can't be disinherited.) You can name the guardian of your children and design creative trusts to achieve your financial goals for them (see the discussion that follows).

*Note:* When you and your husband draft your wills, I recommend that you not necessarily name each other as executor. If at some point in the future you have to deal with the death of your husband, you will have so much else on your mind that it will be a relief to be able to rely on a family member or trusted friend to take on the duties of executor.

## Your Most Precious Assets: Your Children

Many parents put off writing a will because they see it as a downer—a way to dispose of your assets after death. Think of it instead as a way to protect your most precious assets—your children—if something should happen to you and your husband while the kids are still minors.

Parents are often tempted to rely on informal arrangements—"My sister has agreed to take care of our children if we aren't around." But an ad hoc relationship doesn't have the legal standing of a formal guardianship. Most jurisdictions insist on legal guardianship before an adult can enroll a child in school, obtain nonemergency medical care, or include a child on his or her health insurance plan.

If both you and your husband should die without having formally named a guardian, the courts will decide who's going to

## ✖️⏸️▶ An Evolving Document

Once you've drafted your first will, when you're single or when you marry, don't put it aside and forget about it. It isn't set in stone, and you should review it at any number of critical points in your life, including these:

- **After the birth of each child**
- **As you approach middle age and begin amassing significant assets**
- **If you get divorced**
- **If you remarry**
- **If you retire and move to another state**
- **If your spouse dies**

bring up your kids. And you can't count on your wishes being honored. Even after a court investigation, a judge could choose the one relative you wouldn't want.

Worse, a family battle could ensue. Suppose your husband's brother thinks he'd be an even better guardian than your sister. In the absence of a will naming one or the other, both could make a claim. The cost of a court fight would come out of your estate—that is, your kids' pockets.

Avoid hassles by naming a guardian in your will. You should choose as the so-called *guardian of the person* someone who shares your family values.

Because a minor child can't own much property without supervision—usually not more than $5,000—you should also name a *guardian of the property* who would manage your children's assets. You may choose the same person for both roles, or select someone noted for financial acumen as the property guardian.

In addition to specifying your wishes in a will, don't be shy about leaving a letter or tape on which you give detailed instructions about how you want your children to be brought up.

Here's some guidance on how to select the right person for this very special job:

**Look to your generation.** Many older people lack the stamina and desire to start child-rearing all over again. Seek someone near your own age.

## A Useful Tool

Would you or your loved ones know where to find critical documents in the event of an emergency, death, or disability? We often keep our important records in various places—in file drawers, on the computer, in safe-deposit boxes, or in a shoebox on the closet shelf. The important thing is that you—and those with a need to know—can find them. *Your Family Records Organizer* offers a convenient means of writing down and identifying where important information is located. The *Organizer* comes in either a CD-ROM or print version ($14.95, plus shipping and handling; from the Kiplinger Washington Editors; 800-280-7165, operator #97; www.Kiplinger.com\organizer).

**Stick close to home.** The older the children, the more difficult it will be for them to adjust to new surroundings. Modify your plan, if necessary, once your children reach middle school age, so that they can stay on home turf.

**Name one guardian, not two.** Most people think of couples as a unit, but that's a mistake. One spouse could die, or the couple might get a divorce. Just specify the main person.

**Consult the prospective guardian.** Don't assume that the person you have in mind is prepared to accept the job, or even knows what's involved. Potential guardians need to be fully briefed. And don't forget to choose a backup.

**Consult the kids.** At age 14, a child generally has the right to pick his own guardian, and even young children can have strong opinions and keen observations.

**Split the responsibilities.** If you have a relative who's great with kids but can't handle money, enlist a bank or accountant to be co-trustee, or divvy up the responsibilities altogether, naming one guardian to look after the kids and the other to manage the estate. A divorced parent in particular is sometimes more inclined to choose a separate property guardian because the ex-spouse will typically get custody of the child.

**Revisit the plan.** Circumstances change. What seemed an ideal choice yesterday could be a disaster a year from now. Maybe the aunt you designated is now in ill health or married to someone who is bad news. Review your choices every 3 to 5 years to make sure they still meet your children's needs as they get older.

## The Other Pieces of the Plan

In addition to a will, there are several other key pieces to your estate plan:

**A DURABLE POWER OF ATTORNEY.** In this document, a husband and wife can each name the other to handle financial matters if one of them becomes incapacitated.

**A DURABLE POWER OF ATTORNEY FOR HEALTH CARE** (called health care proxies or health care surrogates in some states). This document gives each of you the right to make medical decisions for the other.

**A LIVING WILL.** You can use this document to spell out your wishes about life-sustaining medical treatment if you become terminally ill and are unable to speak for yourself.

**TRUSTS.** You can also set up a number of different kinds of trusts to carry out your wishes. Among the most common:

**Revocable living trusts.** This is a trust that you set up while you're living, and into which you can transfer assets without actually giving up control of them. You can always revoke the trust, take back the assets, or change the terms of the agreement. One advantage is that property held in a living trust avoids the hassle, delay, and expense that are sometimes (but not always) involved with going through probate.

Some financial gurus love to tout the benefits of living trusts, and they can be valuable in certain situations. For example, an elderly woman worried about becoming incapacitated could turn over management of her assets to a living trust. But these trusts have been greatly oversold. For one thing, assets that are owned jointly with the right of survivorship also avoid probate, as do pension and insurance benefits. If your estate is relatively small and simple, the cost of setting up a living trust, and the paperwork involved, probably isn't worth it. And a living trust won't save you any money on taxes.

**Bypass trusts.** You and your husband can already leave all your property to each other without owing any federal estate taxes (that's called the unlimited marital deduction). But if you, as the surviving spouse, pass the property along to your children upon your death, and your estate is substantial, you could hit a snag. You can shelter $1 million in assets in 2003 (and an increasing amount in future years); any assets above the set amount would be hit with estate taxes.

> If your estate is relatively small and simple, the cost (and paperwork) of setting up a living trust probably isn't worth it. And a living trust won't save you any money on taxes.

As mentioned earlier, most people won't ever have an estate that large. But if you're among the fortunate minority, one way to help your heirs avoid the tax bite is for each spouse to set up a bypass trust worth up to the protected amount, rather than leave all of your property to each other in your wills. Thus, if your husband were to die, $1 million in 2003 (or more in future years) would go to the bypass trust instead of directly to you. At your death, the money in the bypass trust would pass free of estate tax to your children. Meanwhile, if you need money during your lifetime, you can use the income thrown off by that $1 million in the bypass trust for as long as you live. (Just in case the estate tax really does disappear in the future, you could set up the bypass trust to disappear, too.)

Remember that any assets used to fund such a trust must be held individually, rather than jointly. That was a potential problem for Lori and Patrick, who, over more than 20 years of marriage, routinely put assets in both of their names. But the total value of the business Patrick owns, the money in his retirement plans, and their jointly owned house and investment accounts was nearing the estate-tax range. To allow each of them to have a tax-saving trust, they retitled the house and investment accounts in Lori's name.

## Help With Long-Term-Care Insurance

There are so many details to be attended to in choosing long-term-care insurance that you may find it easiest to work with a long-term-care specialist who deals with several insurers and knows whose benefits and prices best match your needs and medical condition. (Companies that offer long-term-care insurance coverage include CAN, Fortis, GE Capital, John Hancock, MetLife, Prudential, Transamerica, and UNUM.)

A couple of good resources:

**The Corporation for Long-Term-Care Certification** (www.ltc-cltc.com) is now offering a professional designation, and its Web site may be useful in helping you find a specialist in your area.

**Weiss Ratings'** *Consumer Guide to Long-Term-Care Insurance* ($49; 800-289-9222; www.weissratings.com) provides a personalized list of many companies' prices and coverage details based on your age and zip code.

**Testamentary trusts.** These trusts take effect after you or your husband dies. They're often set up to hold assets for children, and you can give any instructions you wish about how the money should be used and at what age the kids should get hold of it.

One of the newest wrinkles is a so-called incentive trust, which links payouts to specific actions by the beneficiaries. For example, your son might get a bonus if he earned a graduate degree or started a business. By tying payments to what's important to you and your family, you can exercise some control over your money and motivate family members even after you're gone.

# Long-Term-Care Insurance: A Lifesaver for Women

Although long-term-care insurance is an important part of estate planning for both men and women, it's especially critical for women, who are likely to outlive their husbands. A well-chosen policy that pays for both nursing-home care and at-home care can protect the assets you've spent a lifetime accumulating and buy priceless peace of mind.

As a service representative for the Social Security Administration, Louise comes face to face with the financial devastation that long-term-care costs can cause. With the average cost of a nursing-home stay at $60,000-plus a year and rising, "you can be wiped out even if you save and have a good retirement," says Louise. She and her husband, both in their 50s, pay $285 a month for long-term-care insurance, so that they don't have to earmark part of their nest egg for nursing-home bills.

Scottie, a single woman of 50, has also purchased long-term-care insurance for herself. "There are a lot of single women my age who may not have family they can count on to take care of them," says Scottie. "I feel a lot better knowing I would be covered, and that a long illness is not going to threaten my savings."

## How to Evaluate a Policy

Choosing insurance can be confusing and intimidating, especial-ly because you can custom-design a policy to balance the coverage you would like with the price you're willing to pay. You'll feel more at ease if you know the following key points to consider when evaluating a policy:

**BENEFIT AMOUNT.** Your policy will pay a certain benefit per day of any nursing-home stay. To decide how much coverage you'll need, find out the cost of the nursing homes you'd prefer in your area before choosing your daily rate (recently, the average cost nationwide for a private room was in the neighborhood of $170). If you're buying long-term-care insurance in your 50s or 60s, it's essential to include inflation protection so that your benefit amount is adequate if you do not need the coverage until you're in your 70s or 80s. Buying a 5% compound inflation rider gener-ally doubles the cost of your policy, but it can make a huge differ-ence if and when you need care.

**WAITING PERIOD.** You're usually given a wide range of options— from 0 to 365 days—between the time you enter a nursing home and the time that coverage actually begins. The longer the waiting period, the lower your premium. But in the meantime, you'll have to pay your expenses out of pocket. Because those expenses can be significant, it's usually worth the money to stick with a shorter waiting period and pay a higher premium.

## ❌ **Don't Sign These Prenups**

Women are often the ones who leave the work force to raise children or care for ailing parents, and thus are financially vulnerable in a divorce. Be wary of any prenuptial agreement that:

■ **Offers you a poor settlement** because you are starting the marriage with very little money or assets of your own.

■ **Offers you no income** if the marriage ends.

■ **Sets no time limit;** the agreement should basically disappear after the marriage has survived a certain length of time, say, 5 years.

■ **Involves pressure** on you to sign.

You are probably better off not signing any agreement that includes any of the foregoing items, and clearing up any concerns before you marry. Whatever the issues, don't even attempt a prenup without two lawyers, one for each of you, so that you are confident that you have an unbiased advocate of your own.

**BENEFIT PERIOD.** You can usually choose to have benefits continue for a period from 2 years to an unlimited amount of time. Picking unlimited coverage can eliminate the worry of potentially open-ended nursing-home expenses, but it hikes the premium substantially. Most people need nursing-home care for only 3 to 4 years at most, which tends to be the most common benefit period selected.

**HOME CARE.** Choose a policy that pays as much for home care as for nursing-home care, and includes other care options, such as assisted living. That way, you can afford to remain at home, or on your own, for as long as possible, and won't be obliged to enter a nursing home because you can't afford alternative arrangements.

## When to Buy

It's most cost-effective to begin looking at long-term-care insurance at around age 55. At earlier ages, you may have other demands on your available funds—good health insurance and disability insurance if you're still working, and ample life insurance when family members are depending on your income, not to mention saving for your retirement and your kids' college education. At age 55, expect to pay a long-term-care premium of at least $1,000 a year, payable monthly or annually as long as you keep the policy. Although insurers can't raise premiums on an individual policy once it has been issued, the companies can hike premiums for groups of people, such as all 65-year-olds. Before you buy a policy, ask about the company's history of rate increases.

If you're concerned about rate hikes, consider buying a "10-pay" policy, which means that you'll pay more each year but have to pay premiums for only 10 years. If you're 55 when you buy the insurance, you know you'll be finished paying for the coverage by the time you reach retirement. Not all companies offer this option, and some that do don't offer an absolute guarantee that premiums will be permanently suspended. Ask about those details.

(See also the box on page 70.)

# Special Issues for Second Marriages

Helen and Ronald had been married before, and each had children to support. Although they agreed that marriage is a partnership and felt strongly about combining assets, they weren't ready to merge everything right from the start of their own marriage. For example, they decided to keep their children's college-education funds separate. And they also kept their own children as the beneficiaries of their retirement plans. Because each had already been planning independently for retirement, "neither of us felt a tremendous need to provide for the other," says Helen.

Couples who marry in their 20s may be just starting a Roth IRA. But older newlyweds usually have more assets to protect—perhaps a business, an inheritance, some property received in a divorce, or an investment portfolio. The longer you've been on your own, the more likely it is that your money-management habits have become ingrained and harder to merge. In fact, I know of one woman who, when she remarried after being single for 23 years, agreed with her new husband that they would not hold any of their property jointly.

Older newlyweds, and couples marrying for a second time, also should consider a prenuptial agreement. A prenup is a legally

## Cohabitants' Legal Rights

Couples who aren't married don't have the same legal rights as couples who are. In almost every area of personal finance—estate planning, health care, taxes, insurance, and retirement—such couples need to work a lot harder to end up with the same benefits that married people get automatically. And everything has to be spelled out in writing.

**Estate planning.** A will is critical for unmarried couples. Without one, your partner will not inherit any of your assets, and may not be named the guardian of your children, even if he or she has been helping to raise them. Drafting a durable power of attorney also is important, because unmarried couples will be given less leeway than a husband and wife to make financial decisions for each other.

**Health care.** Spouses usually have some say in making health-care decisions on each other's behalf. But unmarried couples have no such rights without a written health-care proxy, also called a durable power of attorney for health care. This document can not only give your partner authority to make medical decisions if you are incapacitated, but can also specify that your partner be allowed to visit you in the hospital or the emergency room—something that otherwise may not be permitted if visits are limited to immediate family.

**Taxes.** With rare exceptions you must file individual returns. If you and your partner own a home together and split the down payment and mortgage evenly, you're each entitled to half of the deductions for mortgage interest and property taxes. The alternative is to make the most of filing as singles. For instance, one person could make the lion's share of mortgage payments and charitable contributions and itemize deductions at tax time, while the other

enforceable contract between spouses-to-be that spells out what will happen to your property when one of you dies or if there is a divorce. An effective agreement can even incorporate long-term financial goals and objectives in areas such as saving, investing, and retirement. If a couple has written both a prenuptial agreement and a will, when one spouse dies, the prenuptial agreement rules unless the will is more generous.

Whether an agreement makes sense for you depends on how valuable your assets are, what kind they are, and whether you want to protect other people, such as children and grand-

partner takes the standard deduction.

**Insurance.** Unless your employer offers domestic-partner health insurance benefits, you can't add your partner to your coverage as you would a spouse. If you do get coverage for your partner, it's considered a taxable benefit to you (spousal coverage isn't taxable). One thing you can usually do with ease is add your partner to your homeowners or renters insurance—a good idea even if you're just sharing an apartment with someone you aren't personally involved with.

**Retirement.** When a couple is married, a spouse who doesn't work can receive social security benefits based on the other spouse's earnings record. Unmarried couples don't have that option. In some states, social security recognizes common-law marriages if an opposite-sex couple has been together for years, but that's not the case for same-sex couples. It's easy to name your partner as the beneficiary of your IRA, 401(k), or other retirement account that you control. But your company pension plan may not let you name an unmarried partner as a beneficiary.

**Ending the relationship.** In the event you break up, a cohabitation agreement can be even more critical for couples who live together than a prenuptial agreement for married couples. For married couples, there are divorce laws and formulas for alimony, child support, and marital assets, but there are no such laws if an unmarried couple splits. If you don't specify in writing who will get what, you could be in for a nasty court battle.

**For more information** about the legal implications of living together, see *Living Together: A Legal Guide for Unmarried Couples* (Nolo Press).

children. The more you have at stake, the more likely you are to benefit from a prenup.

You're a good candidate for a prenup if:

**Both you and your husband-to-be earn a high salary** and have significant assets that you want to protect.

**You have children from a previous marriage** and want to be sure that they will be taken care of after your death. Even if your children are grown and independent, you probably want to know that they will inherit part, if not all, of your assets and property after your death.

**Your new husband is paying child support** for children from a previous marriage. If your marriage fails, you want to be sure that your assets aren't used for those payments.

**You have agreed to pay for the professional education of your soon-to-be husband** and want to be assured that you will benefit from the income that he will receive in the future. In fact, this might be one situation in which you would want to consider a prenup in a first marriage. A friend of mine who used to work in the student counseling bureau of a big state university once told me that the bureau often counseled the ex-wives of professional students who had used their spouses—and their income—to get through school and then dumped them. (See the box on page 72 for reasons not to sign a prenup.)

A prenup goes hand in hand with other estate-planning strategies discussed in this chapter. In addition, second-time-around marriages have another useful tool: a QTIP trust (short for "qualified terminable-interest property"). If you remarry and would like to be sure that children from your first marriage inherit your property without totally cutting your new husband out of the deal, you can set up a QTIP trust. Should you die, income from the trust and even a portion of the principal could go to your new husband. After he dies, the assets will be distributed to whomever you designate—presumably your children.

When Victoria and David married, each had been wed before, and each had children, a successful career, and an independent financial identity. They drafted an amicable agreement clarifying how their children would fare in case of death or divorce. By using trusts and other legal tools, the agreement spelled out how the children would benefit from property kept by each spouse, as well as from property that Victoria and David accumulated during their marriage.

But the real secret of Victoria's and David's success has been their ability to communicate. "When we were married, I enjoyed his joie de vivre," says Victoria. "But I was more thrifty and he was a spender. Part of what drew us together could later have pushed

## Don't Stop Now!

- **Retitle** property—such as your home, vacation home or car—if you and your husband would benefit from a change in the form of ownership.
- **Review** with your husband your financial documents, including retirement and estate plans, credit-card statements, life- and health-insurance policies, and any business-loan documents.
- **Update** your beneficiaries and your will if you or your husband have experienced a major life event.
- **Get** a will and establish guardianship for your children.
- **Look into** long-term-care insurance for your husband and yourself if you're age 55 or older and haven't already done so.
- **Consider** the pros and cons of a prenuptial agreement if you're embarking on a second marriage (or a first one if you and your husband-to-be have high incomes and substantial assets).

us apart." In addition to the prenup, they decided to hold regular "business" meetings to discuss family financial matters before they reached crisis stage. It worked. After almost two decades, their prenup is still in effect—but it has faded into the background.

# Your Children: A New Financial Challenge

**W**hen Susan and her husband, Chris, planned to start a family, they had a definite timetable: The optimum time was when Susan became fully vested in her employer's profit-sharing plan. When their first child was born, Susan quit her job, took with her a "really generous" payout, and rolled it into an IRA invested in mutual funds. Five years and a second child later, Susan is still a stay-at-home mom—and she still has more money in her retirement fund than her husband, who has been concentrating on saving for the kids' college education.

Like Susan, Debbie left her job after the birth of her first child, took with her a payout from her company retirement plan, and rolled it into an IRA. Unlike Susan's kitty, Debbie's was relatively small. But whenever she and her husband Scott have an extra $100 or so, they toss it into her IRA. "My 401(k) and IRA are larger, so we are intentionally funding hers to try to catch up a little," explains Scott. "The idea is as important as the amount." The account may be small, but, at age 29, Debbie already has about $6,000 in her IRA—not bad for a stay-at-home mother of two in a

## Did You Know?

More than half of mothers with children under 1 year old are in the workforce, as are nearly three-quarters of other mothers.

family that's straining to live on one income.

Susan and Debbie, and their husbands, score big points for having the foresight and the discipline to address the first of several money issues women may face when dealing with their children— the cost of leaving the labor force to take care of them. Overall, women work more intermittently than men: By age 45, full-time working women average 3.2 years less work experience than men, according to the Employment Policy Foundation. That situation takes a cumulative toll on wage increases, job advancement, and retirement savings—not to mention providing less income for the kids' clothes, braces, and college tuition.

Even if a woman chooses to stay in the work force, the family budget will take a hit with the big new expense of providing for child care; the cost of paying for services, such as housecleaning, that may not have been required previously; or the necessity of buying a second vehicle to accommodate the increasing—and conflicting—transportation demands of the family.

In addition to the task of coming up with enough cash to support a growing family, parents face the challenge of passing along money-management skills and sound financial values to their kids—both sons *and* daughters—so that they have the money-smarts it takes to think single and be financially secure throughout their lives.

## Working or Not Working?

When you first marry, it may be pretty easy to continue thinking single. You probably still have your own job, income, and benefits. But once you have children, it's a whole new ballgame, with new obligations, new expenses, new demands on your time, and a new degree of interdependency with your husband. Aside from the psychological upheaval, women are confronted with a major financial decision: Go back to work or stay at home with the kids? When you have children, you will have to balance your finances with your feelings—and don't count on your feelings to remain the same after the children arrive. Even the most career-driven women may find themselves longing to extend that 3-month leave into 3 years. "I wouldn't have listened to anyone who tried to tell me I would experience that feeling," says one high-powered manager. "But then you have that new baby and all of a sudden the last thing in the world you want to do is go back to work." (She eventually cut back to part-time hours.)

But for other women, staying at home is simply not an option. They look at the state of their family's finances, or their husband's job situation, and decide that sacrificing their own employment and income would be too risky. Although the second income often doesn't put all that much more food on the table—taxes and other work-related expenses can consume half or more of a second earner's wages—every little bit helps. And, let's face it, you may simply enjoy being on the job—or at least holding your place in the labor force so that you don't fall behind in training or experience. That same manager admits that her "work" day gives her tremendous satisfaction. "I get to exercise my mind, hone my professional skills, and enjoy my professional relationships, but because I'm working part-time, I also get to be at the front door when my son's bus arrives in the afternoon," she says.

**These days, men marry smart, competitive, ambitious women who bring financial resources to the marriage— resources your husband may not want to lose and may even come to depend on.**

Because your marriage is a partnership, your husband may also have something to say about your decision. He may appreciate a traditional stay-at-home wife—or prefer a modern woman who helps bring home the bacon. These days, men marry smart, competitive, ambitious women who bring financial resources to the marriage—resources your husband may not want to lose and may even come to depend on. Shortly after their first child was born, Stephanie's husband returned to school to get a graduate degree and Stephanie became the primary support of the family. To be closer to home, she quit her job and struck out on her own as a full-time freelance writer— saving herself a daily two-hour commute and $120 a month in parking fees. Both she and her husband (who also does occasional freelance work) had to "work harder and take on extra jobs," and they postponed major purchases, such as moving up to a bigger house. But she didn't begrudge the extra effort. "We look at what we're doing as an investment in our future," said Stephanie.

In contrast, Lila was resentful when her husband, Jake, relied on her full-time income (plus overtime) to let him dabble in a series of commission-based sales jobs that never seemed to pan out. The couple finally sought help from a marriage counselor, who got Jake to agree to stay put long enough to set—and meet—sales goals for himself. That agreement took some of the pressure off Lila and let her cut back on her hours.

Every woman will have to assess her family situation and personal preferences, and some sort of compromise may be in order. But when the dust settles, you will have to decide whether to work or not to work—and each decision has financial consequences.

## To Work

This option has lots of financial pluses—probably reflected in the fact that more than half of mothers with children under 1 year old are in the work force, as are nearly three-quarters of other mothers. Aside from earning extra income for your family, you'll continue to enjoy some degree of financial independence, with your own earnings, insurance coverage, and retirement benefits. In this situation, your biggest financial concern is often how to pay for expensive day care (advice on that comes later in this chapter).

## Not to Work

If this is your decision, you face a couple of important financial challenges. The first is to find a way to avoid becoming totally dependent on your husband. Confronted with the prospect of an extended period outside the labor force, Susan, whom we met at the beginning of this chapter, did a masterly job of laying the groundwork for her own retirement before she left her job.

Just because you're out of the labor force doesn't mean you have to be out of the financial picture. You can easily take on the role of household financial manager—not just the day-to-day job of keeping tabs on the household bills (see Chapter 3 for ideas), but also bigger-picture roles of weaving your family's financial safety net (see Chapter 4) and investing for the future (see Chapter 6).

In fact, one of the advantages of staying home is that, just possibly, one of you will have daylight hours in which to focus on those things. One of the disadvantages of the two-earner household is that, with both people out working, neither has the time or energy to "mind the store," which can result in waste, inefficiency, lack of attention, and missed deadlines. ("The money I've spent on overdue fines at the library," laments one working mom.)

But the biggest financial challenge of staying home is being able to afford it. While working moms wonder, "How can I pay for day care?" stay-at-home moms wonder, "How can we live on only one paycheck?"

# Raising Kids on One Paycheck

If you decide to drop out of the work force at least temporarily, you still have two heads and two pairs of hands, if only one paycheck. From people who have been there, the message is clear: You will be more than compensated in parental job satisfaction, but you'll have to be satisfied with less in the way of material goods.

How do successful one-income families do it? It's not rocket science. They don't splurge on clothes or $40,000 SUVs. They make do with a smaller house instead of trading up. They shy away from debt. They don't take expensive vacations. A big evening on the town means going out for a simple dinner or renting a movie. And, like Susan and Chris, they make some smart financial moves before they quit. "When I was pregnant, we saved almost my entire salary for several months," says Susan. "That money definitely paid off later when we needed it."

## Pare Your Expenses

If you (or your husband, if he will become the caregiving parent) leave your job, some savings will be immediate. You won't need to spend money on a work wardrobe, dry cleaning, lunches out, commuting costs, child care, or take-out dinners. Though you may be loath to give it up, you might cut back on or eliminate the cost of cleaning help. You'll also save money on taxes if you end up in a lower bracket.

"I definitely spend less money on clothes," says Susan. "When I worked, I found I used to shop to relieve stress, and that was a big money hole for me. With kids you can't go into a store at your leisure." Now she shops almost exclusively at consignment stores and thrift shops, where even the kids love to buy toys for a couple of quarters. "Here in California, where people throw everything away, the Salvation Army is like a department store." Another option is to look for bargain books, toys, and clothes for kids at yard sales in upscale neighborhoods.

Some expenses may increase: utilities, if you're at home all day; groceries, if you're doing more home cooking or the children are around for lunch and snack times; or health insurance, if your husband isn't covered through his job.

**Consider your last year as a dual-income family a dress rehearsal. Use your second income to slash debt or increase your savings.**

Depending on your family's priorities, spending less may be as simple as cutting back on entertainment, or as major as moving to a less-expensive house or to an area where the cost of living is lower. "You have to decide what you don't need and what you can't live without," says Susan. "It's too hard to remove all the luxuries from your life." In her family's case, "we like to eat out and take vacations," so they continue to do those things. But they don't go to movies or drive fancy cars, and they "accept everything anyone offers us. We have lots of hand-me-downs."

Consider your last year as a dual-income family a dress rehearsal. Use your primary paycheck to cover the mortgage or rent, groceries, and car expenses. Take the second income and start slashing outstanding debt—or if you don't have any debt, follow Susan and Chris's lead and sock away as much as you can. Put your credit card(s) on ice.

Some things may take a little time to arrange. If you're considering refinancing your mortgage to lower your monthly payment, do it while you're still on the job. It will be easier to qualify with two incomes.

Shift medical coverage for you and the children to your husband's plan at the appropriate time. Some plans may make you wait 30 days to be eligible, so timing is critical.

## Borrow With Discretion

In an emergency, some types of debt are better than others, depending on interest rates and tax consequences. For instance, home-equity loans and lines of credit usually have the most attractive rates, and most people will be able to deduct the interest. But apply before you lose your second income.

Credit cards are the least attractive alternative because their interest rates are so high. And although you can borrow from retirement savings, such as 401(k) plans, that course should be a last resort. You're forgoing earnings potential, and if you fail to repay the loan promptly, you'll have to pay income taxes and a penalty if you're under age 55.

## Tap Your Assets, but Address Reality

This could be the rainy day you've been saving for; both Susan and Chris and Debbie and Scott have had to dip into their savings. Still, it can be tough to draw down your bank account or to sell stocks and mutual funds. "It felt funny to write checks when I wasn't putting any money into the account," says Mary, who left an executive job in human resources to stay at home with her toddler triplets. Mary eventually decided to go back to work part-time as a consultant with an office in her home—and she now feels a lot more secure about her finances.

Sometimes families who cut back to one income really do make financial moves that wouldn't ordinarily be considered smart. They withdraw money from their IRAs. They lean on their credit cards. They skimp on financial safety nets, such as retirement savings and life and disability insurance, because there's no immediate pain. Although those may be short-term options, they carry a lot of long-term risk that only increases as time goes on. And the longer you're out of the work force, the more difficult it is to make up income losses and promotions once you return. "Going from two incomes to one works best if you're doing it for a short period," says one financial adviser. "If it's going to be a permanent decision, then major lifestyle adjustments may be in order."

When Pam quit her job in public relations, she had no idea that 9 years and two children later she and her husband Larry would be living in the same modest Cape Cod house. "We always thought we'd move in a few years to a bigger house, but this is a lifestyle that we chose," says Pam. "We are comfortable; we just don't have all the perks of a two-income family." At their house, the rooms are only partially decorated. A big vacation is a trip to

## A Child's IRA?

**Q.** *I'd like to get a head start on saving for my 5-year-old. Can I open a Roth IRA for her?*

**A.** Not unless she's a super model or a child star. Kids can't open a Roth IRA unless they have earned income from a job—which is unlikely at your daughter's age. *Note:* Money that children receive as an allowance or for doing routine chores around the house does *not* count as earned income.

But once your daughter gets older and has steady employment—whether it's flipping burgers at McDonald's or working at a regular babysitting gig—she can and should open her own Roth IRA.

Grandma and Grandpa's house in Florida. Pam and Larry have just one major credit card and live by Pam's 24-hour rule: "I never buy on impulse. I make myself wait at least 24 hours. You'd be surprised how much money you can save that way."

One year Pam had to choose between a new chair for the living room and a root canal for herself. The root canal won. The next year she got her chair. But she and her husband treat themselves to one "date night" a month at a nice restaurant or a concert.

And Pam's husband still contributes to his retirement plan, which his employer matches. An inheritance from an uncle, invested in stocks and mutual funds, will be used as a college fund for the couple's two young children. If they need emergency cash, they are willing to tap their IRAs early and pay the tax penalty. "At first it was difficult," says Pam. "I felt like it was all Larry's money. Asking him for money made me feel incredibly guilty. But now I see it as our money. His check goes into a joint account, and I pay the bills."

# Taking Advantage of Family-Friendly Tax Breaks

When it comes to raising kids, two heads, two pairs of hands, and two paychecks can give moral and financial support to both husband and wife. But child-care expenses can take a big bite out of the income of two-earner families. On average, families in the U.S. pay about 9% of their income for child care, but in some cases the bill can equal or exceed a family's mortgage payment.

Fortunately, you can get some help in paying those bills from tax breaks, compliments of Uncle Sam. In fact, tax changes scheduled to be phased in over the next few years will increase benefits for families.

## The Child Credit

The child credit, available for each child under age 17 whom you claim as a dependent, is $600 in 2003 and 2004 and will rise to $700 in 2005 and $800 in 2009, before hitting $1,000 in 2010. Remember that a tax credit can be even more valuable than a deduction because it's applied directly to your tax bill to reduce the amount you owe, dollar for dollar. The child credit starts to be phased out when adjusted gross income (AGI) hits $75,000 for single taxpayers and $110,000 for married ones.

## The Child-Care Credit

Not to be confused with the child credit, this tax break is based on what you pay for the care of dependent children under age 13. The size of the credit depends on two things: how much you pay for care and what your adjusted gross income is.

There's a limit on how much of your expenses can qualify for the credit. If you're paying for the care of one child under age 13, the first $3,000 you pay during the year qualifies for the credit. If you're paying for the care of two or more children under age 13, the amount doubles to $6,000. But you cannot claim the entire amount:

- **If your AGI is under $15,000,** your credit is 35% of your expenses, up to the $3,000 or $6,000 cap—so the top credit is $1,050 for one child or $2,100 for two or more.
- **Taxpayers with AGI of more than $43,000** get a 20% credit, or a maximum of $600 for one child and $1,200 for two or more.
- **Taxpayers with incomes between these two figures** get a credit based on a sliding scale.

If you're married, both husband and wife must work in order to be eligible for the credit.

## Tuition or Charitable Contribution?

**Q.** I pay $500 a month for my children to attend a church-sponsored school. On one hand, I understand that this is tuition, which is not deductible. But the money I spend for the school does pass through the church's treasury. Can I deduct this from my taxes?

**A.** Sorry, no. When you make a charitable contribution for which you get something in return (other than an "intangible religious benefit"), your deduction is limited to the amount by which the donation exceeds the fair market value of what you're getting.

In other words, if you're getting an education for your child in return for the money you're giving the church, there's no deduction unless you're contributing more than the tuition.

Just about any type of child care qualifies for the credit. When you send a child to a nursery school or a day-care center while you work, you can use the entire cost in calculating your credit—including meals provided as part of the care. The cost of attending kindergarten can count as well, but not the cost allocated to education for first grade on up, if schooling is part of your day-care arrangement. You can include the cost of before- or after-school care, however. In-home child-care expenses count, too. Even if your child-care provider does housekeeping chores and cooking, the entire salary is considered a qualifying expense as long as those services benefit the child being cared for so that you can work.

You claim the child-care credit on Form 2441, and because it is a credit rather than a deduction, you can get the tax benefit whether or not you itemize deductions.

## Child-Care Reimbursement Plans

Offered by employers as a fringe benefit, these plans are also called set-aside accounts or flexible spending accounts (or flex accounts, for short). With these accounts, you can allocate a certain amount of your salary, up to $5,000 a year, to cover child-care costs. Money that you contribute to the account is exempt from federal income, social security, and medicare taxes, and generally from state income tax as well. (They are the same thing as the dependent-care accounts discussed in Chapter 9, only in this case the dependent is a child rather than an elderly parent.)

To take advantage of a reimbursement account, you have to decide in advance how much of your salary to put into it, and you must forfeit any money left in the account at the end of the year. This use-it-or-lose-it provision sometimes scares parents off, but for predictable expenses such as child care there's little danger of having to forfeit any money. You can file a claim for reimbursement from your account periodically throughout the year to improve your cash flow, or cumulatively at the end of the year. Only about 10% of employees who use a reimbursement account leave money behind, mostly in similar accounts earmarked for medical expenses. And the amounts left behind are generally so small that they're far outweighed by the tax benefits of such an account.

**This use-it-or-lose-it provision sometimes scares parents off, but for predictable expenses such as child care there's little danger of having to forfeit any money.**

If you have a choice between the child-care credit and a child-care reimbursement account at work, it's worth taking the time to see which is the better deal for you. The child-care credit may offer more tax savings for lower-income workers, and it can be used by parents who don't have access to reimbursement accounts.

Funds that go through a reimbursement plan reduce dollar for dollar the maximum amount allowed for the credit—$3,000 if you're paying for the care of one child, $6,000 for two or more. But since under current law you can only put $5,000 into a flex account, you can take advantage of the credit if you have an additional $1,000 in expenses.

# Getting Help With the College Bills

Uncle Sam has also become more generous in helping families foot the bill for college. In fact, you may need a cram course to capitalize on all the tax subsidies available for saving and paying for education.

## State-Sponsored College Savings Plans

Also known as 529 plans (after the section of the tax law that bestows all the breaks), these plans are a boon for college-saving parents (and grandparents). Not only do earnings grow tax-deferred, but they are tax-free when the money is used for qualified college expenses.

In most state plans, you choose from a slate of investment options, such as mutual funds offering a portfolio that is heavy on stocks when your children are young and shifts toward bonds later on. You needn't choose your own state's plan. Most states allow any U.S. resident to open an account, and all states let you use the money at any accredited college in the U.S, plus some foreign institutions. In addition to tax-free earnings, many states ice the cake with a state-tax deduction for their residents' contributions. (For more on 529 plans, go to www.savingforcollege.com.)

You can open a 529 plan with as little as $25. Just be sure to avoid plans with hefty fees that will take a big bite out of a modest contribution. And look for plans that give you a wide range of investment options, including stocks (for younger kids) and more conservative fixed-income choices, such as bonds, if your children are older. (For more help in understanding and evaluating the investment component of a 529 plan, see Chapter 6.)

If money is tight in your household, why not enlist the help of Grandma and Grandpa when they ask you for gift ideas that will grow with your child and outlast the latest fashion craze or must-have videogame?

## Coverdell Education Savings Accounts (ESAs)

Formerly known as education IRAs, these accounts are much more attractive now that you can contribute up to $2,000 a year per beneficiary. With an ESA you can invest in any stock, bond, or mutual fund you wish (you're not limited to a menu of choices, as you are with a 529 plan), and you can use the earnings to pay for private elementary or high school expenses in addition to college costs.

A number of major mutual fund companies have chosen not to offer Coverdell accounts because they're relatively small. But plenty of mutual funds and most brokerage firms do offer them. Here's a list of investment companies where you can get an attractive combination of low account minimums (or none at all) and low fees, if any:

## Using a Roth IRA for College Costs

**Q.** *Can you use Roth IRAs—specifically, the entire balance, including earnings—to pay for college bills?*

**A.** You can withdraw *contributions* you make to a Roth IRA at any time, for any purpose, without having to pay income taxes or a penalty. You can also withdraw *earnings* on a Roth to pay college bills without incurring a *penalty*. But in order to avoid paying *income taxes* on the earnings, you must be over 59¹/₂ and meet the "5-year test"— meaning the Roth has to have been in existence for at least 4 calendar years since the year of your first contribution.

- **A.G. Edwards** (no minimum, $10 annual fee)
- **American Express** (no minimum, $10 annual fee)
- **First Union Securities** (no minimum, no annual fee)
- **Franklin Templeton** (no minimum, $10 annual fee)
- **Janus** ($500 minimum, no annual fee if you add $100 annually)
- **J.P. Morgan Chase** ($100 minimum, no annual fee)
- **T. Rowe Price** (no minimum, $10 annual fee)
- **Charles Schwab** ($500 minimum, no annual fee)
- **Scudder** ($1,000 minimum, no annual fee)

You can contribute to both a 529 plan and an ESA for the same beneficiary in the same year. As with 529 plans, you're subject to a penalty—10% of earnings—if you don't use the money for qualified expenses.

## Prepaid College Tuition Plans

These plans allow parents of children who are three or more years away from attending college to lock in today's tuition for the future, by paying a lump sum or by setting up a monthly payment program. Money in the plans grows in lockstep with annual tuition increases and can be used at any public college or university in the state, or transferred to an accredited in-state or out-of-state private or out-of-state public institution. As with 529 plans, earnings are tax-deferred, distributions for qualified expenses are tax-free, and your contributions may qualify for a state income-tax deduction.

## A Small Start to Investing

**Q.** *My daughter would like to start investing in the stock market with her earnings from babysitting and other jobs, but she doesn't have a lot of money and certainly can't afford to pay high brokerage commissions. Where should she start?*

**A.** Try ShareBuilder (www.sharebuilder.com), which lets you invest small amounts of money in thousands of stocks and dozens of index funds for a modest fee. You can even buy fractional shares of stock. Say you wanted to invest $200 in a stock trading at about $15 a share. You could buy roughly 13 1/3 shares. Another way for kids to invest is to buy stock directly from a company. Hundreds of firms will sell shares to investors, letting you bypass a broker. Fees vary widely, and can be steep. See www.netstockdirect.com for a complete list of companies.

Generally speaking, the return on prepaid plans is low compared with the historic return on stocks when your children are young and you have many years before you'll need the money. But when the economy slows and tax revenues fall, as they did in the early 2000s, states are less inclined to subsidize state colleges and more likely to approve tuition hikes, boosting the return on prepaid plans. In fact, some states, unwilling to bear the investment risk, have been cutting back on these plans.

# Teaching Kids About Money

So much for fitting children into your lives—and your budgets—right now. But what about the future—*their* future? How can you instill in them good financial habits and sound values?

To see how it can be done, let's consider a real family—parents Bob and Renae and their children, Danielle, 17, and Jason, 14. Bob is a high school graduate who worked hard to become the successful vice president of a security company. Because he wants to give Danielle and Jason everything he didn't have growing up, when they ask for money, "I pull out my wallet." Danielle buys gas with a Speedpass (Dad pays the bill), and in one month Jason ran up a tab of almost $200 at McDonald's buying Big Macs and

## Grandma's Inspiration

Lynn Roney is a self-taught investor who passed on the tradition to her granddaughter, Danielle Flythe. One day when 3-year-old Danielle and her Nana were having lunch at McDonald's, Roney told Danielle that she was a part owner of the restaurant. "As a 'wannabe' child, I told her, 'I wannabe a part owner, too,'" recalls Danielle. So her grandmother purchased a few shares of stock for her, and showed her how to monitor the price in the newspaper.

When Danielle was 10, Lynn went a step further and helped start a parent-child investment club with her granddaughter. Under her grandmother's tutelage, Danielle built a personal portfolio of 10 individual stocks and two mutual funds. When Danielle was a teenager, she won the Young Investor essay contest, sponsored by the Liberty Young Investor mutual fund, with a paean to her Nana as a successful investor. "Three rules I think every investor should follow," Danielle wrote, "are to start investing early; teach your kids (it's never too early since we are consumers); and contribute to your investments on a regular basis and reinvest your dividends."

McFlurries with a Speedpass (which automatically charged the food to Dad's account).

Bob's freewheeling financial habits were causing friction with Renae, who wanted the family to "act more like a unit and be accountable for the money we spend." But she didn't like playing the role of bad cop.

I met the family when we were all guests on the *Oprah Winfrey Show*. Bob and Renae were looking for advice on how to impose some fiscal discipline on their kids, and I was asked to provide it. What struck me was that in many ways they were a typical American family: financially comfortable, if not wealthy, and eager to spend money on their children—but worried about giving them too much of the good life. As in other families, the kids needed limits, and their parents needed a simple way to set them.

## An Eye-Opening Experience

We started by going through a hands-on exercise to show Danielle and Jason (and Bob and Renae, too) how much money was com-

# What Kids Need to Know—and When

There's no point in overloading your children with financial information they can't understand. When it comes to money, as with everything else you discuss with your kids, your role is to answer their questions in an honest and age-appropriate way, and to build on the foundation you lay when they're young.

**Five things 5-year-olds need to know:**
1. A dime is worth more than a nickel, even though it's smaller.
2. Coins can be exchanged for other good stuff.
3. The toys they see on TV won't look as flashy, or work as well, at home.
4. Saving money can be fun when they can use the money to buy something later.
5. They will not get everything they ask for.

**Five things 10-year-olds need to know:**
1. They will have to pay for their own trading cards, movie tickets, snacks, and other expenses out of their allowance.
2. They will not get an advance on their allowance.
3. They should be able to navigate a supermarket with a cart and a list, and bring home a bargain or two.
4. They should have a savings account in a real bank—and they should learn that although they can withdraw their money, it won't be the same cash and coins they put in. (That's a common misconception kids have.)
5. They will not get everything they ask for.

**Five things 16-year-olds need to know:**
1. They will have to pay for their own gasoline and clothing out of separate allowances for gas and clothes—and earn extra money if they want to buy more.
2. They should have a reasonable idea of your family's finances and realistic expectations for college, so that they know how much you can afford to pay and how much they will have to contribute—and can choose colleges accordingly.
3. They should know how to write a check and balance a checking account.
4. They should save half of everything they earn from a job for major high school expenses, such as a class ring or class trip, or for college.
5. They will not get everything they ask for.

ing in every month and where it was going. Sitting around the kitchen table, the kids got stacks of play money representing Bob's monthly take-home pay. Danielle, who had thought she knew her parents' income, wanted to know why there wasn't more cash. That got her father talking about tax withholding (the kids were suitably shocked by how much the federal and state governments take) and his monthly contributions to his 401(k) plan.

Bob and Renae, a stay-at-home mom, had a stack of their own—the family's actual monthly bills, which the kids proceeded to "pay" with the play money. The mortgage payment was far more than the "few hundred dollars" Danielle had expected, and Jason was floored by the credit card bills: "You bought all that stuff at Wal-Mart?" Jason liked the idea of making just the minimum credit card payment, but his parents explained that at that rate they'd never pay off the bill.

When all the bills were covered, Renae gathered up the $500 remaining on the table. "That's for groceries," she told the wide-eyed kids. "Where do we get money to buy *our* stuff?" Jason wanted to know.

## Hidden Expenses

Because so many of their own expenses were buried in those credit card balances, the kids didn't have a clue about how much "their stuff" actually cost. "Danielle will buy two pairs of jeans online and then complain that she has nothing to wear," said Renae. Instead of having unlimited access to credit cards and Speedpasses, the kids needed to learn how to manage separate cash allowances for gas (in Danielle's case), clothing, and basic expenses.

Bob and Renae had already discussed giving the kids a clothing allowance, but had abandoned the idea when they couldn't agree on a figure. Bob had proposed $1,000 a year per child, and Renae had countered with $200. I suggested $200 for each child twice a year, in the spring and fall, and they thought that sounded reasonable.

Another source of family tension was Renae's car, which Danielle was driving while her parents paid for the gas. Danielle figured that was fair because she helped run errands. But a car isn't an entitlement; it's a convenience. If Mom and Dad are already paying for insurance and maintenance, the least that kids can do is cover

## Different Strokes

**Q.** *We're doing our best to teach our two children how to be financially responsible, but they have very different habits. Our daughter likes to save her money, and our son spends his as fast as he gets his hands on it. Are we doing something wrong?*

**A.** You're doing just fine. No single formula for raising financially responsible children will work for every family, or for every child within a family. Parents should listen to what other families have done successfully, and then choose strategies that make sense for you.

Within a household, I've found that kids who tend to be well organized in general—keeping their rooms reasonably neat and getting their homework done on time, for example—also tend to be more organized with money than their free-spirited siblings. And this isn't a sexist thing; boys and girls can fall into either category.

But it's worth making the effort with all your children. If they all have to put aside part of their allowance to buy the things they want, the child who's most inclined to save may end up with the biggest kitty, but each will learn that thrift is important.

And eventually the lesson may sink in. When the free spirit grows up and starts a business, he or she will at least know enough to hire a good accountant.

the gas. And at 17, Danielle was old enough to earn money of her own. Until she did, her parents could replace the Speedpass with a weekly gas allowance of, say, the cost of a fill-up. Danielle didn't balk at the figure, but, her mother confided, "she's in for a surprise. She doesn't realize she's been spending twice that much."

Jason, meanwhile, was horrified at the prospect of getting a base allowance equal to half his age—$7 a week. "A movie and refreshments cost $14," he protested. I explained that his parents could use that as a guideline and adjust it up (or down), but they didn't have an obligation to cover all his expenses. Besides, he didn't have to go to a movie every week, and he could cut his food costs in half by sticking to a soft drink (with free refills).

## Work Incentives

It's important for kids to take responsibility for some of their own

## Don't Stop Now!

- **Revisit** your financial plan if you're thinking of having a baby, and increase your savings now to give you the financial flexibility you may want later.
- **Don't take** an all-or-nothing approach to work. Instead, investigate alternatives such as working part-time or staggering mom's and dad's work schedules so that one parent can be home with the baby.
- **Call** your benefits department for information about child-care reimbursement plans and be sure to claim any tax credits available to you after the baby comes.
- **Pass along** to your daughters and sons the financial knowledge and sense of personal responsibility you've gained by learning to "think single."
- **Sit down and talk** with your husband to find some common ground if you differ in your expectations for your children regarding money.

expenses so that they can make choices about how to save and spend their money. That responsibility also gives them an incentive to supplement their base allowance by working for pay, either at a regular job or around the house. (Don't pay for everyday chores, but for extra jobs, such as mowing the lawn, that you might hire someone else to do.)

Making the system work requires a certain amount of discipline, something Bob and Renae had struggled with in the past. I suggested that they keep things simple by giving the allowance monthly, instead of weekly, and noting on the calendar when the money had been paid, to avoid disputes—and advances.

With rules to fall back on, the whole family would know what's expected, and Bob and Renae could speak with one voice. "Now they'll know I'm not just being mean," said Renae. Bob "learned a lot" from our exercise, but admitted it would be tough for him to stop "sending a signal that Dad will take care of everything."

Regardless of how old your kids are, your ultimate aim is to turn out independent adults who know how to manage money and have a healthy regard for what it can, and can't, buy. That's as important for daughters as it is for sons. Giving your daughter a smaller allowance than her brother, for example, because "she doesn't need the money as much," or, at the other extreme, indulging her because she's "our little princess," sends the signal that parents—or someone else—will always be there to take care of her. And we've just spent several chapters demonstrating why she should never count on that. Think single. Be independent.

# 6

# Investing: Ways to Meet Your Financial Goals

 **W** hen the stock market plummeted in 2000–01, *USA Today* interviewed a half-dozen investors who had managed to weather the downturn with minimal damage to their portfolios. One investor, Karl, gave full credit to his wife, Joanne. Early in 2000, Joanne had become concerned about the upcoming presidential election. She was also worried that the economic boom couldn't go on forever, and that the stock market could not keep skyrocketing. "As a good husband," said Karl, he heeded her concerns and moved a portion of their stock market investments into safer bonds, which "helped stanch the bleeding" when the market fell. "I'm delighted," said Karl. "Makes you glad you stuck together for 49 years."

Here was a husband who not only listened to his wife on the subject of investing but had the good grace to admit that she was right. And here was a wife who had had a gut feeling and wasn't afraid to go with it.

Judging by the number of press releases that come across my desk, few areas of personal finance have been dissected as thoroughly over the

**Did You Know?**

Even though they express less confidence in their investing ability, women investors often outperform men, largely because they trade less frequently.

## Financial Insecurity

Even among wealthy individuals—those with assets of at least $500,000 to invest—women feel less financially secure than men, and are less prone to attribute their success to their own savvy investing. In a survey by HNW Inc., 29% of the wealthy women interviewed said that they would need more than $50 million in the bank to feel financially secure, compared with just 4% of the wealthy men interviewed. Among the men, 50% said that they had earned their fortune through smart investments; among the women, the comparable figure was 43%.

past decade as the attitude of women toward money in general and investing in particular. The results tend to be remarkably consistent: Far more women than men express a lack of confidence in their ability to invest, which causes the women not to invest at all or to invest too conservatively. In the Women Cents Study, conducted by the National Center for Women and Retirement Research, more than 70% of the respondents said that lack of knowledge about investing is a significant obstacle for them, and more than half said that they put off financial decisions for fear of making a mistake. When they do put money away, 72% choose investments that provide only marginal returns.

The reason is that women tend to be "present thinkers," according to the study, providing for their families' immediate needs and wants, and balancing all the elements of day-to-day life—"multitasking," in popular parlance. They are so busy coping with present needs that they don't always give enough thought to the future. When they do save, it's likely to be for short-term goals, such as a vacation or an appliance, rather than for their own retirement.

Personal experience also plays a big part. As noted in earlier chapters: Women still earn less then men, on average, and work more intermittently. By age 45, full-time working women average 3.2 years less work experience than men, according to the Employment Policy Foundation. For better or worse, women who marry are to some degree dependent on their husbands for their financial security—a risky business in itself when you consider that about 40% of current marriages will end in divorce, and the average age for widowhood among women in first marriages in the U.S. is 58.

No wonder women feel insecure about the future—and are reluctant to risk what resources they have. One of the most striking analyses I've read involves the "bag lady syndrome," as perceived differently by men and women. When a man sees a homeless person, for instance, he's more likely to take a detached view and point out the differences between himself and the homeless person. "I wonder how he got that way," a man might ask himself. A woman, in contrast, looks at the homeless person and thinks, "That could be me someday." One reason for the dramatically different reactions is that men are far more likely than women to feel that they have control over their financial lives, according to the Dreyfus Gender Investment Comparison Survey.

# Women Make Better Investors

As noted in the first chapter, there's no money gene that gives men an edge in financial matters. They're simply more accustomed by culture to dealing with finances, or—what I suspect is just as likely—more inclined to talk as if they know what they're doing even when they don't. As women become more experienced, they also become more confident. The National Center for Women and Retirement Research has picked up a "radical transformation" in women's attitudes toward money and investing since the 1980s. In the Women Cents survey, for example, more than 94% of the sample "mostly" or "strongly" agreed with the statement that "when it comes to money and investing, women can be just as capable as men."

Actually, they can be *more* capable than men. Lack of confidence does not mean lack of competence. In a study of investors at a large discount-brokerage firm during the 1990s, Brad M. Barber and Terrance Odean of the University of California at Davis found that women investors outperformed their male counterparts, earning 1.4 percentage points more each year on a risk-adjusted basis.

What's their secret? Just as women drivers are more likely than men to ask for directions when they're lost, women investors are more likely to do research before they make an investment deci-

## Invest or Pay Off Debt?

**Q.** *My husband recently received an inheritance that is well under $15,000, and he wants to dump it all into the stock market. Here is the problem: Our annual household income is between $40,000 and $50,000, we have $20,000 in credit card debt, we live from paycheck to paycheck, and furthermore, we just put a down payment on a $20,000 vehicle that will take forever to pay off. Do you advise dumping the entire inheritance into the stock market, or do you advise something else? I feel this is a disastrous choice on my husband's part.*

**A.** I agree this could be a disastrous choice, especially if your husband's notion of "dumping the money into the stock market" means taking a big risk on a single "sure thing" that you may never have heard of—not so farfetched, given your family's financial history. Also, you could earn a much better return—equivalent to the 18% or more in credit-card interest charges that you may be racking up—by paying off some of that credit card debt.

At the same time, if you're living paycheck to paycheck, you probably don't have anything set aside in savings, and you don't want to miss an opportunity to take advantage of this windfall, however small it may be. All in all, that's a lot of pressure on a single inheritance of "well under $15,000."

I'd recommend starting a savings kitty by putting, say, $3,000 to $5,000 either in a bank or money-market fund, which would give you access to your cash in an emergency. Put the rest toward your credit card balances and then tear up your cards, or at least put them on ice until the rest of the balance is paid off. If it's possible, get rid of that $20,000 vehicle and buy a used one, or get along with your old car. If you still feel your debts are out of control, see a credit counselor. Once your debts are paid off, you can take the money that would have been going to credit card payments and put it into the stock market.

sion, rather than to gamble on a highflier. Once they decide on a stock, they're more likely to stick with it. They trade less often, Barber and Odean found, and the less often you trade the better your returns will be, because trading costs money, in the form of commissions you pay brokers. Men actually traded 45% more than women—a result that Barber and Odean attributed to over-confidence.

At the extreme, men are much more likely to be seduced by the market and to end up cheating their wives and children by raiding the family savings to support their trading habit. An acquaintance of mine has admitted that he became so obsessed with trading stocks during the technology bubble of the late 1990s that, like a desperate suitor, he borrowed against the ever-dwindling value of his securities, took out cash advances on his credit card, and raided his family's emergency savings and his kids' college fund in a desperate attempt to recover from his losses when the market turned against him. In the end, it was "unrelenting pressure from my wife to get our finances back in order" that ended the affair—although he acknowledges he is a trading addict prone to backsliding. Financially, he gained nothing during the great bull market of the '90s. "The only winner I can identify is my brokerage firm, which made it easy for me to borrow, and rewarded me [with discounted commissions] for stepping up my level of trading."

**Women investors are more likely to do research before they decide on an investment, rather than to gamble on a highflier. Once they decide on a stock, they're more likely to stick with it.**

Fortunately, only about 15% of investors develop an addiction that's akin to gambling, according to estimates by the Council on Compulsive Gambling of New Jersey. Most of them are white-collar professional men with above-average intelligence and an "inflated sense of themselves," says one psychologist. Women, at the other extreme, are often portrayed as financially impaired, unable to understand the most basic financial concepts without having them watered down or sugar-coated. One investment Web site for women featured a financial horoscope. A female financial planner whom I know says she almost walked out of an investment seminar that reminded her of a Tupperware party. Another women-oriented Web site offered a money-back guarantee, letting its brokerage customers sell back their shares commission-free within 30 days—assuming, perhaps, that women would be reassured because they are prone to change their minds or suffer buyer's remorse.

In reality, precisely the opposite is true. Far from being fickle, women are such loyal investors that when the market fell in 2001, 70% of the women responding to a survey on the Women's Financial Network (www.wfn.com) said that the market's behavior had not had any bearing on their decision to buy or sell stocks.

In a survey sponsored by *Microsoft Money,* more women than men described themselves as "bargain hunters," while more men than women described themselves as "risk-takers." That difference suggests that women set out to reach financial goals through practical strategies, whereas men are more inclined to take their chances when they invest and hope to hit it big.

The difference also suggests that, working together, men and women make a socko investment team—and that provides yet another reason why, if you're married, you shouldn't leave all the investment decisions to your husband. The two of you complement each other, enhancing your strengths and compensating for weaknesses.

Take the case of Donna, a stay-at-home mom who handles the family finances, including the finances for an auto repair business that she and her husband, Bob, own. When Bob comes home from work, he takes care of the kids so that Donna can do all her paperwork. They also handle their investments as a team. Bob is the conservative partner; because of his influence, they keep half of their assets in safe bank accounts. Donna is in charge of stock market investments. "She's up on what's going on, and I'm not," says Bob. Donna belongs to an investment club, and spends her free time doing research on stocks and reading mutual fund prospectuses. "It's almost a hobby," she says. "While some people knit or crochet, I research stocks."

## Stocks Are Gender-Neutral

Market research indicates that there's a great Mars-versus-Venus divide when men and women discuss and purchase investment products. When a man tells a financial adviser, "I want to think about it," he usually means, "I don't want it." But when a woman says she wants to think about something, she really means it. When a man asks, "How am I doing?" he usually wants to know his bottom-line investment return versus some outside benchmark—not unlike the sports statistics approach. But women measure their investment performance in terms of progress toward meeting some future goal, such as a child's education or their own retirement. Overall, product information and customer service are more important to women, and financial professionals who don't provide it risk losing women as customers.

Although men and women talk about investments in different terms, investments themselves don't discriminate. Stocks, bonds, and mutual funds are gender-neutral. They work exactly the same way no matter who owns them. If you know how to use them, you can make them work in your favor. Knowledge is power.

Instead of running through a laundry list of investments, most of which you don't need, I'm going to give you the product information you need about investments as people really use them—or should use them—to help you reach your goals within a certain period of time. Goals are divided into short-term and long-term, with 5 years as the dividing line. The further away your goal, the greater the risk you can afford to take with your investments—and the greater your potential reward.

> **Overall, product information and customer service are more important to women than to men; financial professionals who don't provide it risk losing women as customers.**

## Invest for the Short Term

A short-term goal is anything you want to do, buy, or spend money on in fewer than 5 years. Maybe you want to buy a car or a house, or take a vacation. Creating emergency savings would certainly fall into the category of a short-term goal. So, for that matter, would setting aside money for your child's college tuition if the child is in high school and will start college in a year or two. The hallmark of short-term investing is to keep your money liquid—meaning that you can get your hands on it quickly and without penalty if you need it—and to keep it safe. Because you're

## Is It Time for You to Bank Online?

Imagine the convenience of doing your banking from your home computer after putting the children down for a nap, eliminating the need for a stop at the bank while you're running errands around town. If your paycheck is already deposited automatically and you generally use ATMs to get cash, you're halfway there. It may be time to ditch your bricks-and-mortar bank for an Internet bank.

Internet banks are getting better, offering more convenient and cost-effective products and more user-friendly Web sites. You may find that you're able to consolidate all of your financial activities—checking, savings, brokerage needs, an auto loan, and even a mortgage—into a single online summary page.

When evaluating an online bank, look for these features: the ability to open an account with a credit card; reimbursement for fees you accumulate at other banks' ATMs, up to a certain number of transactions or amount per month; automatic deposit of your pay-check; ability to deposit other checks or money orders by mail, at certain ATMs (which you can locate online), by wire, or at branches for bricks-and-mortar banks; free online bill paying; interest-bearing checking accounts; and the ability to download information directly to *Quicken* and *Microsoft Money*.

Some well-regarded online banks are:

- **Citibank** (www.citibank.com; 800-374-9700)
- **First Internet Bank of Indiana** (www.firstib.com; 888-873-3424)
- **NetBank** (www.netbank.com; 888-256-6932)
- **Bank of America** (www.bankof america.com; 800-932-2265)
- **Bank One Corp.** (www.bankone.com; 800-482-3675)
- **ING Direct** (ingdirect.com; 800-464-3473)
- **DeepGreen Bank** (www.deepgreenbank.com; 888-576-9238)
- **Ascencia Bank** (www.ascenciabank.com; 877-369-2265)

not taking much risk, your reward—in the form of the interest you earn—will be fairly low, and that's okay. But there are smart ways to boost your earnings without taking too much of a chance. Several types of investments fill the bill:

## Garden-Variety Bank Savings Accounts

You won't get rich on the interest you earn, especially recently, but savings accounts are convenient and the money is safe as long as it's insured by the Federal Deposit Insurance Corp. (FDIC) or the National Credit Union Administration. *Note:* As mentioned in Chapter 2, credit unions generally offer a higher rate of interest than banks.

## Bank Certificates of Deposit (CDs)

These pay a higher rate of interest than a regular savings account, but in return you'll have to tie up your money for a certain period of time—most commonly 6 months, 1 year, 2 years, or 5 years. If you withdraw your money early, you'll pay a penalty. CDs generally require a minimum deposit of at least several hundred dollars. The more you deposit and the longer the term of the CD, the higher the rate of interest you can earn. Internet banks (see the box at left) are fertile territory for CDs with interest rates that are substantially higher than average.

CDs are particularly useful if you know exactly when you'll need your money and how much you'll need. You can also ladder, or stagger, CDs to come due and make your funds available at regular intervals.

## Money-Market Mutual Funds

To get the best interest rate on a short-term deposit, money-market mutual funds are generally the place to be. Instead of investing in stocks, these mutual funds invest in the "money market," which is a collective name that describes all the different ways in which governments, banks, and corporations borrow and lend money for short periods of time. The interest rate changes every day, but it's typically higher than that on bank accounts, especially when rates are rising. And, in contrast to a CD, you can get your money whenever you want it, as long as the fund has a feature that lets you write checks.

Because most funds set a minimum amount per check—often $500—this isn't a substitute for a regular checking account. And you generally need a minimum of $1,000 to open an account, although some funds will let you in for several hundred dollars or less. (To find funds that meet your needs, go to www.iMoneynet .com, a provider of data on money-market funds.) But if you have already saved several thousand dollars for a specific goal—say, the down payment on a house—a money-market fund can give

## ⊗⊐⊪ More Risk, More Return

Let's say that, at age 35, you invest $10,000 in an account that returns 5% a year, or roughly the long-term annual return on bonds. In 30 years, just in time for retirement, you'd have a tad over $43,000 (not accounting for the effects of any taxes). If you invest the same $10,000 in an account that returns 10% a year, roughly the long-term annual return on stocks, you would have nearly $175,000 after 30 years. At twice the yield, your kitty is four times bigger.

you the ideal combination of yield and liquidity.

Money-market funds are not insured, but they're considered one of the safest uninsured investments around. As mentioned in Chapter 2, on the few occasions when loans in a fund's portfolio have defaulted, the mutual fund company running the fund has absorbed any potential losses.

## Short-Term Bond Funds

These funds put their money into the same types of investments as money-market funds, but they look for slightly longer maturities. That way, you can earn a slightly higher return, especially when rates are low, without taking on too much additional risk.

## Treasury Bills

The U.S. government borrows money by issuing IOUs known as government, or Treasury, securities. They can't be matched for safety, because they're backed by the federal government. The shortest-term securities the government offers are Treasury bills, or T-bills. They usually mature in 3 to 6 months, and the minimum purchase is $1,000. In addition to their safety, T-bills, along with other Treasury securities, have another attraction: Your earnings from them are exempt from state and local taxes. You can buy them by phone at 800-943-6834, or online at www .publicdebt.treas.gov. There is a deeper discussion of bonds later in this chapter.

# Invest for the Long Term

For investment purposes, a long-term goal is anything that you want to do, buy, or spend money on more than 5 years into the future. Of course, "long-term" is relative. Within that time frame you can have medium-term goals of 5 to 10 years. If your kids are in elementary school, their college education would be a medium-term goal. Or you could have super-long-term goals that are more than 10 years away—for example, your own retirement if you are in your 20s or 30s.

To reach any of those goals, you'll need to invest some of your money in stocks, because they offer the best potential return over the long term. Based on the historical performance of stocks since the 1920s, you can reasonably expect a long-term return of about 10% per year on your investments. Because that 10% is an average, the market will do better in some years and worse in others. During the stock market boom of the 1990s, for example, the market's return was higher than average. Many financial analysts believe that returns for the first decade of the 2000s will be lower than average (especially so in view of the bear market that kicked off the decade).

Investing in stocks is riskier than putting your money into bank accounts or money-market funds. And that's one reason I've chosen 5 years as the line of demarcation between short-term and long-term goals. You need at least 5 years to ride out the inevitable fluctuations in the stock market. If you're going to need your money before then, you can't afford to risk it in the stock market; if your goal is further away, you can't afford *not* to risk at least part of it.

Because many women don't feel that they can afford to lose their limited resources, the advantages of investing in stocks are apparently one of the hardest lessons for them to learn. In a survey of single Gen X women by OppenheimerFunds, 35% of the young women interviewed said that bank CDs or money-market funds are the best way to create long-term financial security—almost the same percentage as those who cited stocks or stock mutual funds (37%). If you take one lesson away from this chapter, let it be this: Investing exclusively in bank accounts and money-market funds is too conservative to get you where you want to be, if where you want to be is on a beach enjoying a secure retirement 20 or 30 years from now.

# Invest With Confidence

Of course, as the Enron debacle and other recent business failures have made painfully clear, you don't want to throw caution and good sense to the wind. Fortunately, there are plenty of ways to invest in the stock market without taking undue risk or lying awake at night fretting about your money. Here are three strategies that will help.

## 1. Keep All Things in Proportion.

Remember that investing doesn't need to be an all-or-nothing proposition. An old, rough, and rather conservative rule of thumb states that the percentage of stocks in your portfolio should equal 100 minus your age. Thus, a 25-year-old woman would have 75% of her assets in stocks, versus 40% for a 60-year-old. Or, you can use this range of portfolio mixes as a guideline:

**Stocks:** 40% to 80%
**Bonds:** 20% to 50%
**Cash:** 10% to 25%

That's a fairly wide range that can be tailored to your age, your goal, and your tolerance for risk. If you're 40 and planning for college tuition bills seven years away, you would have less of your money in stocks than if you were saving for your retirement 25 years down the road. You can fiddle with the allocations, but the point is this: At no time does the stock portion of your longer-term savings drop to zero.

Here's how your stock investments might evolve over time:

**YOU'RE YOUNG, WITH NO DEPENDENTS.** You can afford to take a relatively high-risk approach, especially with money you won't need until retirement. Among the investments to consider at this stage of your life are small-company stocks or mutual funds, or mutual funds that invest in developing countries. Balance these aggressive (a code word for risky) assets with less-risky ones, such as blue-chip stocks (the largest, most consistently profitable corporations, so-called for the blue chips used in poker—the most valuable ones) or funds that invest in large companies. Always hold your riskiest investments to no more than 10% or 20% of your portfolio.

## Three Keys to Investing Success

One long-term study of the stock market concluded that there are three keys to successful investing:

1. **Thinking** in terms of portfolios rather than individual stocks—in other words, diversification
2. **Holding** stock for the long term, preferably 10- to 15-year periods
3. **Taking** time to select issues with the potential to grow

**YOU'RE MARRIED WITH CHILDREN.** You still need a mix of aggressive and conservative investments, but as you move into your 40s your portfolio should be weighted more toward large-company growth stocks, or growth-and-income funds, which also invest in stocks that pay dividends. Your financial goals should include accumulating enough money to fund your own retirement and contribute to your children's college education. Remember that your retirement should always come first. When the time comes, you can always pay some of the college bills out of current income, or your kids can contribute by taking out student loans or getting a job. But do you really want to be working at Wal-Mart when you're 75 because you have to? Think single!

**YOU'RE NEARING RETIREMENT OR ALREADY RETIRED.** It's time to adopt a more conservative investment strategy. You'll probably want to tilt toward investments that will produce income, with bonds issued by solid corporations or the U.S. government, or even bank CDs and money-market funds, as mentioned earlier in this chapter. But you still need to hold onto some stocks, whose growing value will offset the effects of inflation that will eat away at your income as the years go by. Hang on to your best conservative stocks or stock mutual funds. Focus your portfolio on stocks noted for generating income, such as blue-chip companies or some utilities.

## 2. Invest Slowly and Steadily.

Invest regularly in small amounts. That way you get used to the idea of investing, but you don't feel as if you have so much on the line.

When Wanda was divorced in the 1970s, she found herself

## ⊗ Stay in the Comfort Zone

The risks you're prepared to take will influence the kinds of investments you make and the expected return. These four rules will keep you in a comfortable risk zone—and let you rest easy at night:

1. **Don't invest until you're ready to invest.** Your investment portfolio should be built on a solid foundation of sure things: sufficient insurance coverage and several months' income tucked securely away in an interest-bearing bank account or money-market fund. Only when you have that cushion are you ready to start investing.

2. **Invest aggressively for the long term and conservatively for the short term.** Stocks are investments for long-term goals. For money you'll need within a few years, stick with bank CDs and other sure bets.

3. **Don't invest in anything that you don't understand, or that you feel uncomfortable about.** That doesn't mean you should never take a flier on something that's legitimate but risky. Just don't take big risks with big chunks of your money.

4. **Don't buy anything you don't know how to sell.** Some so-called investments, such as collectibles and gemstones, are simple to buy but may take specialized assistance and more time to sell because there are no organized national resale markets, as there are for stocks and bonds.

struggling and on welfare. But a credit union manager talked her into saving $5 a month for her daughter's college fund. When she got a job, she increased the amount and gradually broadened her investments. Over the next two decades, Wanda accumulated enough money not only to pay for college but also to buy a house and built a $300,000 nest egg.

Wanda was using a tried-and-true investment strategy called dollar-cost averaging that works like this: You invest a fixed amount on a regular schedule, ignoring the prices of the investments at the time. The amount can be $25 a month, $50 a month, $500 a month—whatever fits your budget. (A study by the Employee Benefit Research Institute found that the vast majority of working Americans could save an extra $20 each week without giving up anything of significance.)

Your fixed number of dollars automatically buys more shares when prices are low than when prices are high. One of the best explanations of dollar-cost averaging I've ever heard came from a young lady named Devon Green, who at the age of 10 was already CEO of her own business, Devon's "Heal the World" Recycling. With her business earnings, Devon put $50 a month into a mutual fund noted for investing in companies that were environmentally friendly. Devon was unfazed by changes in the fund's share price: "If the price goes down I can get more shares for my $50. If the price goes up, I don't get as many shares but the ones I have are worth more. Either way I win."

Dollar-cost averaging won't automatically produce a profit. But by investing on a regular schedule and sticking with it, you're almost guaranteed to do better in a generally rising market, with the usual ups and downs, than investors who try to sell at the top and buy at the bottom. Historically, the odds are strongly against that kind of timing.

> **By judiciously mixing large and small companies in your portfolio or by focusing on larger companies in different industries, you can hedge your bets with a diversified mix of assets.**

## 3. Choose Your Level of Risk.

Even when you're in the stock market, you can control your risk. There are stocks and there are stocks. Small, new companies are riskier than larger companies with a proven track record. *Note:* Penny stocks—the stocks of little-known companies that trade for less than $5 and are often discussed, as well as touted, in investing chat groups online—are pure gambles that should be avoided at all costs.

By judiciously mixing large and small companies in your portfolio or by focusing on larger companies in different industries, you can hedge your bets with a diversified mix of assets. One study indicates that, to be truly diversified, you need a minimum of 10 separate stocks in your portfolio if you're dealing with high-quality companies. Another way to spread the risk would be to buy shares of just a few individual stocks and buffer them with shares in mutual funds, or to stick with mutual funds exclusively. For an investment of as little as several hundred dollars, you can get instant

## Get an Honest Opinion

What with companies being caught cooking their books, and stock analysts skewing their picks in favor of firms with which their employers are doing business, the last couple of years have been a frustrating time for investors in search of an honest guru—and unbiased information—on Wall Street. Prodded by government regulators and a market backlash, things should get better. But if you're looking for independent analysis, consult any of these trusted sources:

- ■ *Value Line Investment Survey* (800-833-0046; www.valueline.com), a one-stop encyclopedia on 1,700 U.S. companies, with an enormous database and trenchant commentaries. It's also the one research tool

you're likely to spot on the desks of mutual fund managers. A subscription costs $598 a year, but you can consult it at no charge from your public library.

- ■ **Standard & Poor's** (800-852-1641; www.spoutlook.com) provides data and commentary on more than 1,000 companies in its *S&P Stock Reports,* which is also available from your public library. An online subscription to *Outlook,* a weekly newsletter, costs $234 a year (the print version costs an extra $64).

- ■ **Morningstar** (800-735-0700; www.morningstar.com) gives you online access to data on thousands of mutual funds, plus 500 individual companies, for $109 a year.

diversification with a mutual fund, which pools money from all its investors to buy several dozen companies.

To get total diversification in a portfolio of stocks or stock mutual funds, you might invest half of your money in stocks of large and midsize domestic companies, one-fourth in stocks of small U.S. companies, and the remaining fourth in stocks of foreign companies. Within each of these broad categories you could split your investments even further, between growth stocks—companies that are expected to generate above-average earnings growth—and value stocks—companies whose share price is cheap in relation to the firm's profits or other fundamental measures of business success (see the discussion that follows). To fine-tune your portfolio to this extent, it's often easier to go the mutual fund route, because you can invest in funds that specialize in each of these categories.

# Pick Stocks

Some people prefer the feeling of control they get by choosing their own stocks instead of investing via mutual funds. When my sister Priscilla joined an investment club with other women teachers in her elementary school, the group never even considered investing their money in mutual funds. "That wasn't the goal of the club," says Priscilla. "We wanted to learn about the stock market ourselves instead of leaving it up to someone else."

Becoming market savvy was especially important for club members who were being offered lump-sum payouts as part of their early retirement packages and wanted to know how to manage the money.

Thanks to the wealth of financial publications and the Internet, "it's no longer necessary to be timid," says Priscilla. "You can get more information about a company than you would ever want to know." Although their technology-heavy portfolio took a hit during the bear market that began in 2000, their goal of becoming educated was wildly successful. "We all wanted to do more interesting things with our money, and now we have a higher comfort level with the market," says Priscilla, who has opened an account with a broker to buy and sell stocks on her own.

How do you sort out the good stocks from the bad? Here are some basic characteristics that the pros look for:

## How Much Does the Company Earn?

This is the famous "bottom line," the company's net income after taxes, expenses, and set-asides, often expressed as earnings per share of common stock outstanding. When a company is described as growing at a certain rate, it's usually the earnings that are being used as the measure. Successful investors look for companies with a strong record of rising earnings.

## How Does the Price Relate to Earnings?

Divide the current price of a stock by its earnings for the past 12-month period and you have the price-earnings ratio (P/E), which is probably the most widely used analytical tool among stock-pickers. It tells you what investors think of a particular stock compared with other stocks and compared with the stock market as a whole. A stock with an especially high P/E in relation to similar stocks or

## Low-Cost Investing for Beginners

One of the questions that many novice investors, both male and female, often ask is whether you can buy small amounts of stock for an affordable price, avoiding brokers entirely. Yes, you can. Here are a couple of methods.

**Direct-investment plans.** Hundreds of companies will sell shares directly to investors, allowing you to bypass brokers and their commissions. Some of these direct-investment plans charge fees of their own or require a minimum initial investment. But they can be an attractive option for do-it-yourself investors. And they make you eligible to join a company's dividend reinvestment plan, or DRIP, which lets you reinvest the dividends you earn or buy additional shares of stock in small increments. For a list of companies offering such plans, check:
- **Netstock Direct** (888-638-7865; www.netstockdirect.com)
- **The Moneypaper** (800-388-9993; www.directinvesting.com)

**The National Association of Investors Corp.** also has a low-cost direct investment plan (248-583-6242; www.better-investing.org).

**Online services.** The newest wrinkle in do-it-yourself investing are online services such as:
- **ShareBuilder** (www.sharebuilder.com)
- **Buy and Hold** (www.buyandhold.com)

Both of those online services are geared toward investors who regularly invest small amounts of money (classic dollar-cost averaging) in a number of stocks. Both let you buy thousands of stocks for rock-bottom commissions, including a *prix fixe* option that lets you trade as much as you wish for a set monthly fee. Because ShareBuilder charges the lowest fee ($4) for a single trade and has no investment minimum or maintenance fee, it's ideal for occasional stock purchases.

One of the best features of these plans is that you can buy fractional shares of stock, making it easy to dollar-cost-average your way into stocks with a lump-sum amount. For example, you might invest, say, $300 a month, divided among three different stocks, and buy as many shares as your money will stretch—even if that means 5.7 shares of a particular company.

There are a couple of catches. You can't pick the price you'll pay for a stock. Both brokers keep commissions low by lumping together lots of trades and placing a single order during limited trading "windows." Buy and Hold executes trades three times a day, and ShareBuilder makes purchases weekly. And you'll pay a higher commission if you want to sell a stock. These services are definitely for buy-and-hold investors, which women tend to be, rather than for traders.

the market as a whole may be the victim of unrealistic expectations on the part of investors. The idea is to buy your stock at the lowest possible P/E, and hope that as other investors begin to recognize the stock's potential, they may bid up the price. (As a point of reference, the historical average P/E for the big companies that make up the Standard & Poor's 500-stock index is 15.)

## What Is a Company's Book Value?

Simply put, a company's book value is the difference between its assets and its liabilities—what it owns and what it is owed, minus what it owes to others. This figure is also referred to as shareholder's equity. Theoretically, book value represents the amount that stockholders would receive for each share they own if the company were to shut down, sell all its assets, pay all its debts, and go out of business. If a company's stock is selling below book value, it may be an undiscovered bargain because the share price is less than what the company is actually worth. Such a stock sometimes becomes a takeover candidate, attracting the attention of other companies that see a chance to buy it on the cheap. And that prospect can drive up the price of the shares.

Of course, it's also possible that the stock is selling below book value because the company or its industry has fallen on hard times, in which case betting on a turnaround is riskier. You need more information before you buy.

## What's the Return on Book Value?

Take a company's total annual net income, express it as a percentage of total book value, and you get a measure of how much the company earns on the stockholders' stake in the enterprise. That measure is also called return on equity. It varies from company to company and from industry to industry, and it fluctuates with economic conditions. One year's return on equity means little, but by comparing several years' results for the company and its industry, you can get an idea of how well, or poorly, a company is doing compared with other firms that are in the same line of business.

## What's the Total Return?

Investors tend to think of their gains and losses in terms of changes

## **www.**

## Join a Club?

Of the more than 30,000 investment clubs that are members of the National Association of Investors Corp. (NAIC), 54% are all female, compared with 38% that include both men and women and 8% that are all male. Women apparently feel comfortable in a group setting, enjoy the camaraderie, and are attracted by the club emphasis on education and long-term investing.

"We started with a male broker, but we never took his advice," says one long-time investment-club member. "We've probably done much better as women [investors] because we do our research and buy things we know about." Adds another member, "It's like playing Monopoly, only 100 times better."

Despite losses during the bear mar-

ket of the early 2000s, many clubs carried on. "It was a tremendous opportunity for us to buy, and to get smarter about how we make our decisions," says the president of one club based in Manhattan. Their perseverance—and enthusiasm—was also bolstered by the members' shared interests beyond investing. They made a point of getting together to watch one of their four actress members perform in a play, or meeting for a concert in Central Park. They also expanded meeting agendas by, for example, bringing in an estate-planning attorney to talk about drafting a will.

For information on setting up a club, contact the NAIC (P.O. Box 220, Royal Oak, MI 48068; 877-275-6242 or 248-583-6242; www.better-investing.org).

in the price of a share of stock. But don't forget dividends, which are profits a company pays out to its shareholders as income. Together, price changes and dividends show your total return, which is the only fair way to compare stocks that pay dividends with stocks that don't, and to compare results from stocks with results from bonds, Treasury bills, and other alternatives that pay interest.

## Find a Stockbroker

Once you have decided to invest in stocks, you'll have to open an account with a stockbroker, who will charge you a fee, or commission, in return for executing your order to buy or sell shares. Online brokers that deal exclusively over the Internet—Ameritrade (www.ameritrade.com), Datek (www.datek.com), and Scottrade (www.scottrade.com), for example—generally offer the lowest commissions. But they concentrate on trading, and don't offer much in the way of service.

At the other end of the spectrum are full-service brokers—A. G. Edwards & Sons, Merrill Lynch, UBS PaineWebber—which offer a wide range of customer services, not to mention access, at least by phone, to a real live broker who can offer advice and counsel if you need it, or reassurance if you want it. Full-service brokers will charge a higher commission that reflects their level of service.

In the middle are discount brokers—Fidelity Brokerage Services (www.fidelity.com), Charles Schwab (www.schwab.com), TD Waterhouse (www.tdwaterhouse.com), for example—which offer some, though not all, the services of a full-service broker, and charge lower commissions. Depending on the size of the transaction, discounts can amount to as much as 80% of what you'd pay a full-service broker, although 20% to 30% is more typical. But some discounters set a minimum fee that can wipe out your savings on small trades. Discount brokers also typically give you the option of online trading; in some cases, you can avoid a transaction fee by executing your own trade online.

If you're married, you may want to open a joint account with your husband, which gives both of you the right to buy and sell and perform other transactions. Married or single, you can open an individual account—which may be a good idea for estate planning purposes, as we saw in Chapter 4.

# Consider the Mutual Fund Alternative

If you don't have the time or inclination to pick stocks, or if you want to buy as much diversification as possible with a relatively small amount of money, mutual funds are for you. Many funds require you to come up with $2,000 or more to open an account, but you can often avoid those minimums by investing a smaller amount each month—sometimes as little as $50. (Most funds also have lower minimums if you're investing through an IRA.)

"If I want to invest in a mutual fund, I don't always have two or three grand to do it with," says Shari, a graduate student and part-time university instructor. Yet even as a cash-strapped student working on a doctorate in social science, she managed to build a six-fund portfolio worth about $30,000 by the time she was 30. Her strategy: She circumvented fund minimums by setting up automatic investment plans, making monthly contributions of about $170. "I would hit one fund's minimum after a year and then move on to some other fund," says Shari.

**Index funds that track the Standard & Poor's index of 500 large-company growth stocks are perhaps the best known, but there are many other index funds.**

Another great thing about mutual funds is that you can invest in them without paying commissions, although you can't escape fees entirely. So-called load funds are sold mostly by brokers and banks and charge commissions of up to 8.5% when you purchase shares, putting less of your money to work right from the get-go. Some funds charge what's called a back-end load when you sell your shares. "No-load" funds charge neither type of commission and are sold directly by the fund companies. Load or no-load, you can expect to pay the fund an annual management fee of 1% or more of your average assets. Some also charge a marketing fee, called a 12b-1 fee. With funds, you want to keep your costs as low as possible, because whatever you pay in expenses reduces your return.

## Different Strokes

No matter what kind of stocks (or bonds) you want to invest in, you can find a mutual fund that will do it for you. Funds generally fall into one of the following types:

**Aggressive-growth funds**—the riskiest type of fund—strive for big profits, generally by investing in small, new companies and developing industries with the potential to grow rapidly. They invest in speculative stocks.

**Growth funds** also look for companies with the potential to grow faster than inflation, so that the share price increases over time. But they focus on less-speculative companies that may be larger or have a longer track record, and thus they're less volatile than aggressive-growth funds.

**Growth-and-income funds** have much the same objective as growth funds, but they try to produce more current income for their shareholders by investing in some bonds or common stocks that pay healthy dividends.

**Sector funds** concentrate their investments in one or two industries or assets, such as energy or biotechnology companies.

**International funds** are U.S.-based but invest in securities of companies traded on foreign exchanges.

You can see that with mutual funds, it would be easy to build an instant portfolio in which half of your stock allocation would be in large and midsize domestic stocks, one-fourth in small U.S. stocks, and the remaining fourth in foreign stocks—a sensible and often-recommended allocation.

## Really Simple Investing

With funds that are actively managed, you are betting that the fund manager is a better stock picker than you or the market— and there's the rub. Although some managers can outwit the market some of the time, few, if any, can do it consistently over long periods—and picking those fund managers from the thousands out there can be like finding a needle in a haystack.

Enter index funds, an even simpler way to invest that can be just as rewarding. Instead of trying to single out which stocks will be best (and risk being wrong), index funds assemble portfolios designed to track one or more broad stock or bond indexes that duplicate as precisely as possible all the stocks in a particular sector of the market, or in the market as a whole. Index funds that track the Standard & Poor's index of 500 large-company growth stocks are perhaps the best known, but there are many others, covering everything from small stocks to international stocks.

One of the most inclusive is Vanguard's Total Stock Market Index fund, which gives you virtually the entire U.S. stock market. In fact, with a two-fund portfolio, 75% invested in Vanguard's Total Stock Market Index and 25% invested in Vanguard's Total International Index, you can invest in stocks of the entire world. (For more information about the Vanguard funds, call 800-635-1511 or visit www.vanguard.com.)

Because index fund managers are merely trying to duplicate a market's average performance rather than beat it, expenses are much lower than with actively managed funds—a real plus for investors, because expenses eat into your returns. Over periods of 10 years or longer, you will almost certainly get higher returns with an index fund than with an actively managed fund, studies show. Although it's true that at any given time some active fund managers can beat the market, it's tough to predict just who those managers will be.

**Expenses of index funds are much lower than those of actively managed funds—a real plus for investors, because expenses eat into your returns.**

Vanguard has a minimum initial investment of $3,000 for most of its index funds, or $1,000 if you open an IRA (another fund, TIAA-CREF Equity Index, 800-223-1200, also invests in the entire U.S. stock market, and has a minimum investment of $1,500 for regular accounts). Index funds are a great way for new investors to get the most bang for their buck. They're also great for experienced investors who don't have the inclination to devote lots of time to managing their own investments—and know that their chances of beating the market are slim anyway. Even professional investment advisers often use index funds to manage their clients' assets. "If you could see our client list, your eyes would pop," says Gus Sauter, who runs all 25 of Vanguard's index funds. "You can't imagine the big-name money managers who invest in our funds."

The dirty little secret of the Wall Street investment industry is that despite computer models, complex technical theories, and reams of stock analysis, it's just about impossible to get better returns than the market with any consistency over long periods of time. One study by the business school at the University of California at Berkeley showed that in 2000, for example, stocks rated least favorably by Wall Street analysts did significantly better than the market as a whole, while the most highly touted stocks trailed the market.

If you'd like to try your hand at beating the market, you can always use a broad index fund as a base and then choose stocks or actively managed funds to fill niches in your portfolio—for example, small-company or international stocks, areas in which financial professionals believe there are more opportunities for active fund managers to find undiscovered bargains.

Remember, however, that index funds are not risk-free. Because you are invested in the stock market, your investments will do whatever the market does, and that means falling as well as rising—a lesson that was learned painfully by index-fund investors during the recent bear market. But the ups and downs should even out over time. If you can make that long-term market return of 10% a year, you'll be sitting pretty when it's time to send your kids to college or retire in style.

# Invest in Bonds

The bulk of this chapter has been devoted to stocks because that's what's lacking in the portfolios of most women, who tend to lean too heavily on more conservative investments, such as bonds. Bonds do have a place in your portfolio. But, just as with proteins or carbohydrates in your diet, too much of a good thing isn't necessarily good for your financial health.

When you buy a bond, you are basically lending money to whoever is issuing the bond—usually the federal government, an individual company, or a state or local government. In return, the issuer gives you an IOU promising to pay back the money, plus interest, over a certain period of time. If you hold the bond till it matures, you'll get your initial investment back. But your money won't grow as it could if you owned a share of stock in a growing company whose stock price was appreciating.

As a result, bonds historically have had a lower return than stocks—in the neighborhood of 5%. And although they're generally considered safer than stocks, bonds do have some risks of their own. For one thing, the bond issuer might run into financial difficulties and be unable to pay you back. For another, a bond's fixed return means that its value can be eaten away by inflation (for a bond alternative with built-in inflation protection, see the box on the following page). And there's yet another risk: Interest rates could rise, in which case your bond would be worth less. Suppose you purchase a bond with a $10,000 face value—the amount you'll be paid when the bond matures—and

## Buy These Bonds

Get a market rate of interest and inflation protection, too, with series I U.S. savings bonds, or I-bonds. These bonds pay a guaranteed rate of return, plus the rate of inflation. Rates are adjusted twice a year, in May and November. Earnings are free from state and local income taxes, and the bonds may also be exempt from federal taxes if they are used to pay for college. Buy them through payroll deduction, or at www.savingsbonds.gov.

an interest rate of 5%. Then suppose that interest rates in the market rise to 6%. Your bond is less attractive because it's paying a lower rate of interest. If you hold on until the maturity date, you'll still get your entire $10,000. But if you have to sell the bond before it matures, you'll get less than that because the bond's price will have fallen.

On the other hand, if interest rates fall, your bond is worth more than its face value—that's how bond traders and investors who are astute (or lucky) make money on bonds. But for most people, bonds come in handy for other reasons:

- **Because they're relatively safe,** they can help balance a portfolio if you're nervous about having too much money in stocks.
- **Because they come in different maturities**—anywhere from several months to 30 years—you can time them to come due just when you'll need the money for some expense in the future, whether it's a down payment on a house in two years or your child's college education in ten years.
- **Because they pay interest,** they can increase your income when you need it—in retirement, for example.

But because they pay a relatively low rate of interest, there is one thing that bonds alone cannot do: build a nest egg that will provide enough money for a financially secure retirement. One financial planner tells of a 40-year-old client—who works for a financial magazine, in fact—who won't invest her retirement plan assets in anything other than a short-term bond fund. In that case, she would better be able to count on supplementing those assets with a fat company pension, a big inheritance, or a rich husband.

## Don't Stop Now!

- **Decide** whether you'd get a better return at this point by paying off debt or investing.
- **Identify** your short-term and long-term goals. Be specific.
- **Talk** with your husband about coordinating your efforts to take advantage of your respective strengths and inclinations as investors so that you can achieve your mutual goals.
- **To get started** the easy way, check out one of the low-cost investing options identified in the box on page 116 or the Vanguard family of index funds discussed on page 121.
- **Join** (or start) an investment club for education and encouragement.
- **Revisit** your 401(k) or IRA, if you already have one, to ensure that you haven't chosen investments that are too conservative or too risky for your goals.

One easy way to balance stocks and bonds in your portfolio is to invest in another simple alternative: all-in-one "life cycle" funds that combine stocks, bonds, and cash in a single package. Fund companies typically offer a range of all-in-one funds, depending on how much risk you want to take and how long it will be before you need your money. For example, in Smith Barney's Allocation Series funds (800-451-2010), stock investments vary from 10% to 90%. Fidelity Investments (800-343-3548) has five Freedom Funds geared to investors entering retirement in specified years. And Charles Schwab's MarketTrack funds (800-435-4000) buy other funds—in this case, index funds holding large U.S. stocks, small U.S. stocks, international stocks, bonds, and cash. A Fidelity executive says the funds are popular with people who "want to make sure they are investing appropriately, but don't want to actively manage the money."

## Assess the Bottom Line

A book format obviously doesn't lend itself to an up-to-date listing of stocks and mutual funds that are good investments. To keep current with that kind of information, see the analysis and portfolios on www.kiplinger.com.

Enough books have been written on the nuances of investment strategy to fill a whole library of their own. If you're interested in learning more about technical analysis, or initial public offerings, or futures contracts, by all means read these guides. But having read and absorbed this chapter, you should know virtually all you need to know about providing for your financial security—on your own.

# Retirement: You Won't Be a Bag Lady

A t age 30, Janet experienced every woman's nightmare: Her husband died unexpectedly, leaving her a widow with two children. To make matters worse, he had no will and no life insurance. His legacy to her was court proceedings to straighten out his legal affairs. "I was terrified that I was going to lose what little money I had," she says.

At age 36, Janet remarried, but vowed that she would never again be so vulnerable. Along with a new husband, she acquired a new career in the financial services industry—and an "insatiable urge to learn about money." By age 41, Janet was deeply involved in her family's finances. She was making college plans for four children, purchasing life and disability insurance, handling the household budget and the upkeep on a farm she and her husband owned—and investing for her own retirement. "I was happy to be a homemaker, but you have to be an active decision-maker, too," she says. "What's at stake is the security of your family, and your own future."

## Did You Know?

Half of workers who are not currently saving for retirement say that it would be possible for them to put away $20 per week. In addition, 7 of 10 workers who are already saving report that they could put aside an extra $20 per week. That adds up to more than $1,000 a year.

Retirement is where all the investing bugaboos that plague women—a lack of confidence, a strategy that's too conservative, and a tendency to rely on a husband to take care of things—come home to roost. At the same time, women have lots of things working in their favor. Realistically, the biggest pot of money many women will control is their retirement assets, the fruits of their financially productive years. Even women who don't work outside the home can have retirement funds of their own, and are entitled to a share of their husbands'. And, as we saw in Chapter 6, women have a great track record as long-term investors. All that adds up to a golden opportunity for women to build security for their golden years.

# Where Do Women Stand?

Throughout this book I've emphasized that although men and women have the same financial opportunities (and risks), the same vehicles for saving, investing, and borrowing, and are subject to the same rules, their circumstances and choices can be very different. This difference is particularly striking when it comes to preparing for retirement. Let's consider a few pertinent statistics and survey results:

- **Less than half of all total wage and salary workers** in the U.S. participate in a pension plan at work, and the proportion is smaller for women than for men.
- **Because they are more likely to move into and out of the labor force,** women are less likely to be entitled to the full benefit of an employer's pension or profit-sharing plan. They are slightly more likely than men to receive preretirement distributions when they leave an employer, and to receive them at younger ages. Yet only one-third of all lump-sum distributions (amounting to about two-thirds of dollars received) are rolled over into another savings vehicle when a worker changes jobs. Women tend to save less of their rollover dollars than do men.
- **Women use 401(k) loans more than men** do to pay for their kids' education and to get out of debt.
- **On average, women in the U.S. live** about 5½ years longer than men, reaching nearly 79½ versus nearly 74 for men. Once men and women reach age 65, women can expect to live

another 19 years and men another 18 years.

■ **In 2000, men age 65 and over had an average annual income** of more than $29,000, compared with just over $15,000 for women.

So let's sum up: Women will probably have to provide for themselves financially for more years of retirement than men will, and for many of those years women are likely to be on their own. Yet women tend to earn less than men and participate in the work force less steadily; thus they lose income and job seniority, and are less likely than men to fully participate in a pension or profit-sharing plan sponsored by their employer. All of those circumstances act as a drag on women's pension assets. When women do build up funds, they tend to borrow against their balances or tap them when they switch jobs or need money.

It's no wonder that across the board women have less confidence than men in their ability to retire comfortably, and have done less than men to prepare for retirement. For instance, 69% of the men interviewed in the 2002 Retirement Confidence Survey (sponsored by the Employee Benefit Research Institute and the American Savings Education Council) said they had saved for retirement, versus 64% of women; 37% of men had calculated how much money they would need in retirement, versus 27% of women; and 39% of men felt that they were on track in saving for retirement, versus 30% of women.

But there's no point in feeling sorry for ourselves. Now that we know what we're up against, there's plenty we can do about it—and we are already working on the problem. The wage gap is narrowing. Women are more likely than in the past to be employed, to have access to a pension plan, and to be saving for retirement. And younger women are investing less conservatively than women have traditionally done.

Mary, a 39-year-old pilot for a major airline, is typical. She already has plans to retire either to a warm climate or to a ski area. To get herself there, she is investing almost all of her retirement plan assets in stock mutual funds, and much of that is in aggressive small-company funds. "I take more of a high-risk approach, given my age and the years I have until retirement," she says. Still, Mary and her male counterparts invest differently. "Some guys, every time they land, they're switching investments around. I stay diversified, and I don't switch my funds."

Remember the mantra chanted throughout this book: Save early, save regularly, save aggressively. Start small, and think big. And if you haven't begun yet, no matter what your age, start now. It's never too late.

# How Much Will You Need?

That's the $64,000 question—or is it the $500,000 question, or even the $1 million question? Those figures are often bandied about as the goal you should aim for in order to retire comfortably. Don't be intimidated—or worse, paralyzed. Everyone's retirement needs will be different, and there are many ways to cut down on your expenses, or to supplement your income from a variety of sources, to see you through.

But instead of saving blindly, at some point it does help to take a realistic look at how much you'll need in retirement and where the money is going to come from. For starters, you can use a few rules of thumb:

- **Figure that in order to maintain your standard of living** in retirement, you'll need 70% to 80% of your preretirement income.
- **For every $1,000 of monthly retirement income you want** to generate from your own savings, you will need about $230,000 in assets, recommends the Schwab Center for Investment Research. For example, if you want $3,000 a month, or $36,000 a year, you would need a kitty of $690,000. That's a conservative estimate, assuming that you earn 5.2% on your investments and live off the earnings without eating into the principal. (Most likely you would not have to depend on your savings for your entire retirement income. You would also be entitled to social security payments and possibly pension benefits through your employer.)
- **If you are in your 20s or 30s,** try to save at least 5% of your income for retirement; women in their 40s should try to increase their savings to at least 10%. If you're meeting those savings goals, you're well on your way to meeting your retirement needs, says Christopher Hayes, executive director of the National Center for Women and Retirement Research.

To estimate how much money you'll need in retirement, try

## Online Help With Your Planning

For help in planning your retirement, try these online sources:

**The American Savings Education Council (www.asec.org).** Its one-page "Ballpark Estimate" worksheet is in an easy-to-use format that helps you identify approximately how much you need to save to fund a comfortable retirement. The worksheet takes complicated issues, such as earnings assumptions and projected social security benefits, and turns them into language and mathematics that are easy to understand. The site also includes answers to frequently asked questions about the worksheet.

For more information on saving for retirement, including handy calculators, see the companion site at www .choosetosave.org.

**FinancialEngines.com,** for a fee, gives you a one-shot personalized analysis of your 401(k) plan.

**Morningstar** (www.morningstar.com) has nifty retirement-planning tools, some for a fee.

**T. Rowe Price** (www.troweprice.com) offers free advice.

the "Ballpark Estimate Retirement Planning Worksheet," at www.choosetosave.org. To get a more precise idea of how much you'll need, use the worksheet on the following pages.

The purpose of doing these exercises isn't to scare you, but to inspire you to start now, start small, and think big. Living below your means, and saving regularly, will put you on the path to a comfortable retirement without your even thinking about it, much less worrying.

Take the case of Connie. Back in 1992, when Connie was 42, her employer went through a series of mergers and reorganizations that placed her job in jeopardy several times over a 3-year period. So she tightened her belt, giving up, among other things, the opera and symphony tickets she loved in order to prepare for what she anticipated would be lean times ahead. Wonder of wonders, she found that she could live on a lot less than she earned. After 3 years, her job situation stabilized, but Connie continued to maximize her savings with an eye toward an early retirement. By the time she resigned in June 2000, she had accumulated about $375,000 in taxable accounts, IRAs, and

# How Much You Need to Save

This worksheet will show you how much you need to save each year to retire in style. It assumes that you are saving in tax-deferred accounts, that inflation will average 3.5% annually and that, prior to retirement, conservative investors will earn 8% annually, while aggressive investors will make 11%. During retirement, conservative investors are assumed to earn 7% and aggressive investors, 9%.

**1. Annual income in current dollars desired during retirement**
Usually you'll need 70% to 80% of your current income.  $ _____

**2. Inflation-adjusted income desired**
Multiply line 1 by the factor in the following table that corresponds most closely to the number of years you plan to work until retirement.  $ _____

| Years until retirement | 5 | 10 | 15 | 20 | 25 | 30 | 35 | 40 | 45 |
|---|---|---|---|---|---|---|---|---|---|
| Inflation factor | 1.19 | 1.41 | 1.68 | 1.99 | 2.36 | 2.81 | 3.33 | 3.96 | 4.70 |

**3. Annual social security benefits**
Multiply the appropriate number from this table by the inflation factor from step 2 to get your approximate benefit in future dollars. If your spouse works, figure his benefits separately, and add both benefits together. Couples with a nonworking spouse should add the benefits for the nonworking spouse to that of the wage earner.  $ _____

| Current income | $36,000 | $48,000 | $65,400+ |
|---|---|---|---|
| Current age, 55 | | | |
| Worker benefits | $13,092 | $14,556 | $16,260 |
| Nonworking spouse | 6,444 | 7,164 | 8,004 |
| Current age, 45 | | | |
| Worker benefits | $11,087 | $12,475 | $14,423 |
| Nonworking spouse | 5,447 | 6,120 | 7,079 |
| Current age, 35 | | | |
| Worker benefits | $8,551 | $9,635 | $11,214 |
| Nonworking spouse | 4,108 | 4,629 | 5,384 |

**4. Annual employer-paid pension benefits**
Ask your employee benefits office for this number. If it isn't adjusted for future inflation, multiply it by the proper factor from step 2.  $ _____

**5. Income from pension and social security**
Add lines 3 and 4.  $ _____

**6. Retirement income needed from your investments**
Subtract line 5 from line 2.  $ _____

**7. Assets needed to generate required investment income during retirement**
Use the tables below to see how long a retirement you need to finance, based on
your age now, your life expectancy, and when you plan to retire. Then multiply line
6 by the appropriate conservative or aggressive multiplier, depending on how you
plan to invest in retirement.                                                                          $ _____

> **How long in retirement?** This table offers a clue to how many years you
> can expect to live in retirement by showing average life expectancies. Subtract
> your planned retirement age from your life expectancy to estimate the length
> of your retirement.
>
> | | | | **Life expectancy** | | | | | |
> | --- | --- | --- | --- | --- | --- | --- | --- | --- |
> | **AGE NOW** | **30** | **35** | **40** | **45** | **50** | **55** | **60** | **65** |
> | **Men** | 78 | 78 | 79 | 79 | 79 | 80 | 81 | 82 |
> | **Women** | 84 | 84 | 85 | 85 | 85 | 85 | 86 | 86 |

| Years in retirement | 15 | 20 | 25 | 30 | 35 | 40 | 45 |
| --- | --- | --- | --- | --- | --- | --- | --- |
| Conservative | 11.52 | 14.21 | 16.48 | 18.39 | 20.00 | 21.36 | 22.50 |
| Aggressive | 10.04 | 11.95 | 13.41 | 14.53 | 15.39 | 16.05 | 16.55 |

**8. Total nest egg for retirement**
Add present tax-deferred and taxable retirement savings (including any real
estate or business that will be sold to fund your retirement) and multiply by
the appropriate number from this table. As in line 7, choose either
conservative or aggressive investments.                                                                $ _____

| Years to retirement | 5 | 10 | 15 | 20 | 25 | 30 | 35 | 40 | 45 |
| --- | --- | --- | --- | --- | --- | --- | --- | --- | --- |
| Conservative | 1.47 | 2.16 | 3.17 | 4.66 | 6.85 | 10.06 | 14.79 | 21.72 | 31.92 |
| Aggressive | 1.69 | 2.84 | 4.78 | 8.06 | 13.59 | 22.89 | 38.57 | 65.00 | 109.53 |

**9. Additional capital needed**
Subtract line 8 from line 7.                                                                               $ _____

**10. Annual savings needed to meet your goal**
Multiply line 9 by the appropriate number from this table, based on how
you plan to invest until retirement.                                                                 $ _____

| Years to retirement | 5 | 10 | 15 | 20 | 25 | 30 | 35 | 40 | 45 |
| --- | --- | --- | --- | --- | --- | --- | --- | --- | --- |
| Conservative | 0.170 | 0.069 | 0.037 | 0.022 | 0.014 | 0.009 | 0.006 | 0.004 | 0.003 |
| Aggressive | 0.161 | 0.060 | 0.029 | 0.160 | 0.009 | 0.005 | 0.003 | 0.002 | 0.001 |

## Investing for Retirement: A Strategy

**1. Save as much as possible.**

**2. Avoid stashing too much of your money in "safe" investments,** such as bank accounts, that won't grow fast enough to keep you ahead of inflation. To find the proportion of your assets that should be invested in stocks or stock mutual funds to help you hedge inflation, one conservative guideline is to subtract your age from 100. (If you feel comfortable investing in the stock market and want to give yourself a larger stake, subtract your age from 110.)

**3. Diversify.** If you're going the mutual fund route, aim for a retirement portfolio of funds that invest in the following types of stocks:

- **Large companies** with fast-growing earnings
- **Large companies** that are undervalued (meaning that their stock price is cheap relative to their earnings because they have been overlooked by the market or are out-of-favor)
- **Small companies** with fast-growing earnings
- **Undervalued stocks of small companies**
- **Foreign stocks**

A sensible breakdown is to have 50% to 60% of your stock investments in large companies, split evenly between growth and value funds. Another 20% to 25% should be in small stocks, again divided between growth and value. The rest of your money belongs in foreign stocks.

Whatever you do, take a lesson from the experience of Enron employees and don't overinvest in your own company stock, which should never exceed 10% to 15% of your portfolio.

To get total diversification, you don't need a slew of mutual funds. In fact, you can plot a simple lifetime investment strategy for your retirement using just three index mutual funds. For the stock portion of your portfolio, consider putting the bulk of your assets in Vanguard Total Stock Market fund, with a slice in Vanguard Total International. For the bond portion, there's Vanguard Total Bond Market (800-635-1511; www.vanguard.com).

her 401(k). A lump-sum payout from her company's pension plan added another $276,000 to her retirement stash. When she retired, she began making monthly withdrawals from the account, and continued to work part-time as a consultant.

# Consider These Golden Opportunities to Save

For generations, financing retirement has been compared to a three-legged stool, the three legs being social security, employer pension plans, and private savings. But it has always been a wobbly stool, because those legs have never been even—especially for women. Social security has always been relatively more important for women than for men, especially before women entered the work force in significant numbers and acquired pension coverage of their own. But social security has always been the shortest leg of the stool, because it was intended to supplement, rather than replace, private saving. That helps explain why women over age 65 today have income equal to slightly more than half that of men, as discussed earlier.

**Current workers overwhelmingly expect personal savings to be their most important source of income when they retire in the future, but the amounts saved are generally small.**

Nowadays, both social security and traditional *defined-benefit* pension plans—in which retirees receive a fixed benefit from their employer, based on their income and years of service—are taking a back seat to *defined-contribution* retirement plans, such as IRAs and employer-sponsored 401(k)s, in which workers contribute to their own retirement kitties, perhaps with a company match.

While today's retirees are likely to rely on social security or employer-provided money as their most important source of income in retirement, current workers overwhelmingly expect personal savings to be their most important source of income when they retire in the future, according to the Retirement Confidence Survey. Yet the amounts actually saved are generally small, with about half of all workers reporting they had accumulated less than $50,000. Although the amount accumulated increases with age, less than one-fourth of workers ages 40 to 59 have saved $100,000 or more.

At the same time, remember those workers who said they could save an extra $20 per week—or about $1,000 per year (highlighted on the opening page of this chapter)? Let's see what you could do with that amount:

■ **If you invest $1,000 a year starting at age 25** in a tax-deferred account, such as an IRA, earning 8% a year, you'd have over $280,000 at age 65.

■ **If you invest $1,000 a year starting at age 40** and earn 8% a year, you'd have $80,000 by age 65.

■ **If you invest $1,000 a year starting at age 50,** you'd have over $30,000 at 65—not as much as the 25-year-old, but $30,000 is nothing to sneeze at, at any age.

Take full advantage of an IRA and you can get even more bang for your buck. In 2003 and 2004, the maximum annual contribution to an IRA is $3,000, and that is scheduled to increase in the years that follow. Annual contributions of $3,000 a year starting at age 40 would give you a nest egg of $240,000 at age 65, again assuming an annual return of 8%.

If you're age 50 or over, the news is even better because of a new "catch up" provision in the tax law. In 2003, anyone who is 50 or older can kick in an extra $500 above the $3,000 maximum (in 2006 that catch-up amount rises to $1,000). Sock away $3,500 a year starting at age 50, and in 15 years at 8% you'd have a nifty $106,000—not bad for a later bloomer. In addition to IRAs, contribution maximums also increase for 401(k), 403(b), and other tax-deferred retirement plans, and there are catch-up provisions for those as well. (See the section that follows.)

So don't be discouraged. Whatever your stage in life and no matter how much you have—or have not—saved until now, you have lots of incentives to start planning for a comfortable—and independent—retirement.

# Run, Don't Walk, to Open an IRA

IRAs are a great deal for lots of reasons. First, they are widely available. Anyone who has income from a paying job can have one, so you don't have to depend on your employer to offer a pension plan; you can start your own. A couple of provisions make IRAs particularly attractive to women: If you are a stay-at-home mom without an income and your husband is employed, he can stash an extra $3,000 a year in an IRA for you, so that you can have your own retirement plan (see the discussion below). Also, alimony payments count as income for purposes of opening an IRA.

Second, money you put into the account grows tax-deferred. That means you don't have to pay tax on the earnings as they accrue, so more of your money is working on your behalf—and reaping the bountiful rewards of compound interest. In the preceding section, we saw that if you begin contributing $3,000 a year to an IRA starting at age 40 and earn 8% a year, you'd have $240,000 by age 65. But if the earnings were taxed annually in the 27% bracket, the account would grow to only about $173,000.

IRAs are so attractive that Leslie and her husband, Richard, couldn't pass them up, even though each is already covered by another retirement plan at work. Leslie, a teacher's assistant, has a traditional pension plan, fully funded by her employer. Richard contributes the maximum to his company's voluntary employee retirement plan, and his contribution is matched by his employer. But the couple, both in their 40s, want to retire at age 62. So each has also been contributing the maximum to an IRA, making their contributions in monthly chunks. They're so impressed with the potential of tax-free growth that they have persuaded their teenage children to open IRAs with their summer earnings.

In fact, the biggest decision you'll have to make is not whether to open an IRA, but which kind to open—a traditional IRA or a Roth IRA. A traditional IRA offers the bonus of an instant tax deduction. Money you contribute to a Roth IRA is not tax-deductible, but withdrawals in retirement are tax-free. Generally speaking, the Roth is the better choice, if you're eligible. Let's review some basics.

## Which IRA, Roth or Traditional?

You can make a contribution to a traditional IRA no matter how much you earn, but the opportunity to use a Roth is phased out as

> **If you are a stay-at-home mom without an income and your husband is employed, he can stash an extra $3,000 a year in an IRA for you.**

## You're the Boss

The growing number of women who are self-employed—working either full- or part-time, often working from home—can set up their own IRA or 401(k) to maximize savings while minimizing administrative hassles.

True to its name, a SIMPLE IRA is the simplest plan. You can contribute as much as $6,500 a year, plus an additional 3% of your annual net profit. To set one up, you don't even have to file any forms with the IRS. You can just go to a bank or investment company.

If your business is growing, an individual 401(k), or "I-401(k)," lets sole proprietors set aside even more pre-tax income. A business owner with no employees can contribute 25% of net profit, as well as the $12,000 401(k) salary contribution allowed in 2003 ($13,000 if you're over age 50), up to a total contribution of $40,000. If your husband is the sole proprietor, you can have an account of your own, as long as you work in the business. (For more information about individual 401(k)s, go to www.individualk.com.)

If you plan to add an employee or two down the road, you could suspend the individual 401(k) and set up a traditional plan instead.

---

your adjusted gross income (AGI) rises from $95,000 to $110,000 on a single return and $150,000 to $160,000 on a joint return. (AGI is basically taxable income before deductions and exemptions are subtracted.) While many individuals can deduct contributions to traditional IRAs, no one can write off Roth deposits.

With both IRA varieties, earnings on the money that you invest are protected from the IRS while they're inside the account. However, every dime coming out of a traditional IRA will be taxed (except to the extent that it represents a nondeductible contribution, as explained below), while cash coming out of a Roth is almost sure to be tax-free in retirement.

Two tests determine whether you can deduct contributions to a traditional IRA:

1. **Are you covered by a retirement plan at work?** If not, you can deduct your contributions, no matter how much you make.

2. **What is your income?** If you have a retirement plan at work, your right to the deduction disappears as your income rises. For 2003, the deduction is phased out as AGI rises from $40,000 to $50,000 on a single return and from $60,000 to

$70,000 on a joint return (those numbers adjust upward in future years). A higher phase-out zone applies if your spouse is covered by a retirement plan but you are not. In that case, your right to the deduction disappears as your AGI rises between $150,000 and $160,000.

If you can't deduct regular IRA contributions, the Roth is definitely a better deal for you. Even if you can, it almost surely makes sense to skip the deduction and choose the Roth, as the following discussion shows.

Of course, a big unknown is what your tax bracket will be when you retire, and that's critical to knowing which IRA will be better for you. All other things being equal, if you will be in a higher tax bracket in retirement than you are now, the Roth will prove to be a winner. You're passing up a tax deduction at your lower tax rates today for a tax benefit when your tax rates will be higher. Even if you end up in the same tax bracket when you retire as you are in now, you'll still probably be better off with the Roth. If your tax rate will be lower when you retire, that's a tougher call. But other attributes of a Roth can tip the balance in its favor:

**After a Roth IRA has been in existence for 5 years, you can withdraw up to $10,000 in earnings for the purchase of a new home and both the tax and penalty will be waived.**

- **You can withdraw the total of your annual contributions** at any time without incurring a penalty or tax. Note that this rule applies only to your Roth *contributions,* not to the account's *earnings.* If your withdrawals reach the point at which you're dipping into earnings, you may owe both taxes and a 10% penalty if you're under age 59½. But even here there are attractive exceptions. After the account has been in existence for 5 years, you can withdraw up to $10,000 in *earnings* for the purchase of a new home (for you, your spouse, your kids, your grandchildren, or your parents), and both the tax and penalty will be waived. You can also withdraw earnings to pay college bills without paying a penalty, although you will have to pay taxes on the amount of the earnings that you withdraw unless you are over 59½.
- **You can make contributions at any age,** and you never have to withdraw funds. With a regular IRA, contributions must end at

## ⊗⊐⊪ A Break for Mom

Women who take time off because of pregnancy, childbirth, or adoption of a child, or because they need to care for a child following birth or adoption, don't have to worry about a break in service. Federal law defines a full year of employment as 1,000 hours or more of service, and a break occurs when an employee works fewer than 500 hours in a single year. However, the law also says that up to 501 hours of child-related leave must be counted as service. That means you can take a full year off without incurring a break, so your retirement benefits will continue to accrue during your absence.

age 70½ and withdrawals must begin. Neither restriction applies to a Roth.

- **Roth withdrawals cannot cause social security benefits** to be taxed, while traditional IRA withdrawals can cause that to happen.
- **The balance in a Roth IRA goes to heirs income-tax-free,** whereas the balance in a traditional IRA is taxed to your heirs in their top tax bracket.

## A Retirement Plan for Stay-at-Home Moms

For women, one of the great features of an IRA is that you can have one even if you don't have a paying job, as long as your husband is employed. In that case, he can contribute up to $3,000 of his compensation to an account for you, besides squirreling away $3,000 in his own IRA. You can open either a traditional or a Roth IRA.

If you open a traditional IRA, you can usually deduct the contribution to the spousal account even if the contribution to the worker's account can't be written off. (If your husband is covered by a retirement plan at work, your spousal IRA deductions are limited by the income test, but a much higher income limit applies to spousal IRAs: A contribution to a spousal account can be fully deducted as long as AGI is under $150,000; a partial deduction is allowed until income hits $160,000.)

You can pass up the deduction altogether and open a spousal Roth IRA. Or you and your husband can hedge your bets and open one of each, traditional and Roth. The point is, you can—and should—have your own retirement savings even if you don't have a paying job outside the home. What's more, you can—and should—manage the money yourself (for an investment strategy, see the box on page 134).

# Take Full Advantage of a 401(k)

In addition to IRAs, the retirement savings account you're most likely to run into is an employer-sponsored 401(k) if you work in private industry, or its twin, the 403(b), if you are a public school teacher or are employed by a nonprofit organization.

Those retirement plans, named after a section of the tax code, put you in charge. Although your employer chooses the plan to set up, you decide how much to contribute and how to invest your money, choosing from a menu of investments that your employer offers. Most employers throw in a company match—50 cents on the dollar is common, and some employers are even more generous.

And Uncle Sam chips in with a double tax break:

1. **Because contributions you make to the plan** come right off the top of your salary, that money is not taxed by the IRS. Putting in $5,000 during the year would cut your take-home pay by just $3,250 if you are in a combined 35% federal and state income-tax bracket.

2. **As with IRAs, earnings inside the plan** aren't touched by taxes; you don't owe any until you begin withdrawing the money.

All around, it's a great deal that's getting better every year. In 2003, you can contribute as much as $12,000, and the ceiling will continue to rise by $1,000 a year until it reaches $15,000 in 2006. After that, it will be adjusted for inflation in $500 increments. In addition, these plans have even better catch-up provisions than IRAs. Workers age 50 and older can add an extra $2,000 in 2003, for a total of $14,000, and bump that up $1,000 each year until it reaches $5,000 a year in 2006.

That's a great opportunity for women who entered the work force late, or delayed starting a retirement plan because they were using their income to pay for the kids' braces, the family vacation, or tuition bills. Don't fret about missed opportunities in the past. Seize the ones you have now. Even if you can't afford to make the

## Max Out Your 401(k)?

**Q.** *After I have reached the limit that my employer will match on my 401(k), should I invest additional retirement savings in a Roth IRA or max out my 401(k)?*

**A.** The ideal would be to max out your 401(k) and contribute the full $3,000 to an IRA (or $3,500 if you're at least 50 years old). If you can't afford to do both, the Roth gets the nod, assuming that you qualify. (The right to contribute is phased out as your adjusted gross income rises from $95,000 to $110,000 on a single return and $150,000 to $160,000 on a joint return.) You have almost unlimited options for where to invest Roth money, and you can tap your Roth *contributions* at any time, tax- and penalty-free.

Your strategy should be to put enough into your 401(k) to take advantage of the maximum employer match, divert the next **$3,000** (or **$3,500**) to a Roth, and then return to the 401(k) for additional retirement savings.

maximum contribution to a 401(k), at least put in enough to capture the maximum employer match. That 50 cents on the dollar is free money—and no one can afford to turn down a risk-free return of 50%.

Companies often make employees wait—sometimes for as long as a year—to join the 401(k). Don't let that requirement deter you. Squirrel away part of each paycheck yourself, in a regular savings account or mutual fund. Then when the 401(k) opens up, double your contributions for awhile and use the money you have saved to make up for the shortfall in your paychecks. You can retroactively capture both the tax savings and the employer match.

# Don't Squander Your Kitty

Because women tend to move into and out of the work force more frequently than men, and spend less time in any one job, it has always been tougher for them to put in enough years to earn the full right to benefits accrued under any employer's retirement plan—what's known as becoming fully vested. You are always vested in any money you contribute. Recent changes in vesting

## The Annuity Option

Annuities can be an important element of your retirement savings, not only as a repository for a large lump-sum distribution from a retirement plan, but also as a place to deposit a large divorce settlement or bequest in return for a guaranteed stream of income over a specified period of time.

Because women on average live longer than men and draw annuity benefits longer, monthly payouts may be smaller than a man's for the same amount of principal.

One way around this problem is to buy your annuity with money from a qualified retirement plan, such as an IRA or 401(k). In that case, the insurer must use unisex mortality tables to determine your payments, and you'd get the same benefits as a man would get.

For the same lump-sum investment, monthly income payments can vary by as much as 10% to 12%, so it pays to shop among insurers for the best combination of competitive rates and top safety ratings. For a free shopping service, check out WebAnnuities.com.

schedules speed up your claim on your employer's matching contributions. A plan may have a vesting schedule that gives you the right to 100% of your benefits after just 3 years of service with an employer. Or your employer may have a gradual vesting schedule that gives you full vesting after 6 years.

But as always, it's important that you don't fritter away the money. As mentioned earlier, statistics show that women borrow from their retirement plans more frequently than men do, usually to finance such things as tuition and to pay off debts. And when they get a distribution because they change jobs, they tend to spend the money instead of rolling it over into an IRA. Whereas both of these strategies may seem to bail you out in the short turn, you're jeopardizing your retirement security.

Don't get suckered into the mistaken belief that 401(k) loans are a free ride. Most plans charge the prime rate plus one or two percentage points. Because the interest you pay goes right back into your 401(k) account, you might think there's really no cost. Not so. In fact, the cost could be significantly higher than the stated interest rate.

Say, for example, that you borrow at 7%, but the money you pull out of the 401(k) would otherwise be earning 10% in a mutual fund. That 10% is the real cost of your loan. If that's better than you could get if you borrowed elsewhere, fine. But don't kid yourself that you've found a free lunch. And remember that if you change jobs, you'll have to repay the loan or the amount you withdrew will qualify as a taxable distribution, on which you will also owe the IRS a penalty for early withdrawal.

When you leave a job, you may want to roll over your 401(k) balance into an IRA. The best way to do that is to arrange a direct transfer from your employer to the rollover IRA. Because you won't actually have the money in your hands, you'll avoid tax consequences—and you won't be tempted to spend the money.

# Plan for His-and-Her Retirement

If both you and your husband are eligible for 401(k) plans, both of you should participate. Figure out how much your joint budget will allow, and split your contributions as close to equally as possible so that each of you has a retirement kitty and takes full advantage of any employer match. Don't get yourself into a situation where all the retirement money is in your husband's name, and all your own earnings have gone toward paying for shorter-term expenses.

Although the theme of this book is to think single, it's not meant to leave your husband out of the loop or to pit the two of you against each other. On the contrary, you should be working as a team. At the risk of repeating myself, there's no gene that automatically makes your husband smarter about money. He doesn't instinctively know how a 401(k) plan works, or where you should invest your money. With the two of you pooling your assets and expertise, you'll be able to build a secure financial future. And a strong financial bond is a strong motivation for sticking together. Statistically, married women do better in retirement because they can draw on their husbands' benefits as well as their own, plus a shared nest egg.

If you and your husband don't think you can afford to put aside the maximum amount in a 401(k), at least contribute enough to take full advantage of the company match in each plan.

If even that seems a stretch, put aside something, no matter how small the amount. Remember, it's always easier to save when the money is automatically invested before it gets to your pocket. What you don't see you don't miss, and you won't spend.

You say you just don't have any spare cash? Here are a few places to find money you didn't think you had:

**YOUR UNCLE SAM.** If you get a tax refund every year, you're paying too much to Uncle Sam. Put that money in your pocket instead of his by filing a new W-4 form with your employer to more closely match the amount withheld from your pay to what you actually owe. Claiming extra W-4 "allowances" will trigger higher take-home pay as soon as your next payday. Stash that extra income in your 401(k).

**YOUR SAVINGS FROM REFINANCING.** If you take advantage of falling interest rates to refinance your home mortgage, share part of the bounty with your 401(k).

**YOUR INSURANCE PREMIUMS.** Life-insurance rates have fallen significantly in recent years. If you're in good health, a few minutes spent reshopping an old policy is almost sure to save you money. You can get the job done quickly at InsWeb (www.insweb.com).

**YOUR CAR INSURANCE.** It isn't unusual for one auto insurer to charge significantly more than another to cover the same driver; you may be able to save hundreds of dollars just by shopping (www.insweb.com can help here, too). Once you've settled on a policy, you can save hundreds of dollars more by taking advantage of discounts you're entitled to if you raise your deductible; consolidate your homeowners insurance with the same company; install a car alarm; and report to the insurer if your teenagers qualify for a good-student discount, or move away from home to attend college.

**YOUR MORTGAGE INSURANCE.** Lenders generally require private mortgage insurance (PMI) if you put down less than 20% when you buy your home. But thanks to brisk house-price appreciation in recent years, your home equity may equal at least 25%

of the property's newly appraised value. That's what lenders require between 2 and 5 years after you take out a loan in order for you to shed PMI and save some serious money—$1,000 to $2,000 a year on a $200,000 mortgage. Call your lender to see what you have to do to pull the plug on PMI.

**YOUR STUDENT LOANS.** When interest rates fall, take advantage of your once-in-a-lifetime opportunity to consolidate your variable-rate loans and lock in a low fixed rate. Cut your rate even further by consolidating with a lender that offers discounts, such as Collegiate Funding Services (888-423-7562; www.cfsloans.com). If payments are automatically withdrawn from your checking account, the lender will cut the interest rate an additional one-fourth of a percentage point. After 5 years of on-time payments, your rate will fall by an additional percentage point.

# What Can Women Expect From Traditional Pension Plans?

For men, the strongest leg of the retirement stool has histori-cally been the traditional defined-benefit pension—a fixed monthly payment pegged to your years of service with the company and your salary level. For women workers, traditional pensions have never provided so much support (unless, of course, you were married to a man with a pension plan) for these reasons:

- **Many women work in the service sector and in small businesses,** where pensions are less common.
- **Many women work part-time.** Companies are permitted to exclude even long-term employees from their pension plans if they work less than 1,000 hours a year.
- **Many women don't stay in a job long enough** to qualify, often because they drop out of the work force for an extended time to raise children.
- **Many women earn less than men** even when they are covered.

Unfortunately, just as women have expanded their presence and longevity in the work force—and might be expected to expand their eligibility for traditional pensions—companies are moving away from defined-benefit plans and toward 401(k)s and other defined-contribution plans, discussed previously.

Still, many women, especially those who work for large companies, are covered by traditional pensions—or would be, if they stuck around long enough. Hence, you need to know what you're entitled to. Beat a path to the benefits director at your place of employment, and ask first if your company has a defined-benefit plan. If so, find out what you have to do to qualify.

If your employer has a plan, federal law requires that you must become a member no later than age 21 (if you're working by then) with 1 year of employment. Once you're a member, you start building up your rights to pension benefits year by year. (The "summary plan description" can give you the precise formula your employer uses.)

Even though you may be building up pension benefits over time, you're not completely entitled to them until you're 100% vested. As mentioned before, a plan's vesting schedule is critical to women, who switch jobs more often. Now that full vesting is available in as little as 3 years, you could qualify for benefits even if you're on the move. If you switch jobs, keep a record of what you're entitled to from each employer—or contact past employers if you have lost track.

Each plan also lays down rules defining your pension status when you have a "break in service"—from a layoff, say, or extended leave—or if you do not work a full year. Federal law says that a full year is 1,000 hours of service, and that a break occurs if you work fewer than 500 hours a year. But the law protects you if you miss an extended period of work because of pregnancy, childbirth, or adoption of a child (see the box on page 140).

# How Can You Make the Most of Your Husband's Pension?

For married women, your husband's pension benefits can provide a big chunk of your financial security—or a comfortable cushion if you also have a pension of your own. This is particularly true in the case of widows. Federal law requires that company pension plans offer survivor's benefits. Electing a survivor's benefit (also called the joint-and-survivor option) reduces the pension you and your husband receive during his life, but you would continue to get payments after his death.

If your husband wants to give up his (and your) right to survivor's benefits altogether in favor of a higher pension during his lifetime, you have to agree in writing. Think twice before agreeing. It's generally not a good idea, unless, because of poor health, you don't expect to outlive your husband.

For your own pension, though, the joint-and-survivor option may not be the best choice. Unless your husband is significantly younger or in better health than you are, chances are he won't survive you; therefore you might as well take full benefits during your lifetime.

In selecting a joint-and-survivor option, you and your husband need to consider your relative ages and financial resources. Say your husband chooses joint-and-survivor 100%. This guarantees that the payments he gets over his lifetime will continue at the same level for you after he dies. If he opts for joint-and-survivor 50%, payments will be somewhat higher during his lifetime but will be cut in half after he dies. Which option is better depends on your personal financial situation and health. If you're substantially younger than your husband and don't have a pension yourself, joint-and-survivor 100% may be the better choice. But if you have your own financial resources, you may want to take advantage of larger payments during your husband's lifetime.

*Note:* If you divorce, the only way you can get access to your husband's pension plan is to build an agreement about this into your divorce settlement (see Chapter 8 for more on this subject). Also, because the joint-and-survivor provision does not apply to IRAs and 401(k)s, it's critical that you be named the primary beneficiary of your husband's plan.

# Test the Social Security Safety Net

In dollar terms, social security is generally the shortest leg of the retirement stool. Never meant to provide a comfortable retirement in itself, it was intended to help prop up other resources. But for women, who in the past have had limited access to other resources, it has proved to be the sturdiest leg. Women tend to be far more dependent on social security income than men. Consider the following statistics:

■ **For 76% of unmarried women who are in retirement,** social security represents more than half of all income, and for 26% of unmarried women retirees, it is the *only* source of income, according to the Social Security Administration. Among the U.S. population as a whole, 23% of all retirees rely on social security as their sole source of support.

■ **For the typical woman of retirement age,** social security accounts for 53% of income, compared with just 38% of income for the typical man in retirement.

And that income is hardly lavish. In 2003 the *maximum* social security benefit for someone who retires at age 65 is $1,721 per month—or $20,652 per year. The *average* benefit paid out is considerably lower—$1,158 per month, or $13,896 per year. Of course, over time that figure does increase with inflation. By the year 2013, the average annual benefit is expected to be about $16,095 (in inflation-adjusted dollars), while the maximum is expected to be in the neighborhood of $25,585.

As a rule of thumb, for the typical worker (which the Social Security Administration defines as someone making about $33,000 today), social security will replace about 41% of preretirement earnings; for the maximum earner it will replace about 27%.

## What You're Entitled To

Basically, you must work and pay social security taxes for at least 10 years to qualify for retirement benefits in your own name. As more women have entered the work force and stayed on the job longer, more women are qualifying, independent of their spouses. You can pick up work "credits" from working part-time and through self-employment, as long as you report your earnings and pay the self-employment tax. To calculate your benefit, the Social Security Administration takes into account your highest-paid 35 years of employment. If you worked fewer years than that because you took time off to raise your family, each year that you took off would count as zero earnings, and your benefits would be reduced accordingly.

If you're married, though, you qualify for benefits even if you don't work. If you've never worked at a paid job, you're entitled to receive 50% of your husband's social security benefit (he gets 100% of his benefit, and you get 50% of that amount). If you also qualify for benefits on the basis of your own work record, you'll receive the larger of the two amounts—50% of his or 100% of your own.

You can even qualify for benefits if you are widowed or divorced—and if you are widowed and have unmarried children under 18, they can qualify for survivor's benefits, too (more details appear in Chapters 8 and 10).

**You can start collecting social security retirement benefits as early as age 62, but the benefit amount will be reduced in comparison with what you'd get if you waited until full retirement age.**

One important thing to remember is that although 65 is generally thought of as the normal retirement age at which people are entitled to full social security benefits, that's no longer the case. The full retirement age is gradually moving from 65 to 67. Starting with people born in 1943, the age at which full retirement benefits are paid is 66. And people born in 1960 and later won't hit full retirement age until 67. You can start collecting social security retirement benefits as early as age 62, but the benefit amount will be reduced in comparison with what you'd get if you waited until full retirement age. If you don't need the money, you're probably better off waiting till 65 (or 67) to start collecting benefits.

The Social Security Administration is happy to figure out what you've got coming. Each year the government sends customized notices to millions of workers, showing an estimate of how much they've paid into the system so far and their estimated benefits when they retire. Each statement will also show the worker's complete earnings history, according to the Social Security Administration's computer records. Take a few minutes to go over the numbers you receive and check for errors. Your benefits will be based on the numbers you see on your statement, so that if earnings are underreported, your benefits will be reduced. If you have misplaced your statement, want an updated one, or wish to correct an error, call the Social Security Administration at 800-772-1213, or visit www.ssa.gov. The site features information for women at www.ssa.gov/women.

## What You Can Count On

For almost as long as any of us can remember, politicians and economists have been debating the future of social security—whether it has a future or will simply run out of money as outgoing benefits exceed the incoming tax revenues needed to pay for them. *Kiplinger's* best guess is, Yes, America, there will be a social security, even for 20-somethings who are just now entering the work force. But changes in the system, necessary to put it on a sound footing for the long-term, will probably mean lower benefits. Here's what you should expect, depending on your age:

**Yes, America, there will be a social security, even for 20-somethings who are just now entering the work force.**

**IF YOU'RE 55 OR OLDER:** You'll be insulated from any major changes to the system. Plan on getting roughly what your social security benefits statement now indicates—maybe a tad less in the event that there are some minor changes down the road, such as smaller cost-of-living adjustments (increases to compensate for inflation) or higher taxes on benefits.

**IF YOU'RE 40 TODAY:** You'll still collect benefits. But at some point, middle-aged and younger workers are going to bear the brunt of putting the system into balance for the long term. If you're 40 now, it's reasonable to assume that in the absence of other reforms, your benefits would be cut by around 10%.

**IF YOU'RE 25 TODAY:** While it's trendy for 20-somethings to say they expect nothing from social security, at the very least you should count on the program as a safety net. But you will probably pay an even higher price than your 40-year-old cousins to eventually put the system into balance. It's not unreasonable to expect a 20% cut in projected benefits.

Of course, if social security adopts some type of private investment account, as has often been suggested, younger workers could make up some, if not all, of any cuts in guaranteed benefits.

# Your Talents Are Your Greatest Asset

Today's workers should expect a greater share of the assets they will need in retirement to come from their own savings and employer-based plans, such as 401(k)s, rather than social security and traditional pensions. But don't panic. Although that situation gives you more responsibility for planning your own retirement, you can also expect help from yet a fourth leg on the traditional three-legged stool: income from a part-time job or a second career. A survey by the AARP found that 80% of baby-boomers say they expect to work at least part-time in retirement, a trend that is particularly pronounced among women. Nearly two-thirds of women questioned by the Women's Retirement Confidence Survey plan to work in retirement.

Sometimes that will be out of necessity, because they simply can't afford to retire cold turkey. That's particularly true of women like Susan, whose story was told in a *New York Times* article about the plight of older divorced women who lack pensions. Susan stopped working when she began having children, and then divorced after 20 years of marriage. Her divorce settlement removed her name from her husband's health insurance, gave her very little income, and left her with no stake in her husband's future pension. She entered the work force, and has had a successful 16-year career. But at 63 she hasn't worked long enough to build a pension that will let her retire completely; hence she's hoping to supplement her income with a part-time job in a new career.

Often women continue working out of choice. Many women now in their 50s and 60s are far from ready to retire, having only entered the workplace in their 40s once their children were in high school or college. In fact, twice as many women (compared with men) perceive their job or career as enriching their life. And a survey by the National Center on Women and Aging found that women age 50 and older who work are healthier and have a more positive attitude than women who don't.

They are women like Carol and Patti, two sisters who, when they were in their 50s, pooled their creative talents to start a business crafting canvas floor coverings and other pieces of Americana folk

## Don't Stop Now!

- **Use** a retirement-planning calculator or the worksheet in this chapter to estimate how money you'll need in retirement.
- **Identify** the extra $20 per week that you could redirect into your retirement savings.
- **Decide** whether a traditional or Roth IRA is better for you and open one.
- **Open** an IRA if you're a stay-at-home mom, and fund it from your husband's income.
- **Stash** at least enough money in your 401(k) to get the maximum employer-sponsored match.
- **Revise** contributions as necessary to even out the amounts in your husband's and your respective accounts.
- **Learn** your pension's rules so that you don't inadvertently penalize yourself.
- **Double-check** your employment history shown on your annual estimate of social security benefits.

art. Not only has their business been a financial success, but it also provides employment for two generations of retirees—the sisters and their 80-something parents. "I would be bored to death," says their mom. "This is much better than playing bridge."

Whatever the reason, labor-force participation by women in their early 60s has been rising, while the proportion of older men in the labor force has been falling. In the future, employers in need of skilled workers will make it even easier for you to stay on the job. One new trend we're already seeing is "phased retirement." Instead of forcing you to leave at a certain age, employers will let you delay full retirement and work part-time or flexible hours, hire you back as an independent contractor, or use you as a kind of floating temp, plugging you into an interim position or giving you a mentoring role.

The point is, in addition to your 401(k) or IRA, you have another major asset that's often overlooked—your earning power. Just like any other asset, you should cultivate it when you're younger—by taking advantage of employer reimbursement for education and training to hone your skills—so that you can draw on it in the future.

# Divorce:
# Get a Fair Deal

 hen Marcie married, it was "before the days of women's lib," she says. "You thought in terms of being a helpmate to your husband. He took care of the finances, and you trusted him." But when Marcie was in her 40s she and her husband were forced to declare bankruptcy. Several years later they divorced, and Marcie faced the prospect of foreclosure on her house and the need to provide stability for her three children. "I got terribly practical and realistic in a hurry," she says. First, she found a bank to extend her a loan and save the house. Then she returned to a full-time job as a teacher to restore her standing in a retirement plan. Several years later, her finances were settled enough for her to start planning for her children's college education and saving for a family trip to Hawaii. "I love calling the shots," she says. "But if I had been ten years older, I don't know if I could have salvaged what I managed to salvage."

Make no mistake about it: From a financial point of view, divorce is a disaster. You have to shell out thousands of dollars in legal fees. Your income is cut in half, or worse. You

### Did You Know?

Hope springs eternal, but perhaps financial relief beckons most strongly: Among people whose first marriages end in divorce, fully 75% will remarry—half within three years.

can't count on receiving alimony or child support. Your ability to pool resources to build family assets for the kids' education or your retirement is severely hampered. You and your ex will have to maintain two households afterward, with additional (and often unanticipated) expenses for travel, duplicate sets of kids' toys and clothes, and possibly a new wardrobe if you (or your ex) have to return to work.

**Divorce can be so financially devastating for both parties, and especially women, that more and more marriage counselors are advising couples to think twice before going through with it.**

Among recently divorced women studied by the U.S. Census Bureau, 21% were living below the poverty line, compared with 9% of recently divorced men. And the recent spike in bankruptcy filings among single women includes "a distressing number" of divorced women with children, says a researcher at the University of Texas. A study by the National Center on Women and Aging found that married women and single women who had never married were much more optimistic about their financial future than women who had been widowed or divorced.

Get the picture? Divorce can be so financially devastating for both parties, and especially women, that more and more marriage counselors are advising couples to think twice before going through with it.

I'd second that opinion. Although the theme running throughout this book has been to think single, it certainly makes sense from a financial point of view to double up. Not only can two live more cheaply together than apart, but two financially savvy partners can also get a leg up on building future assets by merging their funds and their expertise.

And I certainly wouldn't go so far as to talk about "divorce planning." Not only is that a downer, but it's also a contradiction in terms—after all, no couple actually plans to get a divorce.

But let's face it: It certainly helps to be prepared if your marriage breaks up—as about 40% of all first-time marriages in America do, according to the U.S. Census. "When I was married, I thought in terms of being a helpmate," says Marcie. "He took care of all the finances and I trusted him, but I ended up bankrupt and divorced." The lesson, she says, is that "even when you delegate, you have to stay on top of things."

If you've been following the advice in this book, you're already on top of things. You will have credit in your own name, and possibly your own bank accounts. You will be clued in to the family finances, with a handle on what you, as a couple, own and how much you owe. You will have retirement savings of your own— even if you don't work outside the home—and experience in investing that money. You'll be in a good position to land on your feet.

Nevertheless, divorce throws you into a whole new situation with its own set of challenges. As if the emotional issues of untying the knot weren't traumatic enough, divorce can also be one of the largest and most convoluted financial transactions of a lifetime. The attendant money decisions—whether they're made in the heat of anger or the calm of careful calculations—are likely to leave an indelible imprint on your balance sheet. It takes a cool head and careful maneuvering to claim your fair share of family assets and emerge from the experience as financially whole as possible. Obviously, that is an essential goal.

> **It takes a cool head and careful maneuvering to claim your fair share of family assets and emerge from the experience as financially whole as possible.**

Despite the complex feelings that you may have as you end your marriage, and even if you desire fair play for both you and your ex, you can't afford not to ensure the future financial well-being of yourself and your children.

## Don't Go It Alone

Even before one of you has filed for divorce, it's helpful to consult with a lawyer if you feel a split may be imminent. You want someone who's experienced in matrimonial law, but resist the urge to hire a sharklike lawyer to sink his or her teeth into your soon-to-be ex. Although that may be a satisfying thought, nothing is worse than a divorce in which the legal bills consume half your assets. An antagonistic relationship means more time and money spent battling over the little things now—and possibly

## To Find a Mediator

**The Association for Conflict Resolution** (1527 New Hampshire Ave., N.W., Washington, DC 20036; 202-667-9700; www.acresolution.org) offers an online search for family mediators at its Web site. Although the site is dedicated primarily to practitioners, some of the publications and FAQs may be of interest to prospective users of mediation.

into the future if you have children and must continue to make decisions with your ex on their behalf.

In fact, many couples use professional mediation to avoid the lengthy, humiliating, and expensive process of dragging their divorce through the courts. In many cases mediation can be a less expensive and much faster way to arrive at an agreement. The mediator's role is to guide you through the process, not to make decisions for you. Before signing a property settlement, it's a good idea to have it reviewed by a lawyer to make sure that you haven't overlooked something.

Don't let your lawyer orchestrate the whole show. Even the most skilled and attentive lawyer may not lead you to the best financial outcome. Lawyers are trained to interpret the law to get you the settlement you want, but they are not specialists in evaluating whether you're better off with, say, a portfolio of highly appreciated stocks or the beach house. On paper the assets may be equal in value, but their value to you may depend on whether you plan to hold or sell them, and on the taxes and transaction costs you'll pay when you sell. You need to figure out those issues for yourself, perhaps with the help of a financial adviser. (Nowadays there's a whole category of financial advisers known as certified divorce planners; see the box on page 174.)

If your situation is simple, if you don't have any children, and if you're both eager to settle your differences and get on with your lives, you may be able to arrive at an agreement in mediation or through your lawyers, without going to court, or by filing papers on your own, as many people do. But even in a do-it-yourself divorce, you may want to consult with a lawyer or financial professional, or have an expert review the paperwork before you sign off on it. (You can find an abundance of resources on the subjects of divorce and self-help divorce. A good place to start is the book *Divorce & Money: How to Make the Best Financial Decisions During Divorce,* by Violet Woodhouse and Victoria F. Collins with M. C. Blakeman, published by Nolo Press.)

# Get Rid of Joint Debt

I f you know you're headed for divorce and you don't already have your own checking and savings accounts, head straight to your bank and open them. Acquire any new assets in your own name, but try to postpone purchases and conserve as much cash as possible.

Change the signature authority on any joint account so that both of you must sign in order to complete a transaction. You also have the option of withdrawing half the money in the account and depositing it in your individual account. If you (or your husband) should try to get away with all the money, the court would probably order you (or him) to give half of it back. Another option would be to close the joint account and put all the money into a neutral escrow account. Any withdrawal would have to be approved by both spouses and the escrow agent.

With joint brokerage accounts, tell your broker to get both you and your spouse to sign off on any transactions.

If you don't already have a credit card in your own name, apply for one and then close all joint accounts. In most states, both you and your husband are responsible for any debts you incur for necessities—such as food, clothing, shelter, and health care—until your divorce decree is final. Both of you are also liable for joint credit cards, so don't count on getting relief from any big Visa and MasterCard balances. But at least notify card companies and other creditors in writing about your situation, and tell them you won't be responsible for future charges. Ask them to send copies of statements to each of you, so that you can monitor any spending by your husband before the account is closed.

To protect yourself, get a complete list of your creditors by contacting one of the three major credit reporting agencies: Equifax (800-685-1111), Experian (800-397-3742), and Trans Union (800-916-8800). The best strategy is to include a complete payoff of all credit cards and other lines of credit in your divorce settlement. To make sure that all your joint debts really do get paid, consider assuming responsibility for payment yourself, and claim a share of assets to offset the debt.

Since charges sometimes go through on recently closed accounts, notify creditors that you're getting divorced and that you won't be responsible for anything your husband charges. The assertion may not hold up in court should the creditor decide to pursue payment from you, but at least it gives you a shot at making your case. When you're corresponding with a creditor, send all letters by certified mail and keep copies for your files.

The Institute of Consumer Financial Education (ICFE), a nonprofit group in San Diego, reports that most questions it receives about credit problems involve individuals whose credit rating was damaged by a former spouse *after* a divorce. "In most instances, these individuals allowed their former spouse to 'take over' responsibility for paying jointly held debts," says the ICFE. "That's a mistake that may come back to haunt you until the debts are paid in full." (For more information on protecting your credit, see the Web sites sponsored by the ICFE at www.financial-education-icfe.org; and by Myvesta, an independent credit counseling organization, at www.myvesta.org.)

# Who Gets What?

Sometimes it takes a high-profile divorce case to shed light on one of the toughest issues that divorcing couples routinely face—how much of a couple's accumulated assets should be attributed to the breadwinner and how much to the intangible efforts of a non-income-earning spouse.

During the past decade, one of the highest-profile divorce cases was that of Lorna and Gary Wendt. Married for 31 years, Lorna contended that she was part of a 50/50 partnership with Gary, then chief executive officer of GE Capital, and should be entitled to half their accumulated assets. Gary Wendt argued that he would have been just as successful without his wife's support. Apparently agreeing with Lorna, the judge's award exceeded Gary's settlement offer and included the value of some of his stock options and other compensation that he had yet to realize.

**www.**

## Splitting Up the Family Business

If you and your husband own a business together, or if one of you owns a business, it's just as much an asset as your home or your bank accounts—and it may be the most valuable one you own. As with other property, you have several options: sell the business and divide the proceeds, give one spouse the business in exchange for another asset, or let one spouse buy the other out. In any case, it's essential that you get your own independent appraisal of the business so that you know what you're dealing with. Ask your attorney or accountant for a recommendation, or contact the American Society of Appraisers (800-272-8258, www.appraisers.org).

The first significant thing about the Wendt case was that the court sided with Lorna; the second was that in dividing assets, the court went far beyond accounting for the obvious investment accounts and furniture. In any divorce case, a lawyer's advice—and the award you eventually get—is only as good as the information you provide. That means you have to rustle up as many financial details as possible about your income (pay stubs, bank statements, tax returns), and your assets, both financial and real, including which of you owns what, and when you acquired it. Don't overlook any detail when compiling your financial inventory; you'll even need the passwords to any online financial records.

Which assets are on the table in a divorce? Anything acquired during your marriage is considered marital property to be divided according to state law. In the nine community-property states— Arizona, California, Idaho, Louisiana, Nevada, New Mexico, Texas, Washington, and Wisconsin—marital property is divided 50/50. In other states, property is divided "equitably" rather than equally, taking into account the duration of the marriage, the earning capacity of each spouse, and each spouse's contribution to the accumulation of assets, whether by paid work or work in the home. Generally, you're not expected to share inheritances, property you owned before marriage, or gifts directed to only one spouse.

Some assets are obvious: bank accounts, brokerage and mutual fund accounts, the house, the car, a vacation home or rental property, jewelry, electrical equipment, the contents of a safe-deposit

## IRAs and Divorce

**Q.** *My husband and I are getting a divorce, and one of our major assets is his traditional IRA. Can I get that IRA as part of the divorce settlement, or would it have to be cashed in and taxes and penalties paid?*

**A.** This is the one instance—other than death of the owner—that the law allows the ownership of an IRA to be transferred. If the IRA is transferred by a written divorce decree, or a document related to that decree, the transfer is tax-free. The traditional IRA would then be yours; any withdrawals would be taxed to you and, if you are under 59 1/2, subject to the 10% early-withdrawal penalty.

box. Others are less obvious—savings in a retirement plan, stock options and other employee benefits, an upcoming tax refund, frequent-flier miles, and season tickets to sporting events. Lorna Wendt even laid claim to the Macy's credit card—which came with a lifetime 45% discount because at one time Gary Wendt was on Macy's board of directors. If you are uncertain of the value of certain assets, it might be prudent to obtain an appraisal of them.

When the court awarded Lorna Wendt a slice of her husband's stock options, she got her share in cash, so that she didn't have to worry about future movements in the stock price. Faced with a similar choice, or a choice between a lump sum now and ongoing payments in the future (for alimony, for example), go for the lump sum, even if it doesn't quite equal the anticipated future value of the income or assets. Having a lump-sum payment in hand frees you from the risk that an annuity, pension, or shares of stock might be worth less than you expect later on, or that you'll face unforeseen taxes or transaction costs. (See also the discussion of whether to keep the family home, below.)

# Don't Count on Alimony

You don't have an automatic right to alimony, and you should-n't count on getting it. Most divorce settlements don't provide spousal support. When a spouse gets anything, it's usually short-term maintenance that may last for only a few years. Exceptions to that rule are usually older women who have had a long-term marriage and have never worked outside the home. They may be awarded alimony that continues until their death or remarriage.

Nowadays, women may be required to pay alimony to their husbands—especially if the wife was the breadwinner and the husband was a nonworking spouse who had assumed primary care of the children.

No matter what the circumstances under which it is awarded, alimony stops if one spouses dies, or if the recipient remarries or begins living with someone else.

*A note on taxes:* Alimony is taxable income to the person receiving it; the person paying it is entitled to take a tax deduction. Alimony also counts as earned income for purposes of making IRA contributions.

As already mentioned, if you have the option of taking a lump-sum cash settlement instead of alimony, take it. You won't have to worry about your ex making payments, and you won't be cut off if you move in with someone else. Because alimony payments are tax-deductible to the payer while cash settlements are not, your husband might resist the idea (and so might you, if you're the one who's paying). But many women are willing to forgo the tax savings in favor of making a clean break with their former husband.

# Know What to Expect in Child Support

Although child support is more common than alimony, you still can't count on collecting it. Fewer than half of all women who are due child support ever get the full amount to which they are entitled; another quarter or so receive partial payment. (In fairness, however, we should note that fewer than half of all custodial fathers receive the full amount of child support that they are due.) Every state relies on a standardized formula to determine a minimum level of child-support payments. Courts can award more if they choose. Federal law requires states to review child-support agreements from time to time and to adjust them for inflation or changes in parents' income.

Child-support orders generally contain an automatic wage withholding provision, so that your former husband's employer

## Who Claims the Kids?

**Q.** *My husband and I are divorced, and our kids live with me. He is behind in his child support, but he says he should get to claim the kids as dependents on his tax return anyway. I say he should pay up first. Who is correct?*

**A.** The law generally gives the dependency exemption for children to the custodial parent named in the divorce decree. If the decree doesn't name either parent, the custodial parent is the one with whom the children live for the greater part of the year. If your children live with you for more than half the year, you can claim the children as your dependents no matter how much support you receive from your ex.

It's possible for your ex-husband to claim the kids as his dependents if the court decree gives him that right, or if you sign a waiver, Form 8332. You would have to sign that waiver for each year the exemption is shifted to him. Otherwise, you, not he, should claim the children on your return.

can withhold a portion of his pay and send it on to you. But if your ex doesn't have steady income or is self-employed, this tactic may not work. If it appears that your ex will not make good on his child-support commitment, you will have to seek a court hearing. Courts have the option of throwing an offender in jail or of trying to collect the money by some other route, such as confiscating the noncustodial parent's income tax refund.

If the court awards you child-support payments, ask that your ex also be required to purchase a life insurance policy covering the term of the payments, naming you as the owner and beneficiary of the policy. This will protect you in the event of your ex's death. If premium payments are missed, you'll be notified.

Unlike alimony, child-support payments are not tax-deductible for your spouse, nor are they considered taxable income for you.

If you're applying for credit, both alimony and child support can be considered as income when a lender is calculating how much debt you can handle. And they will be considered as income by colleges reviewing your child's application for financial aid.

Because child-support payments usually end when the child

## Trading Dependency

**Q.** *My ex-spouse and I alternate years in which we claim our daughter as a dependent. We agreed to this outside the divorce decree. It was not a big deal, and it's a nice way to pay less tax every other year.*

**A.** It's a pleasure to hear from a couple who have managed to settle this acrimonious issue so amicably and sensibly.

reaches 18, it's a good idea to write an agreement making clear who will pay for the child's college education. Although there's no legal obligation for either parent to pay for college, the Free Application for Federal Student Aid (or FAFSA), which all schools require you to fill out to apply for federal financial aid, asks for information about the income and assets of the custodial parent and, if he or she has remarried, the spouse. However, some schools will award their own financial aid based on the finances of both the custodial and noncustodial parent.

# Look Beyond Child Support

In Chapter 5 I discussed my advice, during an appearance on *The Oprah Winfrey Show,* to one family with teenage kids whose spending habits were out of control. Another of the families on the same show was a recently divorced mother, Susan, and her two teenage daughters. The girls were manipulating their mother's guilt feelings to a fare-thee-well. They had run up a long-distance phone bill of more than $1,000, on which Susan was struggling to pay $100 a month. When she refused to buy them clothes or whatever else they asked for, they frankly admitted to pouting and bugging her until she finally caved in. Susan was afraid to tell them that their financial situation had changed and that they couldn't afford to spend so much money.

Aside from giving Susan practical advice—cut off the kids' long-distance access (or limit it with something like a prepaid phone card), put them on a fixed allowance to help cover their expenses, and say no—my advice to Susan was to level with the kids about the altered state of the family's finances. They were old enough to understand what was going on, and to adapt their

## Health Insurance After a Divorce

**Q.** *My children and I have health insurance through my husband's policy at work, but we're divorcing. Will I have to find new coverage on my own?*
**A.** There are a couple of ways in which you can continue to be covered by your husband's policy.

Under federal law, you can get health-insurance coverage for your children through your husband's employer-provided plan even if he's the noncustodial parent. You will want to negotiate this in your divorce settlement, and you should also request a Qualified Medical Child Support Order, which will require the insurance company to reimburse you directly for any costs that you pay out of pocket for your children's care. This will guarantee that you receive the reimbursement.

Another option: If your husband works for a company with 20 or more employees, federal law requires that the company allow you and your children to continue coverage under the group plan for up to 3 years after the employee dies or divorces. (Some states require smaller companies to continue coverage, too.) You must notify the employer within 60 days of the divorce. The catch is that you'll have to pay the entire premium yourself, which can be a shock if your ex's employer had subsidized the coverage. The employer may also charge you up to 2% extra to cover administrative expenses. If you're in good health, you may find a lower-priced policy on your own. For price quotes on individual health insurance, check out www.eHealthInsurance.com.

behavior to their family's new circumstances.

One of the biggest mistakes divorced parents make is to pretend that nothing has changed—a sure way to dig yourself into a financial hole. It's better to encourage your kids (especially older ones) to brainstorm for ways in which they can help cut back on expenses, or contribute money or sweat equity to the household. Says one divorced parent with custody of three children, "I don't hide the time and money pressures from my kids. We work together to do the household chores, and they no longer beg me for toys I can't possibly afford."

Children will continue to hold you and your ex-husband

together, and financial issues can be even more thorny than when you were together. It's important to sort out as many issues as you can in front of a judge and not the kids. Even if their father is behind on his child-support payments, criticizing him won't necessarily win you any sympathy from the children, because kids can be fiercely loyal to both parents. In fact, some of the biggest bones of contention in a divorce are child-related expenses that were overlooked at the time of the split but surface later.

You can short-circuit future problems by addressing as many child-related financial issues as possible in the divorce agreement:

- **Do your children have special needs or gifts** that will require extra expenditures?
- **Who's going to pay for piano** (or gymnastics) lessons?
- **Is summer camp** still in the picture?
- **If the kids are approaching driving age,** who's going to pay for insurance?

Build into the divorce agreement a procedure for periodically reviewing the settlement through your lawyers, to allow for changes in your children's health, growth patterns, or emotional needs.

Another way to handle these situations is to arrange for both spouses to share more or less equally in child support. One of the most creative systems I've ever encountered is for both parents to draw up a budget for their children's expenses and open a special checking account, funded proportionately in accordance with both their incomes. The checkbook goes back and forth with the kids, and both parents are responsible for handling expenses. That kind of arrangement assumes you're on speaking terms with each other—but maintaining a civilized relationship (and resisting the temptation to get even) can pay off in less financial pressure.

## Should You Keep the House?

Hanging onto the house might seem like a good way to avoid uprooting the kids and to maintain some stability in their world. But keeping the house may backfire, both psychologically and financially. On your reduced income, you may not be able to keep up payments for the mortgage, insurance, taxes, and maintenance. The kids won't feel reassured if they sense you're wor-

## The Importance of a United Front

**Q.** *How would you suggest handling finances for a 13-year-old who spends most of her time with her dad and me (the step-mom), but her mom has primary custody? Her dad is paying child support, but this child is constantly asking us for money. She also expects us to buy her clothes whenever she wants them, and the mom just comes unglued whenever we mention to this child that we are paying child support. Should we give her extra money when she can't get it from her mother? Sometimes she won't even ask her mom because she sees us as doing better financially. For this reason, she feels that we owe her more than just the child support that we pay her mother.*

**A.** If it's any consolation, you are dealing with a classic conflict involving children and divorce. While each family's circumstances are unique, every situation has certain elements in common:

- **Kids are not above playing one parent against another.** They will try to take advantage of parental guilt or resentment toward an ex-spouse to extort money, clothes, and other stuff.
- **Bad-mouthing an ex-spouse won't win over a child to your side.** Kids can be fiercely loyal to both parents. Your stepdaughter doesn't really care about your child-support arrangements with her mother.
- **Divorced parents still share an interest in raising financially responsible kids.** Whether divorced or married, parents should never hand out money or buy clothing on demand, or let kids think you "owe" them something just because you're well off financially.
- **All parents, even divorced ones, should speak to kids with one voice.** That means they need to speak to

ried about making the mortgage payment. If you keep the house and let your ex have some other asset, such as stocks or a retirement plan, you could live to regret the decision. Talk this problem over carefully with your lawyer or financial adviser, and seriously consider trading down your digs. That could ease stress and give everyone a fresh start.

Taxes can also be a factor. Up to $250,000 of home-sale profit is tax-free. That doubles to $500,000 if you file a joint return. To qualify for this exclusion, you must own and live in the house for 2 of the 5 years before the sale. If you are divorced at the end of the year in which the house is sold, you can each exclude up to $250,000 of gain on your individual returns—assuming both of you pass the 2-out-of-5-years ownership and residency tests. In late 2002 the IRS provided an exception to the 2-year rule in cases of

each other first, in a nonthreatening way, to come up with a plan for dealing with the situation.

In your case, Mom and Dad should decide what they are willing to buy for their daughter, and what she should be expected to pay for on her own. If Mom is already buying clothes, Dad needs to know that. If Dad wishes to supplement those purchases, Mom needs to know that.

And they both should agree on a fixed allowance for their daughter— possibly with each contributing a portion—which she has to use for agreed-upon expenses, such as entertainment.

The point is, each parent should know approximately how much the other is spending, so that their daugh-

ter can't double dip.

All this assumes that parents are still on speaking terms. Even if divorced spouses are at odds over everything else, family counselors recommend that they make an effort to communicate regularly about their kids, if only through a phone conversation. If hang-ups become the rule, however, you might seek the services of a divorce mediator. As a result of mediation, one couple reached a written agreement that they and their teenage daughter would discuss extraordinary expenses. "The three of us would decide who would pay for what, and whether the purchase should be made in the first place," says the father. "We paid the mediator $900 to settle something that $75,000 in legal fees hadn't settled."

divorce. If, for example, you owned the house for only one year before the divorce, you could qualify for 50% of the exclusion— or $125,000 on a single return.

If ownership of a home is transferred to you in a divorce, the time that your former spouse owned the place is added to your period of ownership before the sale for purposes of the 2-year test. But you can exclude only up to $250,000 of profit because you're now single.

# Tap Your Husband's Pension

In a story on the retirement woes of older divorced women, *The New York Times* tells the story of Judith, who was divorced from her police officer husband in an amicable arrangement under

## In Defense of the "Innocent Spouse"

When you file a joint tax return with your husband, the law holds each of you fully responsible for the tax due, and Congress has ordered the IRS to collect from whichever spouse it can. This has resulted in some ugly cases in which the IRS has pursued one spouse for taxes owed as a result of misdeeds of the other spouse, such as failure to report income, claims of improper deductions, or failure to pay taxes due.

There are rules that allow the "innocent spouse" to shed responsibility for taxes that are really the obligation of the other spouse. But to do so you have to show that you didn't know or didn't have reason to know that the tax on the return in question was understated. If you find yourself in this situation, you have 2 years from the time the IRS begins trying to collect from you to seek relief by filing Form 8857.

which she did not drive a hard bargain. She received a cash settlement; he kept the house and all rights to his police pension, which he collected until his death. Judith went on to a series of corporate jobs and then started her own business. She created a good life for herself, and a successful one—but not successful enough to provide her with the resources she needs to retire. At the age of 61, she looks back and regrets not having fought for a share of her husband's pension.

When couples divorce, their retirement funds can be their largest single asset. If the bulk of these funds is in your husband's name, it's critical that you take those funds into account in your divorce settlement so that you're not left high and dry. You may decide to forgo a share in your husband's benefits to get some other asset instead. But that should be your choice, and not something that happens by default because you didn't know any better.

To get a share of your ex-husband's retirement nest egg at work, your lawyer must petition for a qualified domestic relations order (QDRO, or "quadro," for short), which tells the pension plan administrator how to divide the benefits between you and your ex-husband. You could be awarded a "cash-out," that is, an immediate payment of benefits that is based on an estimate of the future value of your ex-husband's pension. Or you could opt for a "deferred pay-out" of benefits, which would begin as soon as your ex-husband starts collecting his pension and would be paid out regularly.

## ⊗⊐▯▯ How to File Your Taxes

It's your marital status at the close of December 31 that matters to the IRS. Therefore, even if you are divorced for only one day before year-end, you file as a single person for the entire year. But if you're eligible for head-of-household status, you have the right to use lower-than-single tax rates. To qualify, you must meet two tests:

1. **You must be unmarried at the end of the tax year.**
2. **You must pay more than half the cost of keeping up the principal home** for you and a child or other relative you can claim as a dependent. Even if a child isn't your dependent but is unmarried and living in your home, you can still claim head-of-household status.

Generally, head-of-household status is used by divorced women with small children at home. But it can also pay off for divorced or widowed parents whose grown children return to the nest after college or following a divorce—regardless of how much money the boomerang child makes. In most cases, you and the relative must share the same house for more than half the year.

Unless you think you'd squander the lump sum, a cash-out is safer. If you take a lump sum, you can roll the funds into an IRA or, if you're willing to pay the taxes immediately, keep the cash. If you transfer part of a former husband's IRA into an IRA of your own, you can't tap the account penalty-free until you reach age 59½. But because these are retirement assets, unless you have some overriding need for immediate cash, it's better to let the money continue building up tax-deferred earnings until you're ready to stop working.

In the real world, you won't always have the option of getting a cash-out benefit from a company retirement plan. And your husband may be short of cash, too, given that you're going through a divorce. If that's the case, you may have to rely on a QDRO to spell out the rights and benefits you're entitled to in the future. It's critical that you—through your lawyer—dot every "i" and cross every "t." To be valid, for instance, the QDRO must be signed by the court and approved by the retirement plan administrator—loose ends that often don't get tied up.

Once you have a handle on the value of your husband's retirement assets, you and your attorney can decide whether to fight for a share of them or offer to give up your rights to those assets in exchange for others.

A retirement plan may be more valuable to one spouse than the other. Consider the case of a doctor married to a schoolteacher. Because retirement assets are usually protected from creditors, the doctor, who may face a liability lawsuit some day, may want to keep the plan and the protection that goes along with it. As for the teacher, who may already be covered by a pension of his or her own, having access to a more liquid asset, such as a stock portfolio, could outweigh his or her interest in the retirement plan.

(See also the discussion of changing your designation of beneficiaries on your pension plan, below.)

# Exercise Your Rights to Social Security

As was explained in the preceding chapter, even if you've never worked at a paid job, you're entitled to receive 50% of your husband's social security benefit. And that's true even if you and your husband are divorced.

To qualify for benefits based on your former husband's earnings, the marriage must have lasted at least 10 years, both you and your ex-husband must be at least 62 years old, and the checks can't start until 2 years after the divorce. Figuring out how much you'll receive can be tricky. Here are a few typical scenarios:

**Patty, 54, went back to work after her 27-year marriage ended.** If she is still unmarried when she applies for social security, she will receive half of her former husband's benefits or an amount based on her own earnings, whichever is larger.

**Sharon, 62, was married for 40 years and has been divorced for 3 months.** Her ex-husband is 58. Because she doesn't qualify for benefits on her own, she must wait 4 years—until her ex-husband is 62—to apply for benefits. At that time she will be entitled to 50% of the amount her husband qualifies for, regard-less of whether he retires and files for benefits.

**Phyllis, 53, was married to her first husband for 22 years. Her second marriage lasted only 4 years.** Assuming that she is unmarried at age 62, she can collect benefits that are based on her first hus-band's earnings—but not on her second husband's earnings, because her second marriage lasted less than 10 years. As is always the case with social security, if Phyllis begins to take ben-efits at age 62, they will be lower than if she waits until age 65 to begin collecting.

As a divorced wife, your benefits are not affected if your ex-husband remarries. But if *you* remarry, you lose the right to bene-fits based on your former husband's earnings—unless your sec-ond marriage also ends in divorce. If both marriages lasted at least 10 years, you could elect social security benefits based on either—but not both—of your ex-husbands' earnings, presumably whichever amount is higher.

If you are eligible for spousal benefits and your ex-husband dies, the amount you are due doubles. As a divorced widow, you are eligible for 100% of your ex-husband's benefits, compared with 50% as a divorced spouse. Divorced-widow benefits aren't affected if you remarry after age 60.

*Note:* The same rules apply to ex-husbands as to ex-wives, but men are generally eligible, on the basis of their own earnings, for benefits that are much higher than the amount they'd receive if they applied for 50% of an ex-wife's benefits.

# Revisit Your Estate Plan

Once you've split up the marriage and the property, you may need to make some other estate moves that are easy to over-look. For example, if you and your husband had an advance health-care directive, you probably named him as the person to make health-care decisions for you if you became unable to do so. Likewise, many spouses give each other general powers of attor-ney to manage the other's financial affairs in an emergency. You'll probably want to change those designations.

**www.**

### Expert Assistance

The finances of divorce are so complicated that a whole new group of advisers has sprung up to help clients determine the financial impact of any proposed settlement. Called certified divorce planners or certified divorce specialists, they're usually financial planners, accountants, or other financial professionals who have taken an additional course to learn about financial issues related to divorce, such as tax consequences, division of pension plans, and continued health care coverage.

Note that the role of a divorce planner is to assist an attorney, not replace an attorney. If you're going through a divorce, you still need legal counsel. To find an adviser in your area, contact:

■ **The Institute for Certified Divorce Planners** (800-875-1760; www.institutecdp.com)

■ **The College for Divorce Specialists** (www.cdscollege.com).

You'll also need to rewrite your will, and possibly change the guardianship arrangements you've made for your children. In the event that a custodial parent dies, the ex-spouse will typically get custody of the kids; as a result, you may want to choose a separate property guardian to manage the children's finances.

It's also important to check life insurance policies and retirement plans, and bring the beneficiaries into line with your settlement agreement. If you named your husband as the beneficiary of one or more life insurance policies, consider naming someone else. You'd probably want to name your children as primary beneficiaries. But because minors can't own much property without supervision—typically no more than $5,000—you should also name a property guardian (not necessarily your ex-husband) or set up a trust to manage the funds until your children get older.

If you have young children who are dependent on your income, it becomes even more important to purchase life and disability insurance of your own—and to make sure that the kids are beneficiaries of their father's insurance if he is paying child support.

Pay particular attention to pension plans. Even if your divorce settlement explicitly addresses how these assets should be divided, it can be overridden if you forget to change your beneficiaries. One noteworthy court case involved a divorce decree that had divested a husband of rights to his former wife's retirement plan. But the wife had neglected to change the beneficiary designation on her plan. When she died, her former husband claimed benefits. A federal court ruled that the plan had to follow the beneficiary designation, regardless of the provisions of the divorce decree.

You may still qualify for health insurance through your ex-husband's employer (see the box on page 166).

# Be Informed About Equal Opportunity Divorce

When it comes to divorce, advice to women has traditionally assumed that you were in the role of a dependent spouse trying to get a share of your husband's more substantial income and assets. Not only was that generally the case, it was also fair to women with little or no earnings of their own who had "worked" by maintaining the family home, caring for the children, and contributing to their husband's career.

Today, however, is an era of "equal opportunity" divorce. Women with more income and assets of their own are just as vulnerable to claims by their husbands—even if their husbands did not assume the job of homemaker and caregiver. Despite the increase in the number of stay-at-home dads, studies show that the overwhelming majority of working moms are still responsible for most of the housework.

Nevertheless, when courts try to be objective in dividing assets or assigning alimony, women are vulnerable if they're in the role of main breadwinner. "In my experience, the court just looked at the assets and parceled them out, without regard to who played what role in the marriage," says one professional woman, who, as the financial mainstay of her family, was ordered to pay alimony to her unemployed husband for several years. She agreed to a generous financial settlement to "buy my freedom" from an unhappy marriage. Even so, creditors tracked her down when her husband subsequently declared bankruptcy and reneged on an old debt that she had co-signed.

Ironically, then, much of the traditional advice regarding

## Don't Stop Now!

- **Begin** creating your financial plan before you file for divorce, and seek help from a lawyer, professional mediator, or divorce planner.
- **Establish** a separate bank account if you don't already have one; take steps to separate yourself from your husband's credit obligations; and save, save, save.
- **Find** an outlet for feelings that could cause you trouble at the negotiating table and thereby threaten your financial prospects and the security of your children.
- **Identify** your children's present and future needs.

- **Talk** with your children about how your family's financial situation has changed and what this means for them.
- **Choose** the most prudent form in which to receive your settlement.
- **Decide** whether it's wise to keep the house.
- **Ensure** that you will receive your fair share of your husband's retirement benefits.
- **Know** what you're entitled to through social security.
- **Change** the beneficiaries on your insurance policies and pension plans.

women and divorce is turned on its head, with women increasingly finding themselves in the typically male role of trying to limit alimony and to protect their pension benefits and other assets. A prenuptial agreement would help, but that's not an option in existing marriages. With substantial assets on the line, it's even more important to try to hold your marriage together—or, failing that, to hire a good lawyer.

# Caring for Your Parents: Help Is on the Way

s a single woman with no children and a roomy house, Doreen seemed to be the natural choice among her siblings to take care of her father when he could no longer live on his own. Dad moved in with her, and was able to contribute to the household expenses with his pension income. But Doreen had to change her work hours to accommodate dropping him off at the local senior center during the day, and she worries that she will need to hire household help as he becomes older and more infirm. Not only will her father's care become more complicated and expensive, but Doreen has another concern: "With no children of my own, who's going to be there for me? Watching my father has taught me how important it is that you be financially able to take care of yourself."

Doreen is far from alone. Research by the National Alliance for Caregiving found that nearly three-fourths of all caregivers for persons over the age of 50 are women. What's more, 41% of them are caring for children at the same time they are caring for elderly adults. Even if women have brothers with whom they might share the work, daughters

**Did You Know?**

It is estimated that baby-boomers will spend as many years caring for an elderly parent as raising a child.

## It's Not Too Soon to Talk About It

You thought your parents were nervous when they sat you down to have The Talk about sex. Now it's your turn to have The Talk with your parents—about how they wish to handle their finances as they get older—and your beads of sweat are really flowing. The best course of action is full and mutual disclosure about family finances as soon as possible. How to broach the subject? Try one of the following gambits:

**"Can we talk?"** Taking a direct, Joan Rivers-style approach may work if you have good lines of communication with your parents. And you may be sweating for nothing if they're willing, even eager, to talk with you.

**"We're thinking of rewriting our will and we'd like your advice."** Sharing information about your own estate planning can open a valuable dialogue. Your parents will be pleased that you have consulted them and may feel more comfortable about telling you what, if anything, they've done about estate planning. Take this opportunity to suggest that they draft a durable power of attorney for health care (also called a health care proxy) and a living will to make known their wishes about life-prolonging medical measures.

**"Where do you keep the important papers, so we can get access to them in case of an emergency?"** You could bring this up in the context of a health emergency experienced by a friend or neighbor of your parents. You need to know where your parents keep their wills and other legal and financial documents. Also ask them who has power of attorney, and get the names of their lawyer, accountant, and financial adviser.

**"I read the most interesting book/magazine article the other day..."** "My mom is always saving clippings for me, so now it's time to turn the tables," says one woman who regularly slips her mother copies of topical books or articles.

Be prepared for answers you may not want to hear. "Children shouldn't get stuck on a perfectly equal division of assets," says one lawyer. For instance, a child with a disability may get a greater portion, or a child who has worked for years in the family business may be given voting control of the business.

spend significantly more time providing care for elderly parents than sons do, according to a report on women and retirement prepared for TIAA-CREF.

To accommodate their parents, women often cut back or

change their work schedules, or drop out of the work force altogether. And they sometimes spend their own income on their parents' care. As a result, they have less money to save and invest for retirement. All told, caregivers experience a total lifetime financial loss of about $660,000, on average, if lost wages, missed retirement contributions (and appreciation), and missed social security benefits are included. That estimate is based on research by the National Alliance for Caregiving, the National Center on Women and Aging, and MetLife.

Even when women have the resources, taking care of themselves is not always their top priority. Caught in the sandwich-generation squeeze, they're more likely to devote time and resources to the top layer—their parents—or the bottom layer—their kids. Caregivers surveyed in the MetLife study estimated their own out-of-pocket costs, for such things as their parents' medication and home health aides, at about $20,000, on average.

Called upon to help out aging parents, most adult children respond to the challenge. But generous though the impulse may be, it can also be shortsighted, as Doreen became painfully aware when she considered her own prospects for the future. It may sound heretical, but if you're a member of Generation S (for sandwich), or even if you're dealing with elderly parents alone, it's important to keep your perspective when divvying up financial resources:

**Put yourself first.** You aren't being selfish, just practical, as when the flight attendant tells you to put on your own oxygen mask before helping the child accompanying you. When you're in your peak earning years you need to build your own retirement savings; therefore, don't be too quick to quit your job. If you do, you're doubly penalized: Not only do you lose current income, but you also miss out on accruing social security and pension benefits. Thus your income will be diminished in your later years.

**Your parents come next, because their needs—financial and otherwise—are immediate.** Fortunately, help is available in a variety of forms, ranging from caregiving options to tax breaks for expenses that you incur. And don't discount your parents' own resources. They may be able to arrange a reverse mortgage to

## Give Peace of Mind

When Brenda's mom was in her early 70s, she began to fret constantly that she'd end up in a nursing home. So one Mother's Day, Brenda gave her mother peace of mind: a long-term-care insurance policy that not only will cover nursing-home care, but also will pay for home care to allow her mother to stay in her own house as long as possible. Brenda considers the $2,700 annual premium a small price to pay to put her mother's mind at ease—and her own.

A growing number of people are buying long-term-care policies for their parents; sometimes several siblings will kick in to share the cost of coverage. More employers—including the federal government—are offering the insurance as a benefit to employees. If your employer does, ask whether you can purchase coverage for your parents at group rates. It may be a bit easier for them to qualify for the insurance that way, although they will still need to provide medical records and usually won't qualify if they are already in poor health. Before you buy, compare the cost of the group plan with the price of individual coverage.

For more information on the features and costs of long-term-care insurance, as well as resources for comparison shopping, see Chapter 4.

tap the equity in their house (see page 215 for an example of someone using this strategy), borrow against or cash in a cash-value life insurance policy, or purchase long-term-care insurance (see the box above).

**Consider your kids last, though not necessarily least.** This bottom slice of the sandwich tends to receive the bulk of your attention (and money). But when it comes to big-ticket items such as paying for college, for example, it makes sense to shift some of the load to your children. With their whole working lives ahead of them, they have more earning power, more ability to replace assets and repay loans, and more alternative sources of income.

# Get Help From Your Employer

Cindy is a self-employed graphic designer. When she moved her 82-year-old mother halfway across the country to live with her and her family, she managed to keep her graphic design studio going, although it meant rearranging her work schedule and dropping out of some professional organizations to free up time. Fortunately, her mother had enough retirement income and savings to cover her expenses of about $2,000 a month, including medical care and a daytime caregiver. "I never considered giving up my career to take care of Mom, but if she hadn't been as financially well off as she was, I might have had to," says Cindy.

## The Family and Medical Leave Act

Not everyone is so fortunate. But even if you have to take time off from work or pay for expenses out of your own pocket, there are ways to get help. For example, the Family and Medical Leave Act lets you leave your job temporarily to care for a sick parent without disrupting your career. It allows workers at companies with more than 50 employees to take up to 12 weeks of unpaid leave each year and return to their old job or an equivalent one.

Because the leave is unpaid, it doesn't solve the problem of lost wages while you're away. But it can keep your career on track, and you will continue to be covered by your employer's health insurance during your leave. Even if you decide to quit your job eventually, you should exhaust your leave first. Afterward, you can elect to continue your group health coverage for 18 months longer at your own expense. While you're on the job, you can also continue to participate in an employer-sponsored retirement plan. Afterward, if you're married you can still fund a spousal IRA with up to $3,000 a year.

Many employees who are eligible for family leave don't take advantage of it. It may never cross their minds to ask for a leave, or even to realize they're entitled to one. Don't overlook what could be a godsend for your parents' well-being and your peace of mind. If your parents live out of state, for example, you could take time off to stay with them and arrange for someone to help with their care.

## Flexible Spending Accounts

Another employee benefit—the flexible spending account—can help you with costs you incur in providing for your parents' care. Offered by most major employers, flex accounts are more commonly associated with medical and child-care expenses. But they can also be used to pay for elder care for a physically or mentally disabled parent who lives with you and for whom you provide more than half of his or her support (a section on help from the IRS appears later in this chapter). If your parent qualifies, you can set aside up to $5,000 in pretax dollars. Your employer deducts the money from your paycheck before taxes are applied. Then, as you submit vouchers for qualified dependent-care expenses, you get your money back.

Say that federal and state taxes consume roughly 40% of your wages and you divert $5,000 to a dependent-care flex account. Your take-home pay shrinks by just $3,000 (the rest would have gone for taxes), but you have the full $5,000 in your account.

## Other Employer-Provided Benefits

With an aging population, demand for employer-provided elder-care benefits is expected to skyrocket. Already nearly half of all large employers offer some sort of elder-care assistance. Information and referral services are most common, but a few employers offer gold-plated benefits. For instance, Fannie Mae was the first company to provide its employees with the on-site services of a full-time social worker to guide them through the maze of elder-care services. Fannie Mae also offers flexible work hours; as a result, Linda, a Fannie Mae business analyst, has been able to take time off to accompany her mother to medical appointments. "I think that my career would have suffered if I was working for a company whose culture did not support my caregiving situation," says Linda. (If your company doesn't provide this sort of assistance, you can consult the box, "Resources for Caregivers," at the end of this chapter.)

# Get Help With Your Parent's Care

When Cindy's mother first came to live with her, Mom used the studio apartment Cindy provided in a converted garage. Then when Cindy's older child came back home after graduating from college, the child took over the studio while her grandmother moved into Cindy's house. At first, with her mother in the house, "it felt as if I always had company," says Cindy. "I had to get over the fear of not being the perfect parent, cook, or housekeeper."

## In-Home Care

It used to be routine for elderly parents who couldn't quite manage on their own either to move in with a son or daughter or to enter a nursing home. These days, it's possible to put together a plan that allows your parents to stay in their own home for a much longer time. A combination of services—for example, regular meal delivery and a home health aide who can assist with bathing and housekeeping for a few hours a couple of times a week—might cover the bases for far less than the cost of a nursing home. Cindy used an employment agency that specializes in home health aides to hire people to stay with her mother and fix her meals while Cindy was at work, and occasionally on weekends to give Cindy and her husband an evening out. To hold down the cost Cindy juggled her work schedule so that she didn't get to the office until 10:30 A.M. and was home by 6 P.M. "In the morning before the caregiver comes, I can get in an hour or so of work."

> **The most efficient way to hire a home health aide is to go through a local social services agency, hospital, or geriatric-care manager.**

The most efficient way to hire a home health aide is to do as Cindy did and go through a local social services agency, hospital, or geriatric-care manager. Expect to pay about $16 an hour, the average cost for a home-health aide, according to a study by the MetLife Mature Market Institute. Care can cost more or less depending on the local economy, but if you need intensive, around-the-clock help, you can count on it being more expensive. (For help in locating in-home care, see the box on pages 194–195 of this chapter.)

Surveys show that if elderly people have to leave their home, many prefer to maintain their independence, and avoid being a burden, by moving into a facility that offers some assistance rather than moving in with a relative or friend. If you or your parents can afford such a facility, you have plenty of choices.

## Assisted Living

These facilities provide round-the-clock assistance for residents who can't manage completely on their own. Some may need help bathing or dressing, making meals, paying bills, or performing

## Handling Your Parent's Finances

Handling the paperwork for an aging parent is more convenient if you have a joint bank account. But that doesn't take the place of a durable power of attorney, a legal document in which your parents authorize someone to manage their financial affairs should they become unable to do so.

This might also be a situation in which a living trust is appropriate. Your parents can transfer assets into the trust while they're alive, and continue to control those assets until they're no longer able. At that point, the successor trustee—you or some other family member or friend—can take over to use the assets in the trust for your parent's care and well-being.

Trust documents can give the caregiver specific instructions. In one case, for example, the trustee, a daughter, was directed (1) to hire an accountant to review her mother's financial status each year and report to the family, and (2) to pay a disinterested physician or social worker to check her mother's care and living situation and recommend changes or improvements. Once the trust was in place, says the daughter, "I had access to my mother's accounts and could handle banking and investments online. The financial part of my mother's care was manageable."

This arrangement also avoided financial disputes among siblings. If you are going to hold a joint account with your parent, or have his or her power of attorney, you have a fiduciary responsibility to act within the law and in your parent's best interest. If you don't, you can face civil liability or criminal prosecution.

At the very least, to avoid rancor among family members it's a good idea to have your parent's finances reviewed by an independent third party, or to require more than one signature for large transactions involving a checking or savings account.

other basic daily activities. A nurse is on duty during the day, and medical emergencies are dealt with the same way they would be at home: Somebody calls an ambulance.

Done right, the great appeal of the assisted-living idea is its dedication to preserving residents' autonomy. Residents live in apartments or rooms, either alone or with another resident. Assisted living also offers companionship and security, as well as transportation for shopping, social outings, and appointments with doctors.

Monthly costs for assisted-living residences typically run from about $1,000 to more than $3,000, depending on the size of the rooms, the services provided, and the locale. Residents generally sign a lease for only a year, at the end of which either party may choose not to renew. Assisted-living residences are not nursing homes, and they are reluctant to retain residents who need more care than they can deliver (although some do have special facilities for Alzheimer's patients). Find out what a facility's discharge rules are and how much notice you are entitled to if it decides not to renew your lease. In turn, find out how much notice you must give if your mom or dad is unhappy there and wants to move out.

Assisted living is not governed by any federal guidelines, and although there are varying degrees of state regulation, there are no benchmarks to compare prices, services, facilities, and quality of care. Even the term "assisted living" isn't universal. Facilities are referred to by more than two dozen designations, including residential care, board and care, and personal care.

**The Assisted Living Federation of America (www.alfa.org) has created a "consumer information statement" that helps families compare facilities, services, and prices.**

The Assisted Living Federation of America (www.alfa.org) has created a "consumer information statement" that helps families compare facilities, services, and prices—and the circumstances under which a resident may be forced out. "I used the consumer checklists and my gut instincts," says Anne, a 40-something mother of two who started looking for an assisted-living facility when her own mother began showing signs of dementia: forgetting names, getting lost, skipping her medications. Anne began her search on the Internet, logging onto Senior Housing Net (www.seniorhousing.net) to compile lists of facilities near her mother's home and her own. She downloaded helpful consumer checklists, such as the guide offered by the Consumer Consortium on Assisted Living (www.ccal.org).

When Anne visited facilities, she first listened to the formal sales pitch and then popped back in unannounced. She liked to visit at lunchtime to chat with residents and watch them talk with the staff and one another. If a facility complained about the surprise visit, she immediately crossed it off her list. "If it didn't smell right, if the residents weren't happy, I kept looking," she says.

Ultimately, she chose a facility near her home, where her mother pays $3,800 a month for a one-bedroom apartment with a kitchenette and private bath. The monthly fee includes three meals a day, housekeeping, assistance with her medication, and use of an exercise room and wellness center.

(For more help in choosing an assisted living facility, consult the list of resources at the end of this chapter.)

## *Continuing Care*

Continuing-care retirement communities (CCRCs) offer a range of living options. Residents start in the independent-living portion. If they need more assistance, they can move into an assisted-living facility, and later, if necessary, a skilled-nursing home in the same community.

Most continuing-care facilities charge an entry fee. In some cases it's refundable—either fully or partially—and some states require that refunds be available for long enough to give residents a chance to see whether they can adjust. There may be a penalty for withdrawing, however.

In addition, all CCRCs charge a monthly service fee, which covers the costs of the unit, services such as housekeeping and gardening, meals, and some level of health care. Some contracts cover only the unit and certain services, while health care and other needs are paid for on a fee-for-service basis (which may or may not be covered by medicare or other insurance, depending on the procedure). Residents can usually contract for one of three types of monthly fees:

1. **Extensive agreements** (sometimes called life-care agreements) cover all needs, including housing, services, and unlimited medical care. In effect, residents prepay for services they may or may not need in the future. In return, the monthly fee stays the same except for inflation adjustments and increases in operating costs.

2. **Modified plans** cover the costs of housing, services and a predetermined level of long-term nursing care. Under this plan, residents might be entitled to, say, 60 days of skilled-nursing care if needed.

3. **The fee-for-service agreement** charges a monthly fee that covers housing and services. Residents pay for assisted living and skilled-

nursing care on an as-needed basis. This gets you the lowest monthly fee, in return for assuming the risk of higher medical costs if you need such services (which of these services might be covered by insurance is discussed in the next section).

Of particular concern for couples who enter a CCRC together is the way it handles a situation in which one spouse requires some care and the other doesn't. Will one spouse move into the assisted-living facility while the other stays in independent housing? Or will the facility allow someone to provide services in the independent-living area? Who makes the final decision about when it's time to move into assisted living? If the couple is forced to split up, or residents and families are not involved in making decisions, consider another facility. Dissatisfaction over these issues is the main reason people leave CCRCs.

(For help in choosing a continuing-care facility, consult the list of resources at the end of this chapter.)

## Further Help With the Options

If you feel you need help in evaluating all the options—and in figuring out how to pay for them—consider hiring a geriatric-care manager to assess your parent's situation and recommend a care plan. Many care managers were trained as nurses or social workers; they visit the parent's home to assess his or her needs, and then determine ways to meet those needs locally. A care manager can also mediate disputes among siblings about their parent's care. It isn't unusual for the primary caregiver, feeling overworked and underappreciated, to resent the lack of help from other siblings—and for siblings, feeling guilty, to offer unwanted advice and criticism. That highly volatile combination can lead to a family blowup—and often benefits from the soothing influence of a cool-headed outsider. (For help in locating a geriatric-care manager, see the box at the end of this chapter.)

Care managers can also monitor paid caregivers—which can be especially reassuring for out-of-town children. Carol, a registered nurse who lives in New York, contracted with a geriatric-care manager in Florida to visit her uncle once a month at a small assisted-living home, for which she paid $100 per visit. "It's important to be able to speak to the people who are actually taking care

## Soothing Siblings

Hired to care for aging parents, geriatric-care managers often end up soothing adult children when disputes arise among siblings. Sometimes one sibling wants a parent to continue with home care, while another thinks it's time for the parent to enter an assisted-living facility. Siblings who live at a distance may not have a clear picture of the situation, or "may be in denial," says Connie Rosenberg, who runs Services and Resources for Seniors in Morristown, N.J. "In one of my cases, a parent suffering from dementia was beginning to wander, but one child insisted the parent was just sleepwalking."

Rosenberg's solution is to gather as many family members as possible in her office to give her assessment of the situation, or to put her findings and recommendations in written form. "It helps for it to be in black and white," she says.

When adult children live nearby, the main caregiver may feel resentful that others aren't pulling their weight. If other siblings can't contribute time to a parent's care, Rosenberg sometimes suggests that they contribute money instead. "It's more common for siblings to have small differences rather than major problems," says Rosenberg. "Most are able to work it out."

of your relative," she says, and "when you're far away, it helps to have someone to contact if there's a problem." Expect to pay several hundred dollars for an initial assessment.

(For more information, consult the list of resources at the end of this chapter.)

# Get Help in Paying the Bills

None of these care options comes cheap. When push comes to shove, your parents—or you—are likely to end up paying the bulk of the cost out-of-pocket. There's a lot of confusion among consumers about what insurance does, and doesn't, cover. Here's what to expect.

## Home Care

Don't look for too much help from medicare. Medicare generally pays for home care only when an elderly person needs skilled medical-care services (someone to administer medication, dress wounds, or provide physical therapy); is confined to the house by an illness or injury; and is under the care of a doctor who has prescribed home-care services. (For a source of more information on medicare, consult the list of resources at the end of this chapter.)

Some medigap policies pay for personal-care services up to a certain amount—but only if your parent already qualifies for medicare home-care coverage. To make sure your medicare and medigap claims aren't denied, have the doctor specify in the plan of care that your parent needs personal care following an illness or injury.

> **In a particularly nasty Catch-22, in some cases the same disabilities that trigger insurance benefits also force residents out of assisted living.**

One potential solution is long-term-care insurance that covers home care, as well as a nursing-home stay. These policies pay for the ongoing day-to-day costs of care that aren't triggered by a medical event, such as an illness or injury (as required by medicare), but result instead from the general decline associated with aging. This insurance could be so important that you should consider helping your parents pay for it, or even buying it for them on your own.

## Assisted Living

Most residents pay privately for their care, and those who run out of money usually have to leave. Here again, long-term-care insurance can help. But moving into an assisted-living facility won't automatically trigger your insurance benefits. In most cases, you have to be unable to perform at least two "activities of daily living," such as bathing or dressing yourself, or be diagnosed with dementia, before insurance payments begin. In a particularly nasty Catch-22, in some cases the same disabilities that trigger insurance benefits also force residents out of assisted living.

Some assisted-living expenses are tax-deductible. If a person moves into an assisted-living facility (or nursing home) primarily because of his or her physical or mental condition, such as Parkinson's or Alzheimer's disease, the entire cost of care, including meals and lodging, counts as a medical expense. Such costs are deductible to the extent that total medical expenses exceed 7.5% of adjusted gross income. If an individual chooses assisted living primarily for personal or family reasons—say, to accompany and

## Confusion About Coverage

Not only do people over the age of 45 tend to underestimate the cost of long-term health care, they also tend to overestimate how much insurance will pay, according to a study commissioned by the American Association of Retired Persons (AARP). More than half of people in that age group mistakenly believe that medicare will cover long-term nursing-home stays for age-related or other chronic conditions. Furthermore, 31% of older Americans think they have insurance through work or a private insurer that covers long-term-care costs—yet the Health Insurance Association of America, cited in the study, estimates that only about 6% of Americans actually own a long-term-care policy. The study concludes that "people are confusing long-term insurance with other types of coverage—for example, disability insurance provided by employers or medicare."

continue living with a spouse who has medical reasons for entering assisted living—only the portion of the couple's cost attributable to medical care—excluding room and board—is deductible.

## Nursing-Home Care

Contrary to what many people expect, medicare does *not* pay long-term nursing-home bills for age-related or chronic conditions (medicare offers limited coverage for short-term stays that follow hospitalization and meet strict medical criteria). Neither does regular health insurance. Medicaid, the system run by state governments to provide health care for the poor, has become by default the primary payer of nursing-home bills. (Medicaid pays the bills for more than two-thirds of all nursing-home residents, as more than half of all nursing-home residents run out of money within the first year and turn to the government for help.) By definition, you can't qualify for medicaid unless you are poor, as defined by eligibility rules set by each state. The question is, Can your parents get government help without spending themselves into poverty?

The short answer is yes. Medicaid eligibility rules, though complex, are not so draconian as you may have heard. For married couples, there are numerous safeguards for the spouse who remains at home that protect a surprising amount of assets—including a house, a car, a share of the assets both spouses hold jointly, and a monthly income. Widowed, divorced, and unmarried people have fewer options when it comes to preserving assets while still qualifying for medicaid. To get the best advice about your parent's situation, it probably pays to seek advice from an elder-law attorney who specializes in long-term-care issues. (Consult the list of resources at the end of this chapter.)

The whole purpose of "medicaid planning" is to find legal ways to qualify for medicaid while retaining as many of your assets as the law allows. Such a course of action is perfectly legal, if ethically controversial. You and your parents can sidestep the issue if you have long-term-care coverage. Not only will the insurance pay for a broader range of care options—including home care and assisted living—but it will also assure that your parents have easier access to care as a private-pay patient. If your parent is preparing to enter a nursing home as a medicaid patient, he or she may have a long wait if the facility doesn't have a medicaid bed available.

(For more information about medicaid, consult the list of sources at the end of this chapter.)

## Help From the IRS

If you end up paying all or part of the cost of your parent's care yourself, your best source of assistance could be the IRS. Some of the expenses you incur may generate tax benefits.

**DEDUCTION FOR DEPENDENTS.** If you provide more than half of a parent's support, either in the parent's home or yours, and if that parent's taxable income (not including social security benefits and tax-free interest from investments) is less than the exemption amount—$3,050 in 2003 and adjusted annually for inflation—you can claim the parent as a dependent on your tax return. In 2003 that would save you $824 if you're in the 27% tax bracket.

If you and your siblings jointly contribute more than half of a parent's support, one of you can claim the exemption so long as the others agree not to. The sibling claiming the exemption must file Form 2120, a multiple-support agreement that needs to be signed each year by the other support providers, each of whom must pay for more than 10% of the parent's support. Siblings could take turns claiming the exemption, or perhaps assign the write-off to the one in the highest tax bracket.

**DEDUCTION FOR MEDICAL EXPENSES.** In addition to the exemption, you can deduct the total amount of medical expenses (yours plus your parent's) that exceed 7.5% of your adjusted gross income. To qualify, you must provide at least half of your parent's support, but your parent doesn't have to meet the income requirement just mentioned to be claimed as a dependent on your tax return.

**Among "intense" family caregivers— those providing at least 21 hours of care a week—61% report suffering from depression. It's an easy cycle to fall into.**

Medical expenses may also be deductible if you have a multiple-support agreement with your siblings. You can deduct the amount you pay for medical expenses that's not reimbursed by the other siblings; your siblings, however, aren't permitted to deduct their share of the expenses.

Deductible medical expenses include payments for such personal-care services as bathing and dressing (but not housecleaning or other chores), transportation to and from doctor's appointments, and a portion of nursing-home fees. In addition, you can deduct the cost of modifying your home to help accommodate a disabled parent—installing railings or grab bars in the bathroom, or widening doors, for instance. To document your expenses, have a written contract that spells out your home caregiver's duties and a statement from your parent's doctor describing the type of help needed.

**DEPENDENT-CARE TAX CREDIT.** If you pay for someone to come into your home and care for your parent, or if your parent attends an adult day-care center, you can claim the federal tax credit for dependent care. To qualify for this credit, your parent must live with you, and you must pay more than half of the household expenses, but there is no limit to the income your parent can earn.

There is a limit on how much of your expenses can qualify for the credit. If you are paying for the care of one parent, the first $3,000 you pay during the year qualifies; for both parents, the amount of the credit doubles to $6,000.

But you don't get to claim that entire amount:

- **If your AGI is under $15,000,** your credit is 35% of your expenses, up to the $3,000 or $6,000 cap—so the top credit is $1,050 for one parent or $2,100 for both.
- **Taxpayers with AGI of more than $43,000** get a 20% credit, or a maximum of $600 for one parent, and $1,200 for two.
- **Taxpayers with incomes between those two amounts** figure their credit on the basis of a sliding scale.

Claim the credit on Form 2441 (available at 800-829-3676 or www.irs.gov).

If you have a choice between claiming the credit and using a flexible spending account through your employer, run the numbers on both to see which is a better deal for you. Right now, annual contributions to flexible spending accounts are limited to $5,000. If your expenses are higher, an additional $1,000 is eligible for the dependent-care credit.

# Break the Cycle

Now that people over 85 years of age are the fastest-growing segment of the U.S. population, it isn't surprising that 60% of adults either are or expect to be family caregivers. Among "intense" family caregivers—those providing at least 21 hours of care a week—61% report suffering from depression. It's an easy cycle to fall into. Often one female family member ends up providing care, and paying for it, too. Many caregivers risk becoming frail and poor themselves after sacrificing their own health and money caring for others.

Avoid that trap. Insist on sharing duties with other family members. If you are doing most of the cooking and chauffeuring, for example, try to get someone else to handle the finances (see the box, "Handling Your Parents' Finances," on page 184). Or hire outside help, and split the cost with your siblings.

Take advantage of every avenue of assistance, including those in the list at the end of this chapter. Your church or community may also sponsor support groups for caregivers.

If you're working, stay on the job as long as possible, continue

**www.**

## Resources for Caregivers

### ACCREDITATION AND CONSUMER INFORMATION

**The Assisted Living Federation of America** (www.alfa.org) represents more than 7,000 for-profit and non-profit providers of assisted living, continuing care retirement communities, independent living, and other forms of housing and services. The online ALFA Consumer Information Center provides a directory of its members that you can search by city, state or zip code, or by company, whether a specific residence or its parent firm. You can print out copies of ALFA's "Consumer Guide and Checklist" and the "Assisted Living Consumer Information Statement" to take along when you visit a facility.

**The Consumer Consortium on Assisted Living** (P.O. Box 3375, Arlington, VA 22203; 703-533-8121; www.ccal.org) offers helpful consumer checklists.

**The Continuing Care Accreditation Commission** (2519 Connecticut Ave., N.W., Washington, DC 20008-1520; 202-783-7286; www.ccaconline.org) is sponsored by the American Association of Homes and Services for the Aging (AAHSA). For a list of more than 300 facilities accredited by CCAC, visit the commission's Web site.

**The National Association for Home Care** (228 Seventh St., S.E., Washington, DC 20003; 202-547-7424; www.nahc.org) offers a voluntary certification program for home health aides. Its Web site features a checklist for choosing a home-care provider.

### BENEFIT ELIGIBILITY

**BenefitsCheckUp** (National Council on the Aging, 409 Third St., S.W., Suite 200, Washington DC 20024; 202-479-1200; www.benefitscheckup.org). This online tool identifies government benefits, such as prescription-drug assistance, in-home services, property-tax relief, and nutrition programs. BenefitsCheckUp is a free nationwide service provided by the National Council on the Aging. Most of the 1,000 or so programs listed are targeted to low-income seniors, but some benefits are based strictly on age.

**The Medicare Rights Center** (1460 Broadway, 17th Floor, New York, NY 10036; 212-869-3850;

contributing to your own retirement plan, and buy long-term-care insurance for yourself and possibly your parent.

Encourage your parent to be as independent as possible. If Mom comes to live with you, make sure that she has her own

www.medicarerights.org). Check the Web site of this national nonprofit, nongovernmental organization for an abundance of information about medicare, including phone numbers for state and local agencies on aging that can provide health-insurance counseling to older adults, people with disabilities, and their caregivers.

## PROFESSIONAL ASSISTANCE

**The National Academy of Elder Law Attorneys** (1604 N. Country Club Rd., Tucson, AZ 85716; 520-881-4005; www.naela.org). Check the NAELA Web site for a guide to finding and working with an attorney who specializes in elder law, as well as for referrals to attorneys in your area who specialize in elder law.

**The National Association of Professional Geriatric Care Managers** (1604 N. Country Club Rd., Tucson, AZ 85716-3102; 520-881-8008; www.caremanager.org). Contact this organization for names of care managers in your area.

## SEARCHING FOR CARE

**The Eldercare Locator** (800-677-1116; www.eldercare.gov). For assistance in finding in-home help in your community, contact the Eldercare Locator, sponsored by the National Association of Area Agencies on Aging. The Web site provides links to the information and referral services of your state and area (often county) agencies on aging. The toll-free number provides many more specific references. Both are searchable by state and zip code.

**Senior Housing Net** (www.seniorhousing.net) lets you compile lists of facilities by location.

## SUPPORT FOR CAREGIVERS

**Children of Aging Parents** (CAPs; 1609 Woodbourne Rd., Suite 302A, Levittown, PA 19057; 800-227-7294; www.caps4caregivers.org) provides information, support, and referrals to caregivers. Its Website lists publications and affiliated support groups.

**The National Family Caregivers Association** (10400 Connecticut Ave., #500, Kensington, MD 20895-3944; 800-896-3650; www.nfcacares.org). More information and referrals.

household responsibilities. Give her her own television and cable connection, her own telephone line, and her own newspaper subscription. Put a small refrigerator in her room. Encourage her to participate in community senior-citizen pro-

## Don't Stop Now!

- **Talk** with your parents as soon as possible to discuss their means, abilities and preferences, as well as your own if need be.
- **Encourage** your parents to purchase long-term-care insurance or give it to them as a gift.
- **Take** steps to care for yourself first. You can't help your parents if you sacrifice your own well-being, financial and otherwise.
- **Research** available options for care—in-home or elsewhere—in the community (your's or your parent's) before a need arises.
- **Make sure** you understand how those options will be paid for and take advantage of any tax breaks that you might have coming.
- **Hire** appropriate professional assistance, such as an attorney specializing in elder law or a geriatric-care manager, especially if you live a long distance from your parents or require mediation between siblings.

grams. Change your family's schedule as little as possible.

And don't overlook the benefits of multigenerational living. "Having a loving parent around who can tell family stories and make children aware that older people have a contribution to make is an asset," says one geriatric specialist. In the case of Cindy, the woman cited throughout this chapter who moved her mother halfway across the country to live with her, "my husband and I grew up with grandparents living with us, so this is part of our family history."

# Widowhood: Be Prepared to Carry On

orma, a friend of mine who is a financial planner, tells the story of her aunt, whose husband died unexpectedly. The aunt had always handled her family's finances, but she was so distraught after the death of her husband that she fell behind in the paperwork and Norma offered to help out. She telephoned utilities and other creditors to see whether late charges could be waived or items returned.

But the most immediate financial problem turned out not to be getting the power turned back on, or paying for the funeral, or even investing the insurance settlement. The biggest headache was figuring out what to do with shipments of herbal supplements Norma's uncle had ordered from Home Shopping Network to treat arthritis. "Three months went by before I was aware of the problem," says Norma. "The Home Shopping Network had a 30-day return policy and insisted on payment for all but the last item shipped, which we were allowed to return."

**Did You Know?**

According to the Census Bureau, women in their 50s and 60s are three times more likely to be widowed than men in the same age group; women 70 years and older are twice as likely. The higher likelihood of widowhood among women reflects higher mortality rates for men and the fact that husbands are generally older than their wives.

The moral here is that despite the trauma caused by the death of a spouse, life goes on. And often it's life's little details that can cause the biggest hassles and trip you up financially. Faced with tragedy, some people find it therapeutic to bury themselves in the minutiae of everyday tasks, while others, like Norma's aunt, can't bear to face them. If you belong to the latter category, you will need a friend or family member to help you through those first critical months. Eventually you may even want to consider getting advice from a professional financial adviser (see the box on page 202–203).

**If you follow the advice in this book, you won't have to worry about any major financial problems during those first psychologically devastating months; plans you have set in place will kick in automatically.**

But the biggest help of all is to have as many details as possible taken care of in advance. If you follow the advice in this book, you won't have to worry about any major financial problems during those first psychologically devastating months, because plans you have set in place will kick in automatically. You will have savings of your own so that you are not totally dependent on what your husband may (or may not) have left you. You will know what assets he had, and what you are entitled to through his pension or retirement benefits. If you have children, you will get a life insurance settlement, and you will have confidence in your ability to invest it. Your husband will have left a will that provides clear instructions about how his property is to be divided.

Just as important as having the proper paperwork is knowing where to find it. Your life will be so much simpler if you can put your hands on copies of your husband's will and insurance policies, a list of bank accounts and other assets, the key to the safe deposit box, the telephone numbers of people you will need to contact—your lawyer, the executor of your husband's will, your accountant (For help in keeping track of important records and names of contacts, see the box on page 67 of Chapter 4.)

And the bills have to be paid. In the initial shock of bereavement, don't sweat the big stuff, but keep the small stuff going. That means making a number of contacts (by phone, mail, or in person), or relying on a friend or family member to make them for you. Those include:

**Your husband's employer** (or former employer, if he was retired). If your husband was still working, you need to know about such things as accrued but unpaid bonuses or vacation time, and the value of any life insurance policy or retirement benefits. Under the federal COBRA law, you can continue coverage on your husband's health insurance plan at work for up to 36 months after his death, although you'll have to pay the premiums. Also get in touch with any previous employers to see if he was entitled to retirement or other benefits that he wasn't already receiving.

If he was retired and receiving a pension, the benefits should continue, although possibly at a reduced level (see the section on pensions later in this chapter and earlier, in Chapter 7, beginning on page 146).

**The Social Security Administration, and the Department of Veterans Affairs** if your husband was a veteran. Whether you are an older widow or a young widow with dependent children, you are likely to qualify for benefits if your husband was eligible for social security (social security is further discussed later in this chapter; for more information, call 800-772-1213, or go to www.ssa.gov). If your husband was in the military, you may be entitled to funeral and burial benefits (for more information, go to the Department of Veterans Affairs' Web site at www.cem.va.gov; to reach the regional veterans office in your area, call 800-827-1000).

**The issuer of your husband's life insurance policy.** Life insurance benefits are tax-free, and eventually you'll have to make some decisions about what you want to do with the money—but for now, that can wait.

# Make Settlement Easy

Granted, Abraham Lincoln had a lot on his mind. After all, he was busy fighting a war, holding the union together, and putting an end to slavery. But he neglected to write a will. When he died without one, his estate was divided (as an estate still would be in some states) into thirds—one-third for his widow and a third for each of their two remaining sons. At the time of his death, one son was grown and the other was 12 years old, so the arrangement may not have been considered ideal by Abe's widow, Mary.

But you should be better off than Mary Lincoln. Having followed the advice in Chapter 4, you and your husband will have purchased insurance, written wills, and otherwise put your temporal affairs in order; hence, things should proceed with little legal trauma at his death. It's up to the executor named in the will to see to the distribution of your husband's estate by beginning probate, and to make sure any taxes, debts, and other obligations are paid.

> **But the horrors of probate have been overstated. Sensitive to criticism, most states have adopted a streamlined system for small estates, with informal procedures.**

(As I mentioned in Chapter 4, for your own convenience and peace of mind, I recommend that the executor be someone other than yourself. When your husband drafts his will, he could choose another family member, a friend, or an outside professional, such as a lawyer or accountant—anyone whom you trust and feel comfortable with. In exchange for his or her services, an executor is entitled to a commission, which in most states is figured as a percentage of the estate. But in the majority of cases, an executor who is a family member waives compensation.)

Probate is the procedure by which state courts validate a will's authenticity, clearing the way for the executor to collect and pay debts, pay taxes, sell property, distribute funds, and carry out other necessary tasks involved with settling an estate. The process can be slow and expensive, and probate fees can absorb as much as 10% of the estate's assets.

But the horrors of probate have been overstated. Sensitive to criticism, most states have adopted a streamlined system for small estates, with informal procedures requiring little court supervision. Sometimes all that's necessary is for the appropriate person to file an affidavit with the court and have relevant records, such as title to property, changed.

Each state has its own definition of what is considered a small estate; in general, limits range from several thousand dollars to

$50,000 or more. But that figure excludes many of your husband's assets that don't have to go through probate at all. Among the items exempted are life insurance proceeds payable to a named beneficiary, property left in certain kinds of trusts, and assets such as homes and bank accounts held with you as joint tenants with rights of survivorship.

For typical estates, in which most property is held jointly and major assets such as retirement plans and insurance policies have named beneficiaries, settlement should proceed simply and without incident. But in the absence of a will, there's potential for all kinds of mischief. There may be disagreement about how to divide property your husband held in his own name. Creditors might show up with claims you were unaware of. A hostile relative might be able to acquire a share of the estate, or a relative who is already well-fixed might take legal precedence over needier kin. And you might find yourself depleting the estate's assets by fighting costly court battles. If your husband didn't have a will, the court will appoint an administrator to settle the estate.

It's up to you to eventually notify banks, brokers, other financial institutions, credit card companies, the motor vehicle department, and anyone else with whom you held joint accounts that the accounts should be changed to your name if only to keep things simple administratively. Each of these institutions may request a death certificate; make sure that you get a dozen or so from the funeral director to have on hand if you need them.

# Sit Tight With Your Money and Say No

It was supposed to have been the best of times for Kay and her husband, Louis. It ended up being the worst. When Louis retired, he and Kay were looking forward to traveling together. But 4 months after his retirement, Louis suffered a heart attack, and 2 months later he died. "It was chaotic," recalls Kay, and the turmoil extended to her finances.

She knew that her pension and social security benefits would be reduced when her husband died. But the point wasn't driven home until she had written checks to cover expenses and then

## Get Professional Advice

Becoming a widow may be the life event that persuades you to hire an adviser to help sort out your finances and plan for your future. Women place a premium on trust in such a relationship. That's tough to quantify, so it's difficult to give precise guidelines on how to choose an adviser. Word of mouth from other women whose opinion you respect may be as good an indicator as any. But there are some objective criteria to consider:

**Experience.** Your financial adviser should have, at a minimum, a few years of experience in financial planning or related fields, such as accounting, securities analysis or trading, or law.

**Professional credentials.** Many practitioners have managed to pull themselves above the crowd by taking courses and passing examinations that lead to a professional designation. It's no guarantee that his or her advice will be any better, but it is a sign that

an adviser takes the business seriously, and takes time to keep up with continuing education.

At a minimum, look for the certified financial planner (CFP) designation. That's a license, as opposed to being exclusively an educational credential; therefore, if a CFP does something unethical his or her license can be taken away. (Find CFPs near you through the Financial Planning Association, 800-282-7526; www.fpanet.org.)

**Compensation.** Some financial planners are paid solely on commission from products they sell. Some are paid through a combination of fees and commissions (often called fee-based). And fee-only planners simply charge a fee, either a flat rate or a percentage of your assets. You may feel more comfortable with a fee-only planner because such planners don't get a cut of the products they're trying to sell you. (Find a fee-only planner through the National Association of Personal

learned there would be a delay in getting her benefits because the amount was being recomputed. She couldn't bring herself to sell the new car that she and Louis had bought for their traveling, or her major financial asset: shares of stock in the company where her husband had worked for 30 years. Explains Kay, "I felt it was letting go of something that belonged to my husband."

It took 6 months before Kay started making some major financial moves. And that was a good thing. Because of insurance settlements or other inheritances, new widows often end

Financial Advisors, 800-366-2732; www.napfa.org.)

A fee-only planner may work by the hour (charging, for example, $100 or $200 per hour, depending on the plan's complexity and the client's means); $500 for a limited plan for, say, a single mother; or $1,000 and up for a more comprehensive family plan and follow-up service. If a fee-only planner is too expensive for your budget, consider a commissioned or fee-based planner. Such planners are likely to suggest financial products for which they get paid a fee. That's not necessarily bad—just be aware that it's going to happen, and evaluate products accordingly.

**An interview.** Once you get referrals, visit several planners in person. Ask to see the registration they're required to file with the Securities and Exchange Commission. Be sure to ask for both part I, which contains disciplinary history, and part II, which describes the business and how the planner gets paid. Ask each planner about educational credentials, continuing education, any specialties, what kind of reports clients get and how often. Verify what the costs will be.

You're looking for knowledge, but you're also looking for your own sense of comfort. Be wary of anyone who tries to sell you something the minute you step in the door. A good planner should be questioning you, too, quizzing you thoroughly about your assets, your goals, and your tolerance for risk. Before clients come in for the first time, some firms send out lengthy questionnaires asking such questions as, "What is your most pressing concern?" or "What do you think we can do for you?"

Don't be intimidated into silence. "Planners almost always control the discussion," one adviser laments. "Sometimes we'd like to shake people and say, 'What are your questions?'"

up with more money than they've ever had to deal with. You may be tempted to take a cruise or give it to the kids, and you'll be besieged by people who want to sell you something. After 3 years, Kay was still getting calls and literature from "anybody and everybody." Your best response: Say no.

## Take Your Time

Losing your husband creates enough emotional turmoil without adding any more financial distress than necessary. Don't make any financial decisions for a while. Don't invest any lump-sum insurance settlement or pension payout for at least 6 months, and possibly even a year. You don't have to decide right away what to do with insurance money. Your insurer can hold it in an interest-bearing account until you want it. Or you can keep the money in a very liquid (and safe) investment that gives you easy access if you need it, such as a money-market fund, a short-term certificate of deposit, or a Treasury bill (these investments were discussed in Chapter 5).

## Manage Carefully

When you get the life insurance benefits, be sure to set aside enough to get yourself through the first year, including any major expenditures you can anticipate will be necessary, before making any long-term investment decisions. Take time to become accustomed to your new pattern of income and expenses. You'll know fairly quickly what you can expect to receive from social security and your husband's pension, but it will take longer to assess how much income you'll need from employment or investments. Resist the temptation to make expensive purchases that aren't essential. Don't take that cruise right away—and don't give your money to the kids.

## Take a Lump Sum or Invest in an Annuity?

When you receive an insurance settlement, you'll have to decide whether to take the money as a lump sum and invest it yourself, or to convert it into some form of annuity. When you buy an annuity, you pay money to an insurance company and receive in return a guaranteed income, starting right now or later on. The income can continue for a specified period of time—say, 10 years—or for as long as you live. The size of the payments will vary accordingly.

Annuity contracts have a tax advantage—no federal or state income taxes are owed on any interest or investment earnings until the money is withdrawn. But there are drawbacks. You'll usually pay a 10% penalty tax on amounts you withdraw or borrow from an annuity before age 59½. Annuities generally have stiff charges for surrendering (cashing in) the contract within the first several years of its purchase. And with inflation, any kind of fixed income you sign up for will buy less and less as years go by.

## Revisit Your Investment Plan

In deciding what to do with the money, your best strategy is to follow the investment advice outlined in Chapter 5: Consider what your goals are—short-, medium-, or long-term——and what your tolerance for risk is. If you are already retired and have no dependents, a guaranteed lifetime income may give you the security you crave. But if you are a young widow with small children, you may need to invest all or part of your insurance proceeds so that the money grows enough to cover the cost of college for the kids—and that means being more aggressive and investing in stocks.

Don't be afraid to invest the money on your own (with advice from someone you trust, if you feel you need it) because you gain flexibility to choose your own investments, instead of being locked in to a fixed annuity payout.

## Consider Kay's Example

When Kay was finally able to face up to making financial decisions, she began selling her stock bit by bit and investing in money-market funds, bond funds, and an annuity that provided both immediate payments and an investment feature to keep her assets growing and protect her against future inflation. Because she had owned the stock (and other assets) jointly with her husband, she had to file papers (including a death certificate) to prove the change of ownership. There's no rush to do this immediately after a death, but you have to do it eventually to simplify the process if you want to sell the assets.

Kay was never tempted to sell her home, and she ended up keeping the car, too. And she's glad she didn't make any rash decisions. "It was very hard, but it worked out," she says. "After a while I could look forward instead of backward."

# Get Support From the Widow's Safety Net

When you're widowed, you can get critical financial support from social security and from your husband's pension—support that can continue even if you remarry.

## Social Security

If your spouse was entitled to benefits, you can collect widow's benefits starting at age 60, or 50 if you're disabled. (If your husband dies at, say, age 55, before he's actually eligible to collect benefits, you're still entitled to benefits that are based on his earnings record when you turn 60.) As a widow, you can generally receive the greater of your husband's social security payments or your social security payments; the specifics depend on your age and eligibility.

If you still have young children, they also may be entitled to survivor's benefits. Unmarried children under 18, or under 19 if they are full-time students at a secondary school, are eligible. So are unmarried children who were severely disabled before age 22 and who remain disabled. In addition, you can claim a widow's benefit at any age if you are caring for a child who is under age 16 (or disabled) and who is receiving benefits based on his or her deceased parent's earnings.

Furthermore, if you are 60 or older you can remarry and still collect benefits on your deceased husband's record. You can choose the greatest of:

■ **your deceased husband's full benefit**
■ **50% of your new spouse's benefit**
■ **your own benefit based on your own work history.**

If you remarry before age 60, you lose your deceased husband's benefit. But if your second husband also dies, then you are entitled to either your deceased husband's full benefit or your own benefit, whichever is greater.

In addition, spouses and dependent minors can receive a $255 death benefit from the Social Security Administration. That sounds laughably small compared with the cost of a funeral, but there's no reason to turn it down. Eligibility depends on age. Call Social Security (800-772-1213) or visit its Web site (www.ssa.gov) to get information about survivor's benefits of all kinds and to have application forms sent to you.

## Pensions

For widows, your husband's pension income can be a godsend. As discussed in Chapter 6, federal law (under the Employee Retirement Income Security Act, or ERISA) requires that company pension plans offer survivor's benefits. Electing a survivor benefit (also called the joint-and-survivor option) may reduce the pension you and your husband receive during his life, but ensures that you continue to get payments after his death.

If your husband wants to give up his right to survivor's benefits in favor of a higher pension during his lifetime, you have to agree in writing. Most women are advised not to agree—and you'll realize the wisdom of that advice if you're widowed. (The only time it might make sense to give up your right to survivor's benefits is if you don't expect to outlive your husband, because of poor health, for example.)

Depending on which option you and your husband have chosen, your pension may or may not be reduced in retirement:

- **If you have chosen joint-and-survivor 100%,** for example, the payments he gets over his lifetime will continue at the same level for you after he dies.
- **If he opts for joint-and-survivor 50%,** payments will be somewhat higher during his lifetime but will be cut in half after he dies.

*Note:* The joint-and-survivor option does not apply to 401(k) plans or IRAs. You must be named the primary beneficiary in order to get access to those plans when your husband dies.

If you're a surviving widow, you won't lose your survivor's pension benefit because you remarry. Also, if you are the named beneficiary on a company-sponsored 401(k) or other retirement plan, you won't jeopardize this inheritance by remarrying.

However, you do need to be concerned if your deceased husband retired from the military or the federal government. In those cases, you may forfeit pension benefits if you remarry before the age of 55. After 55, your benefits are safe. However, some police and firefighters' plans cut off benefits if a survivor remarries at any age.

## IRAs

Of particular interest to women are inheritance rules for IRAs and Roths. If you are the beneficiary of your husband's traditional IRA, money left in the account at his death will be taxable to you in your top tax bracket. In contrast, what's left in a Roth goes to you (or other heirs) tax-free.

To avoid paying immediate income taxes on an inherited IRA, the surviving spouse does have an important option: You can simply treat the IRA as your own. No payouts would be required until you reached age 70½. (If you are the beneficiary of your husband's 401(k) plan, you can also roll over part or all of a distribution into your own IRA.) Alternatively, you could leave the funds in your husband's account until the year he would have reached age 70½, at which time withdrawals have to begin; the amount of the withdrawal is based on your life expectancy.

> **To avoid paying immediate income taxes on an inherited IRA, the surviving spouse does have an important option: You can simply treat the IRA as your own.**

Here's the difference: If you treat the IRA as your own, you don't have to start making withdrawals until *you* turn 70½; if you leave it in your husband's IRA, you have to start making withdrawals when *he* would have turned 70½. Your decision depends on how long you'd like the money to continue to grow, and when you think you'll need it. But there are a couple of advantages to rolling the money into your own IRA. If you're younger than your husband, your money will continue to accumulate tax-deferred earnings for a longer period of time. And when you do begin to make withdrawals, payouts will be based on more favorable distribution rules.

If you need the cash right away, you have the option of cashing in part or all of the account without worrying about the early-withdrawal penalty, but you'll still have to pay income tax.

Note that you don't get any of these options unless you're actually listed as the beneficiary of your husband's account. You don't want to find yourself in the position of Caroline (described in Chapter 4), whose husband neglected to change the beneficiary of his retirement plan from his mother to his new wife when they married. When he died a premature death, Caroline had no claim on the account.

That's why it's critical for beneficiary designations to be up to date—not just on your husband's IRA and 401(k) accounts, but on your own, so that your money goes to your spouse and/or your children, or whomever else you choose, should something happen to you.

# Deal With Death and Taxes

Nothing, they say, is as certain as death and taxes. Even when mourning the death of a spouse, you—or your accountant or some other financial professional—must consider tax issues. Fortunately, there's good news here. Many of the tax law provisions involving the death of a spouse can save you money (or at least not cost you any), so it pays to be familiar with the high points.

## Insurance Proceeds

Proceeds you receive from your husband's insurance policy are not subject to federal income tax. In general, other inheritances are not subject to the income tax either. If you inherit a certificate of deposit, for example, the principal is not taxable. Only the interest earned from the time you become its owner is taxed.

A major exception to the general rule that inheritances are not subject to the income tax is that money in a traditional IRA, or a company retirement plan such as a 401(k) or 403(b), falls into a special category called "income in respect of a decedent" and is taxed to the heir. But, as has already been explained, you can avoid paying immediate income taxes on this money by rolling it into an IRA of your own.

## Estate Tax

In what's known as the "unlimited marital deduction" your husband can leave any amount to you, his wife, without incurring the federal estate tax. On top of that, he can leave a total of $1 million (in 2003) to other beneficiaries without incurring the estate tax, an amount that is scheduled to rise annually until the tax disappears altogether in 2010 (although it may be reinstated in 2011).

Given the increasing size of the exclusion amounts, few families will have to worry about the federal estate tax. If yours is one that does, an estate tax return will have to be filed within 9 months after your husband's death. The executor of the estate must file the return.

## Income Tax

The chore of filing your husband's final income tax return also

## If You Remarry

It's a happy time for you, but it's also a time to assess any property you may have inherited, or accumulated on your own, so that you can preserve it for yourself or for children from your prior marriage. (See also Chapter 4.)

■ **Consider a prenuptial agreement.** You may not have wanted or needed one the first time around, but a prenup may make sense this time if you want to keep assets separate so that your new husband doesn't have automatic inheritance rights to your estate.

■ **Take care of the kids.** Talk to an estate-planning lawyer about a quali-

fied terminable interest property trust—QTIP, for short. With a QTIP, you can give your new husband the income from property you put into the trust, and let him use some of the assets, such as a home. But when your spouse dies, the assets go to the beneficiaries you have chosen, possibly your children. (QTIPs are discussed in Chapter 4.)

■ **Know your rights.** As outlined earlier in this chapter (see pages 205–207), you may still be able to collect social security and pension benefits from your first marriage.

falls to the executor of the estate or to you (or your accountant). You'll have to report any income your husband earned between the beginning of the year and the date of his death. Write "deceased" after your husband's name, and enter the date of death. The return is not due until the traditional filing date of April 15 of the following year, no matter what time during the tax year your husband died. Furthermore, you can continue to file a joint return for the year in which your husband died, even if he died on January 1, and you can claim the full standard deduction if you don't itemize.

In the 2 years following your husband's death, if you have dependent children you can file as a qualified widow and use joint-return rates. After that, if you still have dependents living at home, you can file as a head of household. In all of these cases, your tax rate will be lower than if you filed as a single person.

If an executor or estate administrator (appointed by the state) is involved, he or she must sign the return for your husband. You sign for yourself. If you're filing the joint return on your own, you should sign the return and write "filing as surviving spouse" in the space for your husband's signature.

If a refund is due, there's one more step. You should also complete and file a copy of Form 1310, *Statement of Person Claiming Refund Due a Deceased Taxpayer.*

## Medical Expenses

You are eligible to deduct medical expenses if they exceed 7.5% of your adjusted gross income. If that's the case, deduct all medical bills incurred by your husband during the year in which he died, even if you don't pay them until up to 12 months after your spouse's death.

What if there's money left in your husband's medical reimbursement account (flexible-spending account)? Can you use up the balance and deduct his medical expenses, too? Yes, so long as you don't double dip. Say there are $10,000 worth of expenses and only $3,000 left in the flex account. You could run $3,000 of expenses through the account and be reimbursed, and deduct the other $7,000 on your income tax—provided that that amount still exceeds 7.5% of your adjusted gross income.

## Capital Gains

When you inherit stocks, mutual fund shares, or other assets, the capital-gains tax on any appreciation in the value of your husband's share of the property prior to his death is forgiven (in tax-speak, your husband's share of the assets is given a "stepped-up" basis—the basis being the base value of the asset for purposes of computing capital gains or losses when the asset is sold):

- **If your husband held the asset in his own name,** you can sell it immediately and not have to pay tax on the capital gain.
- **If you owned the property jointly,** you can sell it and there will be no tax on his half of the profit.
- **If you hang on to the property and sell it in the future,** the capital gains tax on your husband's share of the asset will be figured only on appreciation since he died and you inherited the property.

# Take Care of Yourself

Although your immediate attention is on your husband's finances, eventually you'll have to turn to your own. Widowhood is one of those critical life events—along with

## A Widow's Tale

Susan lost her 38-year-old husband on September 11, 2001, in the World Trade Center tragedy. She agreed to talk to Kiplinger because she wanted other couples to know the importance of sharing financial information—not just the big-picture goals of education and retirement, but the nitty-gritty details of daily life.

After Susan got over the initial shock of her husband's death, one of her first thoughts was, "How am I going to pay the bills?" It wasn't that she worried there wouldn't be enough money. She had cash in the bank, her husband had had life insurance, and his Wall Street employer agreed to continue paying his commissions and bonuses through the end of the year. She just didn't know how, and when, he actually paid the household bills.

With friends and relatives on hand to watch her two small children, the New Jersey homemaker locked herself in her husband's home office and pored over financial records. A bank representative walked her though the online bill-paying system her husband had set up. She found a clear record of which bills had been paid and which were pending.

While Susan's immediate financial future was secure, she worried that her life insurance benefits would cover only about 4 years of living expenses. She can collect a modest amount in worker's compensation for life (unless she remarries). She and her children also receive social security survivor benefits. She'd like to keep her house for the kids' sake, and for sentiment's sake—because it meant so much to her husband. She'll go back to work if she has to, but if it becomes necessary to move, she'll do that, too. "I have learned that I can probably handle anything," she says. "I am more self-reliant. That's the one good thing that has come out of this."

divorce, remarriage, and the birth of a child—that require a major reassessment of your estate plan.

For starters, you must redo your own will and change the beneficiaries of your insurance policies and retirement plans. Not only was your husband almost certainly your primary beneficiary, he may also have been named as your executor and the person to whom you gave power of attorney in the event that something happened to you. All of those designations need to be changed.

If you haven't had a will or a power of attorney, now is certainly the time to draft one—especially because you may have received an insurance settlement that boosted the value of your estate. Even if that's not the case, because you're on your own now, it's critical that you give someone the power of attorney to act on your behalf.

If you have young children, you need to name guardians and decide whether you want to set up trusts for them. Because your children are likely to be more dependent on your own income, you may have to increase your life and disability coverage (the guidelines for establishing guardianship for your children and for buying insurance were presented in Chapter 4).

**For starters, you must redo your own will and change the beneficiaries of your insurance policies and retirement plans.**

As mentioned earlier, if you were covered by your husband's health insurance, you can continue group coverage for you and your children for 36 months, although you may be required to pay for it. You may also be able to pick up coverage through your own employer. (If you or your children haven't previously been enrolled in your employer's health insurance plan, you may be able to join it outside the usual enrollment period due to your spouse's death.) Depending on your age, your career may become a bigger factor in your life, and because you're now on your own it's essential that you take advantage of any retirement plans and flexible-spending accounts that will let you set aside pretax earnings to pay for child care and medical expenses.

## Don't Panic

Finding yourself widowed and alone can snowball into full-blown panic about facing the future in straitened circumstances. One of my goals has been to give you a strategy for remaining calm by taking control of your own financial security before widowhood becomes reality:

- **Save for your own retirement.** If you're in the work force, take full advantage of 401(k) plans, IRAs, and Roth IRAs. If you're a stay-at-home mom, take advantage of spousal IRAs.
- **Don't leave estate planning to your husband.** Because you and your children are the ones who are most likely to benefit, make sure that your spouse has enough life insurance, and know what other assets you can expect.

■ **Get your share of other benefits.** Don't sign away the survivor benefits you're entitled to through your husband's pension plan. Make sure you're the beneficiary of his IRA and 401(k). Know what other benefits you can count on from social security and other sources.

Even if you do all these things and are comfortably well off, your assets will still be vulnerable if you have to pay for someone to help care for you in your home—or in a nursing home, where the average cost of a stay is $60,000-plus a year and rising, and where most residents are women.

Mary came face-to-face with that fear whenever she visited her elderly aunt in a nursing home. "She ran out of money and had to file for medicaid," says Mary. "It was devastating for her. She had worked her entire life and was independent. I don't want to go through that myself." Mary probably won't have to. Soon after her experience with her aunt, she and her husband, ages 55 and 64 at the time, bought long-term-care insurance to protect the savings they had worked so hard to build.

If you anticipate having less than, say, $100,000 in assets, you may quickly qualify for medicaid, and paying a hefty premium for long-term-care insurance may not be cost-effective. At the other extreme, if you have more than $1 million in assets, you may be able to pay for nursing-home care on your own—especially if you aren't concerned about leaving a legacy to your heirs—and won't need insurance. For everyone else in the middle, long-term-care coverage can buy both financial security and peace of mind. And being able to pay for your own care gives you more options than depending on medicaid (for a fuller discussion of long-term-care insurance, see Chapter 4).

# Don't Underestimate Your Own Resources

Depending on your age when you're widowed, your own resourcefulness may be your greatest asset. Recall from Chapter 7 the case of Janet, widowed in her 30s and bequeathed a financial mess by her husband, whose experience led her to

## Don't Stop Now!

- **Be sure to get** plenty of copies of your husband's death certificate when you are making his funeral arrangements.
- **Ask** a family member or friend to make some of the necessary business calls.
- **Don't rush** to invest insurance proceeds or any other payout. Take your time.
- **File** a joint tax return for the year in which your husband died, use up any balance left in a flexible-spending account, and take advantage of any medical tax deductions you may be entitled to.
- **Revise** your own will and related documents, such as a power of attorney.
- **Don't overlook** any resources that are available to you, such as social security or veteran's benefits, pensions or retirement plans, health-insurance coverage, or the equity in your home.

start a new career in the financial field.

Or consider the case of Marty, a feisty 89-year-old widow who confronted every woman's fear—outliving her money. She tells her story in her own words:

"My husband was a metallurgical engineer and I was a legal secretary. When we first retired, we wanted for nothing. We had lots of bonds, mutual funds, and certificates of deposit that were paying 11% or 12%. We took trips and cruises, built our home, paid cash for new cars.

"Even before my husband died, the income was no longer coming in. The CDs were paying 3%, and the mutual-fund dividends kept dropping. Then, when my husband died, I lost his pension and a portion of our combined social security. I could have lost the house, too. It costs me $300 or $400 a month just for prescriptions. What I most needed was to get back to the level of income my husband and I had prior to his death.

"Then I read about reverse mortgages [which let you borrow against your home equity and repay the loan with proceeds from the eventual sale of your house]. I started doing my own research on the computer. My kids got their lawyers and accountants involved, and I contacted a banker. I decided to take monthly payments equal to what I had lost when my husband died. I also have a line of credit that I can access at any time. Now I don't have to worry if I have to replace the air conditioner or fix the roof.

"It's hard to shake the habits of the past couple of years. I still have to force myself to spend money on things. But the worry is gone. I don't wake up at 4:30 in the morning anymore, fretting about my future."

The point here is not to suggest that a reverse mortgage is the solution to every widow's financial situation (for more information on such mortgages, contact the Department of Housing and Urban Development, 800-217-6970; www.hud.gov/buying /rvrsmort.cfm).

What's most significant about Marty's case is that, even at the age of 89, she took the initiative to think single and act independently.

# Index

## A

**AARP.** See American Association of Retired Persons
**Adjusted gross income**
dependent-care tax credit, 193
IRAs and, 137–138
**Adult day care,** 192
**A.G. Edwards & Sons,** 90, 119
**Aggressive-growth funds,** 120
**Alimony**
IRAs and, 137
not counting on, 162–163
tax issues, 163
**Alzheimer's disease,** 185, 189
**American Association of Retired Persons**
part-time work in retirement study, 152
study of the cost of long-term health care, 190
**American Express,** 90
**Ameritrade,** 118
**Annuities,** 143, 204
**Assisted-living facilities**
choosing, 185–186
comparing, 185
description, 183–184
help with paying for, 189–190
monthly costs, 184–185
**Assisted Living Federation of America, "consumer information statement,"** 185
**Association for Conflict Resolution,** 158
**Association of Independent Consumer Credit Counseling Agents,** 21

## B

**"Bag lady syndrome,"** 101
**"Ballpark Estimate Retirement Planning Worksheet,"** 131
**Bankruptcy**
divorce and, 155
filing by single women, 19, 156
**Banks**
applying for a loan to create a credit history, 23–24
certificates of deposit, 107
FDIC insurance, 106–107
getting rid of paperwork you don't need, 6
joint ownership of accounts, 59
online, 106
savings accounts, 25–29, 30, 42–43, 106–107
**BenefitsCheckUp,** 195
**Bonds**
historic return on, 123
interest rates and, 123–124
"life cycle" funds, 125
separate ownership of, 60–61
short-term bond funds, 108
U.S. savings bonds, 124
**Book value of stocks,** 117
**Break in service rules,** 140, 147
*The Budget Kit: The Common Cents Money Management Workbook,* 46
**Budgeting**
commonsense tool, 46
worksheet, 12–13
**Business loans,** 58
**Bypass trusts,** 69

## C

**Capital gains tax,** 211
**Capital One cards,** 25
**CardWeb,** 25
**Caring for your parents**
assisted-living facilities, 183–186, 189–190

avoiding traps, 193–196
care payment options,
    188–193
continuing-care
    retirement
    communities, 186–187
elderly persons as the
    fastest-growing
    segment of the U.S.
    population, 193
estimate of number of
    years you may spend,
    177
flexible spending
    accounts, 181–182
geriatric-care managers,
    187–188
help from your employer,
    180–182
home health aides, 183
in-home care, 183,
    188–189
keeping your perspective,
    179–180
Medicare and, 188–189
multigenerational living
    benefits, 195–196
nursing-home care,
    190–191
resources for caregivers,
    194–195
talking to your parents
    about how to handle
    their finances, 178
tax issues, 191–193
total lifetime financial
    cost to caregivers, 179
underestimating the cost
    of, 190
**Cars**
car loans, 21
separate ownership of,
    60
used cars, 28

**Cash flow calculation, 8,
    10–11, 14**
**CCRCs.** *See* Continuing-
    care retirement
    communities
**CDs.** *See* Certificates of
    deposit
**Certificates of deposit,**
    107
**Certified divorce
    planners, 158, 174**
**Charles Schwab**
Coverdell accounts, 91
discount broker service,
    119
MarketTrack funds, 125
**Checking accounts.** *See*
    Banks
**Child-care credit, 87–88**
**Child-care
    reimbursement plans,**
    88–89
**Child credit, 87**
**Child support**
automatic wage
    withholding provision,
    163
standardized formula, 163
tax issues, 164
time limit, 164–165
**Children.** *See also* Caring
    for your parents;
    Motherhood
allowances for, 95–98
child-care reimbursement
    plans, 88–89
child-care tax credit, 52
child support, 163–165
church-sponsored school
    tuition, 88
claiming as dependents
    after divorce, 164, 165
death benefit from social
    security, 206

differences in spending
    habits, 196
financial challenges,
    79–98
financial implications of
    divorce and, 165–167
hands-on exercise on
    how family money is
    spent, 93, 95
health insurance and, 84,
    166
investing and, 92, 93
life insurance and, 62–63
naming guardians for,
    65–68, 173–174, 213
parental united front
    after divorce and,
    168–169
parents' health insurance
    and, 32–33
prenuptial agreements
    and, 75–76
raising on one paycheck,
    83–86
Roth IRAs for, 86
social security benefits,
    150, 205–206
tax issues, 86–89
teaching about money,
    92–98
testamentary trusts, 70
what kids need to know,
    and when, 94
work incentives, 96–98
**Children of Aging
    Parents, 196**
**COBRA.** *See*
    Consolidated Omnibus
    Budget Reconciliation
    Act
**Cohabitants' legal rights,**
    74–75
**Cohabitation agreement,**
    75

**College**
college students and
credit card debt, 19–20,
22–23
Coverdell Education
Savings Accounts, 90–91
divorced parents and
payment for, 164–165
prepaid tuition plans,
91–92
Roth IRAs for, 91
state-sponsored college
savings plans, 89–90
student loans, 19, 146
**Community property
states,** 60, 161
**Consignment stores,** 28
**Consolidated Omnibus
Budget Reconciliation
Act,** 33, 168, 199
**Consumer Consortium
on Assisted Living,** 185,
194
**Consumer Credit
Counseling Service,** 21
**Continuing Care Accredit-
ation Commission,** 195
**Continuing-care**
retirement
communities, 186–187
**Council on Compulsive
Gambling of New
Jersey,** investing as
addictive behavior, 103
**Coverdell Education
Savings Accounts,**
90–91
**Credit bureaus,** 22
**Credit cards**
building a credit history,
23–24
cards to avoid, 24
child support payments
and, 164

college students and,
19–20, 22–23
direct-mail offers, 24
divorce and, 159–160
financing a calamity and,
25–26
getting rid of paperwork
you don't need, 6
important documents, 58
rule of thumb on
installment debt, 20
secured cards, 24–25
separate credit cards for
married persons, 49–50
shotgunning credit, 24
switching to a low-rate
card, 20
**Credit counseling,** 21
**Credit history,** 22–25
**Credit rights of women,**
22, 48
**Credit unions**
checking accounts with,
28–29
FDIC insurance, 106–107
higher rate of interest
from, 107

**D**
**Datek,** 118–119
**Death certificates,** 201
**Debt.** See also Credit
cards; Loans
credit counseling, 21
divorce and, 157–160
installment debt rule of
thumb, 20
paying off debt versus
investing, 102
secrets to eliminating,
20–22
**Defined-benefit pension
plans,** 135, 146

**Defined-contribution
pension plans,** 135
**Dependent-care tax
credit,** 192–193
**Direct-investment plans,**
116
**Disability insurance,**
35–36
**Disabled persons,** social
security for, 205–206
**Discount stockbrokers,**
119
**Divorce**
alimony, 162–163
bankruptcy and, 155
certified divorce planners,
158, 174
child support, 163–165
children and financial
implications, 165–167
community property
states, 161
credit cards and, 159–160
dividing assets, 160–162
do-it-yourself divorces,
158
equal opportunity
divorce, 175–176
estate planning and,
173–175
family businesses and, 161
filing taxes after, 171
financial advisers for, 158
financial implications of,
155–156
health insurance and, 166,
175
homeownership and,
167–169
husband's pension and,
169–172
IRAs and, 162
joint accounts with a
stockbroker, 159

joint debt and, 157–160
lawyers for, 157–158
mediation for, 157–158
Medicaid and, 190
money issues as the
  leading cause, 41
notifying creditors, 160
parental united front
  after, 168–169
percent of marriages that
  end in, 100–101, 156
qualified domestic
  relations orders, 170
remarriage and, 155
social security and, 150,
  172–173
spouse's pension plan
  and, 148
statistics, 18
**Documents**
getting rid of paperwork
  you don't need, 6
important documents for
  married persons, 58
knowing where your
  elderly parents keep
  important papers, 178
organizer for, 67
**Dollar-cost averaging,**
  112–113
**Dreyfus Gender
  Investment
  Comparison Survey,**
  women's feelings about
  control over financial
  affairs, 101
**Durable powers of
  attorney,** 68, 74, 178,
  184, 212–213

**E**

**Education IRAs.** See
  Coverdell Education
  Savings Accounts

**Elder care.** See Caring for
  your parents
**Eldercare Locator,** 196
**Elderly persons.** See
  Caring for your
  parents; Widowhood
**Employee Benefit
  Research Institute of
  the American Savings
  Education Council,**
  Retirement Confidence
  Survey, 129, 152
**Employment Policy
  Foundation,** survey of
  women's work and
  earnings patterns, 18,
  80, 100
**Equal Credit Opportunity
  Act,** 22, 48
**Equal opportunity
  divorce,** 175–176
**Equifax,** 22, 159
**ESAs.** See Coverdell
  Education Savings
  Accounts
**Estate planning.** *See also*
  Wills
children and, 65–68
cohabitants, 74
divorce and, 173–175
durable powers of
  attorney, 68, 173, 184,
  212–213
for elderly parents,
  178
health care proxies, 68
life insurance, 62–64
living wills, 68, 178
questions about, 61
trusts, 68–70
widowhood and,
  211–213
**Estate tax,** 59, 209
**Experian,** 22, 159

**F**

**Family and Medical Leave
  Act,** 181
**Family businesses,** divorce
  and, 161
**Fannie Mae,** staff social
  workers to coordinate
  elder care, 182
**Fidelity Brokerage
  Services,** 119
**Fidelity Investments**
  Freedom Funds, 125
**Financial advisers**
divorce and, 158
widowhood and,
  202–203
**Financial management**
cash flow calculation, 8,
  10–11, 14
financial goals, 14–15
important documents, 58
money personalities and,
  4–5
monthly budget
  worksheet, 12–13
net worth calculation,
  10–11
shopping savings tips, 28
survey, 1, 7, 9, 29
thirty-something financial
  check-up, 34
tips, 26–27
**First Union Securities,** 91
**Flexible spending
  accounts,** 181–182, 211
**403(b) plans**
catch-up provision, 136
maximum contribution,
  136
single women and, 30
tax issues, 209
**401(k) plans**
beneficiaries, 64, 208, 214

borrowing from, 25–26, 143–144
catch-up provision, 136
I-401(k) plans, 138
individual spouse accounts, 45
maximum contribution, 136, 141
maxing out your plan, 142
single women and, 30
tax issues, 30, 141, 209
Franklin Templeton, 91

**G**

Gender gap, 5, 7, 9
Geriatric-care managers, 187–188
Growth-and-income funds, 121
Growth funds, 120
Guardian of the person, 66
Guardian of the property, 66, 174
Guardians for children, 65–68

**H**

Health care proxies, 68, 178
Health insurance
children and, 84
COBRA coverage, 33, 166, 199
cohabitants, 74
divorce and, 166, 175
important documents, 58
job changes and, 34–35
for a limited time, 33
parents' policy coverage, 32–33

self-employed persons, 33–34
single women and, 32–35
**Health Insurance Association of America**, estimates of how many Americans own long-term-care insurance policies, 190
**HNW Inc.**, survey of wealthy women, 100
**Home-equity loans**, 84–85
**Home health aides**, 183, 188–189
**Homeownership**
divorce and, 167–169
getting rid of paperwork you don't need, 6
joint ownership, 59–60
joint tenancy, 59–60
reverse mortgages, 179–180, 215–216
single women and, 36
tax issues, 168–169
tenancy by the entirety, 60

**I**

I-bonds, 124
Imoneynet.com, 29
In-home care for elderly parents, 183, 188–189
Incentive trusts, 70
Index funds, 121–123
Individual retirement accounts. See also Roth IRAs
adjusted gross income and, 137–138
alimony and, 137
availability, 136
beneficiaries, 64, 208, 214

"catch-up" provision, 136
divorce and, 162
early withdrawal penalties, 139, 144
I-401(k) plans, 138
individual spouse accounts, 45
inheritance rules, 207–208
maximum annual contribution, 136
rollovers to, 79, 143, 208
Roth IRA versus traditional IRA, 137–140
SIMPLE IRAs, 138
stay-at-home moms and, 136, 140
tax issues, 137, 138
**Institute of Consumer Financial Education**, credit ratings damaged by former spouses after a divorce, 160
**Insurance**
cohabitants, 75
disability, 35–36
health insurance, 32–35, 58, 74, 84, 166, 175, 199
life insurance, 58, 62–64, 199, 203–204, 209
long-term-care insurance, 70–73, 180, 189, 191, 214
**InsWeb**, 63
**International funds**, 121
**Internet**
banking, 106, 107
help with retirement planning, 131
investing services, 116
life insurance, 63
money-market funds, 29
Sallie Mae Web site, 21

secured credit cards, 25
Senior Housing Net, 185
stockbrokers, 118–119
**Investing**
as an addictive behavior,
103
assessing the bottom line,
125–126
bonds, 123–125
book value of stocks, 117
children and, 92, 93
choosing stocks, 115–118
clubs for, 118
controlling risk, 113–114
differences between
women and men, 7
direct-investment plans,
116
diversification, 113–114
dollar-cost averaging,
112–113
finding a stockbroker,
118–119
getting rid of paperwork
you don't need, 6
independent analysis
sources, 114
keeping your portfolio in
proportion, 110–111
keys to success, 111
lack of knowledge about
as an obstacle to, 100
"life cycle" funds, 125
long-term, 109
low-cost for beginners,
116
loyalty of women
investors, 104
money-market funds, 29
money-market
mutual funds,
107–108
mutual funds, 119–123
paying off debt and, 102

reasons why women
make better investors,
101–104
for retirement, 134
return on book value,
117
risk versus return, 108
rules for confident
investing, 112
short-term, 105–108
single women and, 31–32
slow and steady rate of,
111–113
stocks, 31
stocks as gender-neutral,
104–105
strategies for, 110–114
total return on stocks,
117–118
traits of male investors,
101–103
Treasury securities, 108
widowhood and, 204–205
**Investment clubs,** 118
**IRAs.** See Individual
retirement accounts

**J**

**Janus,** 91
**Joint-and-survivor option
for pension plans,**
147–148, 206–207
**Joint ownership of
property,** 56–57, 59–60,
64
**Joint tenancy with the
right of survivorship,**
57, 59, 64, 201
**JP Morgan Chase,** 91

**K**

**Keogh plans,** 64

**L**

**Lawyers**
for divorce, 157–158
elder-law specialists, 191
**"Life cycle" funds,** 125
**Life expectancy of**
women, 2, 129
**Life insurance**
amount you need, 63
beneficiaries, 64, 174
child support payments
and, 164
children and, 62–63
important documents, 58
purpose of, 62
recalculating needs, 64
tax issues, 199
term insurance, 63
widowhood and,
203–204, 209
**Living together,** 74–75
**Living trusts,** 68–69, 184
**Living wills,** 68, 178
**Load funds,** 120
**Loans**
borrowing from your
401(k) plan, 25–26,
143–144
business loans, 58
car loans, 21
home-equity loans, 84–85
student loans, 19, 21, 146
**Long-term-care insurance**
assisted living facilities
coverage, 189
average cost of a nursing
home, 71
buying for your parents,
180
evaluating policies, 71–72
home care coverage, 189
inflation protection, 71
nursing homes and, 191

premiums, 73
when to buy, 72–73
widowhood and, 214
**Lutheran Brotherhood,**
survey on savings
accounts, 25

# M

**Marriage.** *See also*
Motherhood;
Widowhood
building a credit rating in
your own name, 50
cohabitants' rights, 74–75
credit cards and, 49–50
credit rights of married
women, 48
dysfunctional couple
scenarios, 39–40
estate planning, 61–70
getting financial issues
out in the open, 40–42
goals and, 42, 53
golden rules for fending
off fights, 44
holding "business"
meetings, 77
joint accounts with a
stockbroker, 119, 159
keeping assets separate,
41
keeping secrets about
money, 39
keeping your name, 50
one spouse as
bookkeeper, 43
overseas weddings, 28
paying for the
professional education
of your spouse, 76–77
percent of marriages that
end in divorce,
100–101

pooling your money,
45–49
prenuptial agreements,
41, 72, 73–76
property ownership
options, 56–61
remarriage, 155, 207
risk-taking, 43–45
saving one spouse's
salary, 84
second marriages, 73–77
slush funds, 43, 52
solutions for
dysfunctional couple
scenarios, 52–53
spending too much,
42–43
tax issues, 50–52
wills and, 64–68
**Mediators for divorces,**
157–158
**Medicaid**
nursing-home care
coverage, 190–191
widowhood and, 214
**Medicare,** 188–189
**Medicare Rights Center,**
195–196
**Medigap policies,** 189
**Merrill Lynch,** 119
**MetLife,** total lifetime
financial cost to
caregivers of caring for
a parent, 179
**MetLife Mature Market
Institute,** study on
home-health aide
costs, 183
*Microsoft Money,* traits of
women investors, 104
**Money-market funds,** 29
**Money-market mutual
funds,** 107–108
**Money personalities,** 4–5

**Motherhood.** *See also*
Children
borrowing carefully,
84–85
break in service rules,
140, 147
paring expenses, 83–84
raising children on one
paycheck, 83–86
stay-at-home moms and
retirement, 136,
140–141
using assets to pay bills,
85–86
working versus
nonworking mothers,
80–86
**Multiple-support
agreements,** 191–192
**Mutual funds**
index funds, 121–123
load versus no-load, 120
minimum investment,
119
money-market mutual
funds, 107–108
12b-1 fees for, 120
types, 120–121

# N

**NAIC.** See National
Association of
Investors Corp.
**National Academy of
Elder Law Attorneys,**
196
**National Alliance for
Caregiving**
total lifetime financial
cost to caregivers of
caring for a parent, 179
women as caregivers for
elderly parents, 177

**National Association for Home Care,** 195

**National Association of Investors Corp.,** 116, 118

**National Association of Professional Geriatric Care Managers,** 196

**National Center for Women and Retirement Research**
savings needed for retirement, 130
"Women Cents Survey," 4, 15, 100, 101

**National Center on Women and Aging**
optimism of women about their financial future, 156
survey of older women who work, 152
total lifetime financial cost to caregivers of caring for a parent, 179

**National Family Caregivers Association,** 196

**National Foundation for Credit Counseling,** 21

**Nellie Mae,** college students and credit card debt study, 19

**Net worth calculation,** 10–11

**No-load funds,** 120

**Nursing-home care,** 190–191

# O

**Online sources.** See Internet

**OppenheimerFunds**

credit card debt, 19
financial management survey, 1, 7, 9, 29
single women's attitudes toward investing in stocks, 109

# P

**P/E.** See Price-earnings ratio

**Paperwork.** See Documents

**Parents.** See Caring for your parents; Children; Motherhood

**Parkinson's disease,** 189

**Penny stocks,** 113

**"Phased retirement,"** 153

**Powers of attorney,** 58, 68, 74, 173, 178, 212–213

**Prenuptial agreements**
reasons not to sign, 72
reasons to sign, 75–77

**Price-earnings ratio,** 115, 117

**Property ownership issues**
cars, 60
community property states, 60, 161
dying intestate, 200–201
estate planning, 61–70
joint ownership, 56–57, 64
joint tenancy with the right of survivorship, 57, 64, 201
living trusts and, 68
savings and checking accounts, 59
stocks and bonds, 60–61
tenancy by the entirety, 57
tenants in common, 58–59

wills and, 57–59

# Q

**QDROs.** See Qualified domestic relations orders

**QMSCOs.** See Qualified Medical Child Support Orders

**QTIP trusts,** 76

**Qualified domestic relations orders,** 170

**Qualified Medical Child Support Orders,** 166

**Qualified terminable-interest property trusts,** 76

*Quicken* money management software, 47

# R

**Rainy-day funds,** 25–29

**Remarriage,** 155, 207

**Retirement.** *See also* specific retirement plans
annuities, 143, 204
average annual retirement income of men and women, 129
borrowing from plans, 25–26, 143–144
break in service rules, 140, 147
case study, 131, 134
cohabitants and, 75
defined-benefit pension plans, 135, 146
defined-contribution plans, 135
divorce and, 148, 169–172

his-and-her retirement
planning, 144–146
important documents, 58
joint-and-survivor option
for pension plans,
147–148, 206–207
life expectancy of women
and, 128–129
making the most of your
husband's pension,
147–148
online help with planning,
131
part-time work and,
152–153
"phased retirement," 153
plan beneficiaries, 64, 148,
174–175, 208, 214
Roth IRAs, 31, 86
rules of thumb for how
much you will need,
130–131
saving $20 a week for,
127, 135–136
savings needed, 130,
132–133
second careers, 152–153
single women and,
29–32
social security, 148–151
spending distributions
instead of rolling over
into an IRA, 143
statistics and survey
results, 128–129
stay-at-home moms and,
136, 140–141
typical woman, 129–130
unexpected places to find
money, 145–146
vesting schedules, 128,
142–143, 147
working in retirement,
152–153

**Retirement Confidence
Survey,** savings for
retirement, 129, 135
**Reverse mortgages,**
179–180, 215–216
**Risk**
bonds and, 123
index funds and, 123
investing and, 108,
113–114
marriage and, 43–45
**Roth IRAs**
for children, 86
for college costs, 91
early withdrawal
penalties, 139
inheritance rules, 207–208
Roth IRA versus
traditional IRA,
137–140
single women and, 31
stay-at-home moms and,
140–141
tax issues, 138, 140

**S**

**Sallie Mae Web site,** 21
**Sandwich generation,**
179–180
**Savings accounts**
automatic deductions for,
42–43
interest compounding, 30
joint ownership of, 59
rainy-day fund, 25–29
saving $20 a week for
retirement, 127,
135–136
savings needed for
retirement, 130–131,
132–133
as short-term investment,
106–107

**Savings bonds,** 124
**Schwab Center for
Investment Research,**
recommendations for
retirement assets, 130
**Scottrade,** 119
**Scudder,** 91
**Sector funds,** 121
**Self-employed persons**
health insurance, 33–34
SIMPLE IRAs for, 138
social security and, 149
**Senior Housing Net,** 196
**Shopping savings tips,** 28
**Shotgunning your credit,**
24
**SIMPLE IRAs,** 138
**Single women.** See also
Divorce; Widowhood
attitudes toward investing
in stocks, 109
bankruptcy filings by, 19,
156
buying a home, 36
earning power, 18
financial to-do list for
later, 37
insurance issues, 32–36
Medicaid and, 190
paying off debts, 19–22
rainy-day funds, 25–29
retirement accounts,
29–32
statistics, 18
steps to financial
independence, 19–36
thirty-something financial
check-up, 34
**Slush funds,** 43, 52
**Smith Barney**
Allocation Series funds,
125
**Social security**
average benefit, 149

dependency on for
retirement, 148–149
divorce and, 150, 172–173
earnings replacement
percentage, 149
eligibility for, 149–150
estimate statements, 150
maximum benefit, 149
retirement age, 150
survivor's benefits, 150,
205–206
what you can expect
from, 151
**Social Security
Administration**
address, phone number,
and Web site, 150
death benefit, 206
notifying of the death of a
spouse, 199
**States**
community property
states, 60, 161
Medicaid eligibility rules,
190
prepaid tuition plans,
91–92
regulation of assisted
living facilities, 185
standardized formula for
child support, 163
state-sponsored college
savings plans,
89–90
will probate, 200–201
**Stockbrokers,** 118–119
**Stocks**
book value, 117
company's net income
and, 115
finding a stockbroker,
118–119
as gender-neutral,
104–105

historical performance of,
31, 109
independent analysis
sources, 114
penny stocks, 113
price-earnings ratio, 115,
117
return on book value,
117
selection criteria,
115–118
separate ownership of,
60–61
total return, 117–118
**Student loans,** 19, 146
**Surveys**
credit card debt, 19
daughters caring for
elderly parents,
177–178
earning power of single
women, 18
financial management, 1,
7, 9, 29
gender gap, 4
keeping secrets about
money, 39
performance of women
versus men as
investors, 101
personality traits that
influence money
choices, 15
savings account amounts,
25
single women's attitudes
toward investing in
stocks, 109
teenage spending, 5–6
traits of women
investors, 104
women and job changes, 7
women as caregivers for
elderly parents, 177

women's feelings about
control over financial
affairs, 101
women's feelings of
financial insecurity, 100
work and earnings
patterns of women, 80,
100

**T**

**T. Rowe Price,** 91
**T-bills,** 108
**Tax issues**
adjusting withholding,
51
alimony, 163
annuities, 204
assisted-living expenses,
189
capital gains tax, 211
child-care credit, 52,
87–88
child-care reimbursement
plans, 88–89
child credit, 87
child support, 164
children and, 86–89
church-sponsored school
tuition, 88
claiming children as
dependents after
divorce, 164, 165
cohabitants, 74
dependent-care tax
credit, 192–193
dependent deduction,
191–192
disability insurance, 35
estate tax, 59, 69, 209
filing jointly, 51
filing separately, 52
filing taxes after a
divorce, 171

flexible spending
accounts, 182, 211
403(b) plans, 209
401(k) plans, 30, 141, 209
getting rid of paperwork
you don't need, 6
homeownership, 168–169
"innocent spouse" and
tax responsibility after
divorce, 170
IRAs, 136, 137, 138
life insurance, 199
marriage, 50–52
marriage penalty, 50–52
medical expenses, 52,
192, 211
multiple-support
agreements, 191–192
prepaid tuition plans,
91–92
Roth IRAs, 138, 140
state-sponsored college
savings plans, 90
tax software, 47
trusts, 69
widowhood, 209–211
*TaxCut* software, 47
TD Waterhouse, 119
Teenage Research
Unlimited of
Northbrook, Ill., survey
on teenage spending,
5–6
Telephones, savings on
long-distance calls, 28
Tenancy by the entirety,
57, 60
Tenants in common,
58–59
Testamentary trusts, 70
TIAA-CREF
daughters caring for
elderly parents survey,
177–178

Equity Index fund, 31, 122
Total return on stocks,
117–118
Trans Union, 22, 159
Treasury securities, 108
Trusts
bypass trusts, 69
important documents, 58
incentive trusts, 70
qualified terminable-
interest property
trusts, 76
revocable living trusts,
68–69, 184
tax issues, 69
testamentary trusts, 70
12b-1 fees for mutual
funds, 120

U

UBS PaineWebber, 119
Unmarried partners' legal
rights, 74–75
U.S. Census Bureau
likelihood of widowhood,
197
study of recently
divorced women, 156
U.S. Department of
Veterans Affairs, funeral
and burial benefits, 199
U.S. savings bonds, series
I, 124

V

Vanguard
Total International Index
fund, 121–122
Total Stock Market Index
fund, 31, 121–122
Vanguard.com, 63
Vesting, 128, 142–143, 147

W

Warehouse clubs, 28
Web sites. See Internet
Widowhood
average age, 18
COBRA coverage, 199
death certificates, 201
delaying financial
decisions, 201–205
divorced-widow social
security benefits, 173
estate planning, 211–213
filing income tax returns,
209–210
financial advisers,
202–203
the first months, 197–199
having the proper
paperwork and
knowing where to find
it, 198
health insurance and, 213
income tax refunds,
210–211
investment plan and,
204–205
IRA inheritance rules,
207–208
joint-and-survivor option
for pension plans,
147–148, 206–207
life insurance and,
203–204, 209
likelihood of, 197
long-term-care insurance
and, 214
Medicaid and, 190
organizations you need to
contact, 198–199, 201
personal account, 212
remarriage and, 207
reverse mortgages,
215–216

settling the estate,
199–201
social security and, 150,
205–206
survivor's benefits,
147–148
taking control of your
financial security
before, 213–214
tax issues, 209–211
using your own
resourcefulness,
214–216
wills and, 199–201, 212
**Wills**
divorce and, 173
dying intestate, 64–65,
199–200
executors, 200
guardianship of children,
65–68, 173–174
important documents, 58
living wills, 68, 178
probate, 200–201
property ownership and,

57–59
updating, 66, 212
**Women.** *See also* Single
women
attitude toward money,
99–100
"bag lady syndrome," 101
credit rights, 22, 48
earning power, 18, 100
feelings about control
over financial affairs,
101
feelings of financial
insecurity, 100
financial situation
differences from men,
2
frequency of job changes,
7
gender gap and, 5, 7, 9
life expectancy, 2,
128–129
personality traits that
influence money
choices, 15

as "present thinkers," 100
reasons why women
make better investors,
101–104
stereotype of, 2
thinking single, 3–4
"Women Cents Survey,"
4, 15, 100, 101
**Women's Financial
Network,** survey on
loyalty of women
investors, 104
**Women's Institute for
a Secure Retirement,**
7
**Worksheets**
"Ballpark Estimate
Retirement Planning
Worksheet," 131
cash flow, 8
how much you need to
save for retirement,
132–133
monthly budget, 12–13
net worth, 10–11